Offshore Citizens

When it comes to extending citizenship to some groups, why might ruling political elites say neither "yes" nor "no," but "wait"? The dominant theories of citizenship tend to recognize clear distinctions between citizens and aliens; either one has citizenship or one does not. This book shows that not all populations are fully included or expelled by a state; they can be suspended in limbo – residing in a territory for protracted periods without accruing citizenship rights. This in-depth case study of the United Arab Emirates uses new archival sources and extensive interviews to show how temporary residency can be transformed into a permanent legal status. Temporary residency can informally become permanent through visa renewals and the postponement of naturalization cases. In the UAE, temporary residency was also codified into a formal citizenship status through the outsourcing of passports from the Union of the Comoros, allowing elites to effectively reclassify minorities into foreign residents.

Noora Lori is Assistant Professor of International Relations at the Pardee School of Global Studies, Boston University. She was a scholar at the Harvard Academy for International and Area Studies and received the Best Dissertation Award from the Migration and Citizenship section of the American Political Science Association (2014). She has published several works on citizenship and migration including in the *Oxford Handbook on Citizenship* (2017).

Offshore Citizens

Permanent Temporary Status in the Gulf

NOORA LORI
Boston University

CAMBRIDGE
UNIVERSITY PRESS

CAMBRIDGE
UNIVERSITY PRESS

University Printing House, Cambridge CB2 8BS, United Kingdom

One Liberty Plaza, 20th Floor, New York, NY 10006, USA

477 Williamstown Road, Port Melbourne, VIC 3207, Australia

314-321, 3rd Floor, Plot 3, Splendor Forum, Jasola District Centre, New Delhi - 110025, India

79 Anson Road, #06-04/06, Singapore 079906

Cambridge University Press is part of the University of Cambridge.

It furthers the University's mission by disseminating knowledge in the pursuit of education, learning and research at the highest international levels of excellence.

www.cambridge.org
Information on this title: www.cambridge.org/9781108705561
DOI: 10.1017/9781108632560

First published 2019
First paperback edition 2021

A catalogue record for this publication is available from the British Library

ISBN 978-1-108-49817-3 Hardback
ISBN 978-1-108-70556-1 Paperback

Contents

Figures

Tables

Introduction

"ISLANDS OF THE MOON"?

It was a humid evening in Dubai, but since it was early December it was just cool enough to sit outside and sip our tea. The occasional breeze carried the wafting scent of the jasmine plants that snaked up the walls of the outdoor coffee shop. Despite the pleasant surroundings, the interview was not going well.

Ibrahim's voice – inflected with the Emirati dialect – was laced with anger and exasperation, and now some of it was being directed at me. I knew that "but where are you *really* from?" was quite possibly the worst question to ask, but I blurted out the words without thinking. All of my training had receded into the background as I tried to process a story that seemed stranger than fiction.[1]

Dressed in a crisp white *dishdāshah*,[2] Ibrahim leaned back in his seat, crossed his legs and looked at me defiantly. Pointing at himself from head to feet, he asked, "Do I look African to you?"

"No," I thought to myself, "you do not," but I stayed silent.

"I am Emirati, where else would I be from?" He continued, "I was born here and I am not a foreigner." He pointed behind us in the direction of

---

[1] Interview with Ibrahim, December 11, 2010. Ibrahim is a pseudonym (as are all other interviewee names in this book). These quotes and descriptions come from transcribed and translated interview notes. Unless otherwise specified all interviews were conducted in Arabic. The quotes were transcribed from memory shortly after the original interview and translated into English. All interviews are anonymized. With the exception of one extended interview (which was filmed in the United States) none of the interviews were taped.

[2] A long (usually white) robe traditionally worn by men in the Persian Gulf.

Dubai's international airport. "Even at the airport, the border officials know that I am Emirati. They look at me like they know."

A heavy silence hung in the air between us as I tried to make sense of the story and engage him again.

"*Bas mā fahimt* [but I don't understand]," I said and asked, "*qamar mitl gumar?*" [moon like moon?]"[3]

I pointed up to the sky as I switched to English: "You got a passport from the 'Islands of the *Moon*'?"

He chuckled and admitted he had to look online to find out that *Juzur al Qamar* was "Comoros Islands" in English: a small island archipelago situated off the coast of East Africa, near Madagascar.[4]

Ibrahim now holds a passport from the Union of the Comoros, but has no connections to the country. He was born in Dubai, a bustling city-state in the United Arab Emirates,[5] to an Emirati mother and *bidūn* father.[6] His father was also born in Dubai, but unlike his mother (whose own father securely belonged to a recognized Arab tribe), Ibrahim's father comes from a family of "unknown origins." The Emirati woman who introduced me to Ibrahim referred to him as "Persian" but Ibrahim never self-identified as such. In his narrative his family lineage has always been Arab and his father's family has been in Dubai for as long as they can trace, but they don't have the crucial document that proves one is Emirati – the federally issued *khulāṣat al-qayd* or "family book."[7]

By the time I met Ibrahim in 2010, he had spent his whole life – over twenty years at that time – applying and waiting for Emirati citizenship. He explained the relief he finally felt in 2001, when he was issued an Emirati passport and was told by civil servants that it would be only a matter of time before he would receive a family book. Five years later, in 2006, he received a scholarship from the Ministry of Education to

---

[3] *Qamar* is moon in *fuṣḥā* Arabic and *gumar* is moon in the *khaleeji* (Gulf) dialect.
[4] The Comoros Islands (*Juzur al Qamar*) form an archipelago of four volcanic islands located on the southeast coast of Africa, just north of Madagascar. Politically, the islands are divided into two entities, the Union of the Comoros, a sovereign state, and Mayotte, an overseas department of France (and technically part of the Schengen visa zone).
[5] The UAE is a federal state that comprises seven emirates, including Abu Dhabi (the capital), Ajman, Dubai, Fujairah, Ras al Khaimah, Sharjah, and Umm Al Quwain.
[6] *Bidūn* refers to stateless populations in the Gulf, particularly in Kuwait and the UAE. The term literally means "without," deriving from the Arabic *bidūn jinsiya*, which means without nationality.
[7] While Emirati passports identify individuals as nationals externally, internally the *khulāṣat al-qayd* or family book is the key document that identifies an individual as a citizen of the UAE.

pursue his higher education in the United States. The American embassy instructed him to renew his passport in order to apply for a student visa, but when Ibrahim attempted to renew his passport, it was withheld and never returned to him. The only explanation he received from naturalization officials was that they were following *awāmir* (orders) from higher up in the Ministry of Interior (MOI). Without his UAE passport, Ibrahim lost his scholarship, job, and bank account.

In 2008, Ibrahim became one of approximately 80,000–120,000 people impacted by the UAE federal government's identity registration drive. This national campaign was designed to "place everyone in a category," by registering all individuals who did not have a family book, regardless of whether they had been previously granted an Emirati passport or naturalization decree. The MOI encouraged all people without a family book to come forward for clemency. There was a two-month window for registration, after which time all of the people who had not registered would be considered "illegal" and would be apprehended by the authorities. Those who, like Ibrahim, followed the directions of the MOI were issued new IDs called *Biṭāqa masjīl lā yaḥmilu awrāq ṯubūtiya* (registration card for undocumented persons).

Then, in 2009, Ibrahim was called into the federal Ministry of Interior in Abu Dhabi about his citizenship case. He was instructed to go to a separate two-story villa where he was issued a new passport. This time, however, the document was not an Emirati passport but one from the Union of the Comoros. In a confused state he examined the identity document he had in front of him: a crisp new passport from a country in Africa he had never heard of, it already had his picture, biometrics, and a frenchized version of his name that now had a slightly different spelling in the Latin script. He was told that if he could identify any Emirati friend or family member who may act as his *kafīl* (national sponsor), then he would be able to apply for a valid UAE residency visa.[8] As long as he had a national sponsor, he would be able to legally reside in the UAE, but as a foreign resident under the guest worker program. He was given vague assurances from a ministry official that this was just a temporary step in the naturalization process, and that at some unidentified point in

---

[8] In the *kafāla* (guest worker) system that operates across the Gulf, the residency of a foreign worker is merged with and tied to their labor contract. Each noncitizen must be sponsored by a *kafīl* (national sponsor). The *kafīl* must be a citizen of the country. A company can also act as a *kafīl* if it is at least 51 percent owned by citizens.

time – contingent upon his good behavior – he would very likely be granted Emirati citizenship once again.

I refer to this passport outsourcing arrangement as creating "offshore citizens" because the UAE government transferred citizenship cases to an offshore site, while the individuals themselves never actually moved. Working with Comoros Gulf Holding (a private-public company) and the presidency of the Union of the Comoros, the UAE's federal government purchased Comoros Islands passports to effectively gerrymander its domestic minorities into "foreign residents." These outsourced passports do not entitle the recipients to any diplomatic protection or the right to reside in the Comoros Islands; on the contrary, they are explicitly banned from being able to reside there. Instead, the passport holders are expected to continue residing in the UAE, but as "guest workers." This arrangement thus invents and codifies a permanently "temporary" legal status; one that enables residents to legally reside in their country of birth, but without ever accruing any form of citizenship rights.

How is it possible for the same individual to oscillate between mutually exclusive legal categories – citizen and foreign "guest worker" – without ever moving between states? How and why did the UAE's federal government outsource naturalization cases to the Union of the Comoros? And what impact has this outsourcing of passports had on the individuals who have become citizens of a state they never applied for citizenship in? To address these questions, this book's population of study is neither the foreign residents who make up approximately 90 percent of the UAE's population nor the Emirati citizens who are now a minority in their own country – but rather those who (like Ibrahim) are suspended in an ambiguous zone in between the official categories of citizen and alien.

ARGUMENT: LIMBO STATUSES AND THE SUSPENSION OF NATIONAL INCORPORATION

By outsourcing national passports, the UAE's federal government may have taken a novel approach to issuing national identity documents, but the problem it faced – how to incorporate domestic minorities – is an old and common one. The "imagined communities" of the world's peoples are not exhaustively encompassed by, or aligned with, the current configuration of internationally recognized sovereign states. Ruling political elites have traditionally held three options when responding to internal others: incorporate as citizens, expel, or ignore. This case shows how national governments have used outsourcing to create a fourth option in national incorporation: the power to transform domestic minorities into documented "foreign" residents.

I argue that this passport outsourcing arrangement was not designed for the purposes of incorporation (citizenship and secure residency) nor expulsion (deportation and nonresidency), but rather to codify the *conditional* inclusion of a population with contingent and revocable residency rights. This citizenship status codifies a form of exclusion that falls short of expulsion. The agreement creates a population that is suspended in a limbo state – they have been rendered readily deportable, but instead of being deported, they inhabit an ambiguous legal position under the guise of renewable "temporary" residency. This represents the first (and at the time of publication only) case of one state purchasing citizenship documents en masse from another state in order to document its own internal minorities. Through this arrangement, minority groups can be documented, accounted for, and issued working visas, but will be, regardless of duration or location, perennial guests.

While the UAE's outsourcing of passports to the Union of the Comoros is novel and puzzling, I use the subsequent chapters to show that this use of outsourcing represents the formalization of a strategy that was already occurring informally. Even before receiving Union of Comoros passports, people like Ibrahim inhabited an informal limbo status due to bureaucratic delays in their citizenship cases. By constantly postponing naturalization cases, the federal authorities have stalled the entry of internal minorities into the national citizenry since the state was formed in 1971. Instead of following the written naturalization laws that identify duration of residency as a path to citizenship, delays are used to evade and suspend the question of national incorporation. Meanwhile, as these internal minorities have been suspended in limbo, the UAE's federal authorities have had to respond to massive influxes of migrant workers and one of the fastest demographic growth rates of the twentieth century. Again, the way the UAE government counts time is critical to its ability to exclude this migrant population from becoming citizens. Regardless of the length of their duration in the UAE, foreign residents are treated as temporary workers who are not eligible for citizenship. Even though economic and social practices make it so that foreign residents are far from temporary in practice, on paper they are on temporary residency visas and their time spent does not enable them to accrue permanent rights. People can thus fall into a limbo status in one of two ways in the UAE – when naturalization cases are constantly deferred or temporary residency visas are continually renewed without ever translating into any possibility for citizenship.

The innovation of offshore citizens is an extension of these practices, codifying "temporary" residency into a permanent citizenship status. I argue that the use of limbo statuses should not be seen as an intermediate step in the implementation of a larger policy design, but as a policy and practice in its own right: the practice of making people wait. A key component of conditional inclusion is the deployment of time as a strategy of exclusion; limbo legal statuses enable states to place certain populations at the cusp of both entry and exit for extended time periods. The populations who inhabit limbo statuses experience a form of residency that is structured by the contradictions of conditional inclusion: an ever-present possibility of deportation intertwined with a constant hope for inclusion.

Though a variety of alternative explanations have been provided for explaining settled citizenship outcomes (inclusion or exclusion), much less attention has gone into explaining limbo legal statuses – the suspension of any settled citizenship outcome. The UAE case illustrates why limbo legal statuses are a useful political strategy – limbo statuses provide political elites with a means of evading larger impasses about the boundaries of the national body politic. Such national dilemmas emerge when there is a contestation among competing domestic political actors over the incorporation of ethnic minorities, refugees, or labor. In such cases, policy-makers often find it more politically expedient to postpone the larger questions about belonging and address the more immediate issues of identity management by creating short-term, renewable legal statuses.

This is because when it comes to issuing documents to resident populations, ruling political elites face two (often competing) dilemmas or pressures. The first is the national dilemma, or the question of who should be considered a citizen. The second is the security dilemma, or the question of effective identity management that allows authorities to fortify their territorial borders and control which populations should gain access to particular services and rights within the territory. On the one hand, liminal and ambiguous citizenship statuses are politically strategic because they allow decision-makers to address the national dilemma through deferral. This strategy allows ruling elites to ignore minority groups and placate competing factions that seek to expel or incorporate a specific population by postponing rather than resolving the issue. On the other hand, irregular legal statuses produce identity management challenges for a growing bureaucracy – as the UAE has developed as a federal state, private and public institutions do not know how to process people who are not citizens nor guest workers. The innovation of offshore citizenship addresses both of these dilemmas by continuing to postpone the national inclusion of this domestic population, while artificially documenting them as "foreign residents" who can fit into the UAE's extant binary population categories of citizens and guest workers.

Conditional inclusion has advantages for the state over full inclusion or expulsion. In the UAE case, incorporation would make this indigenous population eligible for the robust monetary and social benefits of Emirati citizenship. There are different levels of incorporation experienced by the local resident population in the UAE. At the formation of the federal state in 1971, some resident populations became full Emirati citizens, with access to not only a passport but also the more important *khulāṣat al-qayd* (family book) document, whereas others only had a passport or local forms of identification (including birth certificates or driver's licenses issued by individual emirates). Only the Emirati citizens who have family books issued by the federal government can have access to the robust resources associated with citizenship. This includes free healthcare (including specialized treatment abroad) and education (including higher education locally and abroad for specific degrees). The government subsidizes housing for citizens through housing projects, land grants, and zero-interest home loans. Citizens are exempt from taxes, including income taxes, property taxes, or the "housing fee" that noncitizens must pay. Citizens are also eligible for free or discounted utilities (gasoline, electricity, and water), as well as social security/retirement funds, unemployment benefits, child support, marriage grants (to supplement wedding costs), and single-parent financial assistance. Citizens may also apply for food subsidies, earnings from food co-ops, and free parking permits. It is difficult to calculate the exact amount that each citizen costs the state because costs vary between male and female citizens, the costs of different benefits vary greatly, and some benefits are recurring (such as subsidized utilities) whereas others are sporadic (such as land and marriage grants).[9] Citizens also benefit from national quotas and nationalization policies in the private sector, as well as the right to work in the public sector. Indeed,

---

[9] According to one estimate calculated by Kenneth Wilson from Zayed University in 2007, the average male Emirati receives benefits worth about 204,000 dirhams ($55,500) per year (*Economic Times* 2007).

government employment is a key rent-sharing tool and material entitlement that can lead to over-bloated bureaucracies and underemployment. As Joppke aptly describes, "a better description of Gulf State social citizenship would be the 'right *not* to work,' because work is what migrants do" (2017: 389). Citizens also benefit from sporadic influxes of increased income or cash "gifts."[10]

It should be noted that citizenship in the UAE is highly stratified, and even before the creation of offshore citizens, not all citizens had equal access to these benefits. There were (and continue to be) important internal hierarchies among UAE citizens (Jamal 2015). As Dresch and Piscatori (2005) explain, "there are three strata: Abu Dhabi citizens, the citizens of other emirates and citizens by naturalisation (*mutajannasīn*)" (143). Abu Dhabi citizens are routinely privileged over the citizens of the other emirates when it comes to the material benefits of Emirati citizenship and access to superior jobs. And all naturalized Emiratis, even those who now have family books, are lower on the totem pole. A naturalized citizen carries evidence of this change of status on their family book and passport, and this status is transmitted over generations. In other words, "not only are wives of a naturalized citizen (*muwāṭin b-il-tajannus*) themselves naturalized citizens unless Emirati by male descent, but the children of a naturalized citizen are naturalized citizens (*mutajannasīn*) in turn, and so on, presumably through the generations. They never become fully Emirati" (Dresch and Piscatori 2005: 143). Naturalized citizens can never be appointed to office, and they may also have their status revoked if they are considered to be a security threat.[11] This stratification of citizenship is not unique to the UAE; Longva's (1997) work on citizenship in Kuwait, for example, highlights how important such degrees of citizenship are to the redistributive politics of rentier states.

By stratifying access to identity documents, governments can strategically redistribute the robust benefits associated with citizenship in rentier

[10] The minimum wage of public sector employees was raised in the aftermath of the Arab Spring protests. It more recently increased again with a bonus payment to all public sector employees in celebration of 2018 as the "year of Zayed" (marking 100 years since the birth of the founder of the nation, Shaikh Zayed bin Sultan Al Nahyan).

[11] The federal nationality law states that no naturalized citizens would "have the right of candidature, election or appointment" – circumscribing (already limited) political rights to the individuals who were incorporated in the founding national pact and can trace their lineage to 1925. This clause comes from article 13 of Federal Law No. 17 for 1972 Concerning Nationality, Passports and Amendments Thereof.

states. While domestic minorities in the UAE could previously gain access to some benefits of Emirati citizenship when they carried local documents, the identity regularization drive and issuance of new national biometric IDs has since foreclosed that possibility. The Union of Comoros passport recipients are not eligible for any of the benefits associated with Emirati citizenship. And they also can no longer act as national sponsors for noncitizens.[12] See Table I.1 for an overview of the rights associated with citizenship statuses in the UAE.

Conditional inclusion is strategic because while denials prevent people from residing in the country, by contrast delays enable the state to legalize certain dimensions of a population's residency (such as labor) without allowing those individuals to accrue full citizenship rights. Limbo statuses thus deprive people of claimant rights – the right to state resources and social benefits, the right to own property, voting rights (when applicable), and the right to all other rights guaranteed under the country's rule of law for citizens. If, as Sadiq (2005) shows in his work on Malaysia, central governments can strategically count noncitizen residents (including "illegal" immigrants) as citizens for the purposes of political gerrymandering, then this case demonstrates how a central authority can strategically count would-be citizens as noncitizen residents for the purposes of economic gerrymandering.[13]

While the UAE's federal government can reap economic benefits by excluding domestic minorities from Emirati citizenship, the postponement rather than explicit denial of these cases is politically strategic. The outright denial of the right of these populations to gain Emirati citizenship would create several problems for the federal government in Abu Dhabi. First, since the people in this limbo zone carry local identity documents but are missing the key federal nationality document (the family book), the formal denial of these citizenship cases would mean that the rulers of Abu Dhabi do not recognize the historical right of the rulers of the

---

[12] Chapter 6, Section 6.6 provides a longer explanation of the differences between carrying a Union of Comoro passport versus a local ID.

[13] Sadiq's research on the region of Sabah shows how authorities from the central government in Malaysia collaborate with their regional partners to utilize census practices and documentation to incorporate an "illegal" immigrant population from the Philippines. Despite their "illegal" status, immigrants are able to use the census by giving self-reports that deny their residency status and also obtain local IDs that subsequently function as a proof of citizenship. In this way, by tempering of the boundaries of the citizenry at the subnational level, officials from the central government and ruling party are able to enfranchise "illegal" immigrants, while disenfranchising poorer minorities who are citizens (but do not have documentation), to more effectively consolidate political control.

TABLE 1.1 *Rights associated with legal status in the UAE*

	Citizen (with family book)	Local ID or passport (no family book)	Offshore citizens (Comoros passport with UAE foreign residency visa)	Foreign resident (with valid visa)
Social	• Public primary, secondary, and higher education • Direct and indirect subsidies for families: housing, marriage, childcare • Subsidized utilities • No housing fees • Preferential employment policies (quotas) • Can sponsor noncitizens	• Public education (primary & secondary only) • Public healthcare • Some subsidies at the local level • Cannot receive a national ID card • Access to national-level subsidies foreclosed after introduction of national ID card	• No public education • No healthcare • No longer eligible for national employment quotas • Can no longer sponsor nonciti-zens (including foreign spouses)	• Limited healthcare • No public education • No land subsidies • Pay housing fees (tax) • Cannot own land • Partial rights to sponsor other non-citizens (varies by wage level and sectors of employment)
Civil	• Freedom of speech, except against the rulers or perceived support for Islamist groups	• Freedom of speech, except against the rulers or perceived support for Islamist groups	• Freedom of speech, except against the rulers or perceived support for Islamist groups	• Freedom of speech, except against the rulers or support for Islamist groups • Freedom of religion

| Political | • Consumption of alcohol forbidden (not systematically enforced)
 • Voting rights: Only for half of Federal National Council
 • Cannot vote for leadership: presidency/ prime minister | • Consumption of alcohol forbidden (not systematically enforced)
 • No voting rights in UAE | • Consumption of alcohol forbidden (not systematically enforced)
 • No voting rights in either the UAE or Union of the Comoros | • Permission to consume alcohol (with license) if non-Muslim
 • No voting rights in the UAE
 • Depending on national origin, may be eligible to vote in sending country |

remaining emirates to define the boundaries of their citizenries.[14] The
pattern of the pending citizenship cases reveals key political dynamics
between the elite rulers in the federation, with all of the stalled cases
originating from outside the capitol of Abu Dhabi. Those who have an
Arab ethnic tribal background and apply for citizenship from Abu Dhabi
are successful, whereas those who apply for citizenship from the remaining emirates are not rejected but are kept waiting. Until 2008, this act of
postponement and bureaucratic foot dragging appears to be an ad hoc
coping strategy of the federal government, but the outsourcing of passports turned the tactic of postponement into a deliberate strategy. By
keeping the citizenship cases of the smaller emirates pending, as opposed
to excluding or including those individuals, the federal government does
not outwardly reject people who have been recognized as citizens by the
rulers of Dubai, Ras al Khaimah, Sharjah, Ajman, Fujairah, and Umm Al
Quwain, but it does not incorporate them as full citizens either. Saying
"no" would mean acknowledging that Abu Dhabi does not recognize the
emirates' sovereignty to define the membership in their jurisdictions.
Instead of being rejected, the cases are left pending, and in many cases
are still being processed four decades after the formation of the union.

Second, if the federal government explicitly denies this population from
receiving Emirati citizenship, then it would render this population de jure
stateless. Meanwhile the Comoros Islands passports have made this population effectively de facto stateless, while allowing the security forces to
enumerate and count this population. This solves the problem of statelessness from the state's perspective, since the formal denial of citizenship
would strip people of documentation and challenge the state's ability to
have a comprehensive registry of its population.

As a political tactic, conditional inclusion is more powerful than either
acceptance or rejection. Political gains are reaped from pending inclusion –
from making people wait, hope, and keep trying. Since the federal MOI
officials informed recipients that the Union of Comoros passports are an

---

[14] Naturalization applicants must apply for citizenship through the emirate of their residency, and because citizenship was historically determined at the emirate level, emirates
approved some families for passports who were not approved by Abu Dhabi for family
books. Only the federal ministry of interior in Abu Dhabi can issue "family books." These
family books trace an individual's family lineage in one of the UAE's emirates since 1925,
providing evidence that the ruling tribes identified this family as constituent member in
the founding of the state. See Federal Law No. 17 for 1972 Concerning Nationality,
Passports and Amendments Thereof, article 2(a). For more on the importance of family
books, see Al Qassemi (2010).

interim step in the Emirati naturalization process, the recipients continue to hope and wait for Emirati citizenship and believe that – contingent upon their "good behavior" and their submission to further security checks – they might finally become secure Emirati citizens. Outsourcing thus enables the federal government to assert that this is not a rejection of all naturalization cases, but rather a temporary measure required for more extensive security checks. Doing so extends the waiting time of a population that continues to be only precariously and conditionally included, all the while ensnaring this population into a structured performance of allegiance that must be constantly repeated.

The uncertainty of waiting for citizenship is an important part of this process – waiting is a political tactic in its own right. Though far more attention has gone into the study of the repressive tactics of states, waiting is a subtle but powerful form of political domination. In her book on the political value of time, Cohen (2018) shows that states assign durations of time political value and use time as a form of exchange value to accord or deny rights. Waiting can thus be used by the state as a form of exclusion when people reside in a territory without accruing membership rights over time. This work is particularly useful for emphasizing the relationship between political time and social justice. As Cohen explains, "racialized incarceration practices, delayed naturalization, and obstructionist abortion waiting periods are all instances in which select people's time is appropriated as a means of denying them rights that others enjoy" (2018: 4–5). Meanwhile, the previous work of sociologist Schwartz (1974; 1975) also draws a correlation between the distribution of time and power in social systems, and more recently, Auyero (2012) demonstrates how delays are used as part of the state's poverty regulation strategies. All three authors critically link the deployment of delays to power relations and the management of resources. As they argue, speed is a marker of privilege; the powerful do not wait, they are waited upon. There are psychological and material costs to serving this waiting time, which is why though delays have not received extensive treatment in the social sciences, they have been studied in psychological and industry-driven research (Janakiraman, Meyer, and Hoch 2011; Larson 1987; Leclerc, Schmitt, and Dubé 1995; Maister 1985; Mann 1970).

The empirics of the UAE case illustrate how the deployment of time through postponements can be an active political strategy rather than simply a characteristic of the sloth-like nature of bureaucracies. If bureaucratic inefficiencies explained delays in this case, then the delays in citizenship cases would be randomly distributed across the UAE's population.

This study finds that, on the contrary, there is a clear pattern of who must wait for citizenship, reflecting how the UAE's federal government privileges its subnational populations. There are key differences in the pattern of citizenship outcomes across the nation. Specifically, all of the pending cases originate from emirates other than Abu Dhabi. These findings are based on three evidentiary sources that are presented in the forthcoming chapters: (1) the pattern of pending naturalization cases from interviews with both naturalization applicants and civil servants in naturalization departments; (2) the pattern in the origin of cases of those who received Comoros Islands passports from interviews and archives; and (3) the divergent citizenship outcomes of the same refugee community that was resettled to Dubai and Abu Dhabi in 1973 – the refugee group in Dubai received Comoros Islands passports while the group in Abu Dhabi was resettled elsewhere.

Postponement is a strategic and political act and not just an indication of bureaucratic ineptitude. What likely began as the federal government's ad hoc evasion of the question of national incorporation has turned into a deliberate strategy of suspending that question indefinitely. The UAE's federal government did not *ignore* people with pending naturalization cases. There is no evidence demonstrating that officials did not have the capacity to count or process these cases; on the contrary, the evidence suggests that they went to great lengths to regularize these cases and count domestic minorities as foreign residents instead of citizens. First, the Ministry of Interior registered the population with new stateless IDs, and then the government invested resources to involve a private company and foreign state and purchase foreign national IDs to issue to this domestic population. The federal government invested time and money to go out of its way *not* to naturalize these individuals, but rather to create a new category of permanently "temporary" residents. Since these Comoros passports (and the UAE residency visas that recipients must obtain) have to be continually renewed, this new legal status is instantiated and reaffirmed by the state's bureaucratic apparatus. These cases are processed *as* ambiguous; with "offshore citizens" the ambiguity of having a limbo status is not a consequence of pitting informal practices against formal laws, but rather found in the formal legal status itself.

The postponement of incorporation through the adoption of limbo statuses is both a consequence of inter-emirate conflicts and a deliberate strategy of wearing people down. The federal government never issued a decree stating that individual rulers cannot define who their subjects are. On the contrary, naturalization cases cannot be initiated through the federal state; they must still go through the emirate level first and be approved locally before they are referred to the federal authority. Formally the rulers of each emirate retain the right to define their citizenry; informally this right is never realized because the cases outside of Abu Dhabi are constantly postponed. Postponement may thus appear to be an unintended consequence of inter-emirate conflicts rather than a deliberate strategy of wearing people down, but just because a strategy might be developed for one issue does not mean it does not gain value as a political tactic in its own right. In other words, this policy is a deliberate attempt to wear people down so that they relent and opt out of the naturalization process if they can (by, for example, purchasing black-market passports). That is one concrete benefit to the regime that comes out of the material and psychological costs of waiting – delays are a way of culling the pool of applicants and policing national boundaries. Another concrete political gain from making people wait is that these security checks function as "allegiance checks," creating a structured performance of deference to the head of state and the construction of the nation. The psychological costs of waiting include being suspended in a constant state of uncertainty, repeating the same actions (reapplying for citizenship) with the hope for different results. There are also material costs to waiting, including application fees, transportation costs, childcare costs, and taking time off work. Delays thus produce both costs (to those who wait) and benefits (to those who are waited upon).

There are important differences between outright denial and expulsion on the one hand, and limbo statuses or postponement on the other. My central argument is not that there are *no* domestic elites or political factions (such as the rulers of Abu Dhabi in this case) who would like to exclude certain groups from the citizenry permanently. On the contrary, the evidence shows that exclusion was (and continues to be) their goal, and that they have attempted to achieve that goal through outsourcing. The analysis of the impact of these passports on the recipients also shows that if the intention was to exclude, it was successfully achieved because in many ways this population has been stripped from having any meaningful rights. The point, however, is that this attempt to exclude a population from the national body politic has not led to the expulsion of that same group from the territory. This population is not being systematically deported, or forcibly displaced. The recipients are not told that they are no longer eligible for citizenship. On the contrary, they have a legal residency permit to continue residing in the UAE, and are told by the Ministry of Interior authorities in Abu Dhabi that the Comoros passports are simply an interim step in the federal security and vetting process of becoming an Emirati citizen. By continually postponing the outright denial of citizenship, this population is neither fully excluded nor included, but instead suspended in a limbo state. Indeed, for the refugee groups in Dubai who have been mired in the naturalization process for decades, a formal denial of their citizenship cases might be a willing reprieve, because it would mean becoming eligible for refugee status and resettlement elsewhere. Limbo statuses are lived as a form of exclusion, but that exclusion is never fully realized.

CASE SELECTION: UNITED ARAB EMIRATES

This case is important because it confounds dominant narratives about the existence of a clear citizen/noncitizen binary. In the formal policies and laws of all modern states, citizens are a circumscribed group who are clearly distinct from aliens. This formal/legal claim about a citizen/non-citizen dichotomy has been largely reproduced in the media, political debates about migration, and the academic literature on citizenship. The prevailing political theories of citizenship tend to recognize clear distinctions between citizens and aliens; either one has citizenship or one does not.[15] When it comes to the question of national incorporation, the existing literature has thus extensively examined why states choose to either include or expel minorities and new migrants. Policy-makers differentiate between groups that they (attempt to) assimilate, culturally accommodate, or expel, based on long-standing ideas about nationhood and political culture (Brubaker 1992), the need for labor or military conscription (Weil 2001), and strategic calculations about national security threats and foreign relations (Greenhill 2010; Mylonas 2013; Weiner 1992).

This book uses the UAE case to show that in the same way that there is a buffer zone around the territorial boundaries of states, demographic boundaries are not binary. Through the skillful deployment of citizenship

---

[15] See, for example, Michael Walzer's (1983) defense of kinship ties as being a necessary way of determining the boundaries of membership. John Rawls (1999) defines citizenship rights as being determined by racial and ethnic descent, and Koopmans and Statham (2000) argue that ethnic and cultural differences pose a challenge to national citizenship. Collectively, these and other works assume that there are preexisting national citizenries and one can clearly delineate insiders from outsiders. Approaching the alien/citizen divide from a different perspective, Honig (2003) has argued that foreignness is a necessary and key component of democratic politics and national foundings. For a critique of this citizen/noncitizen dichotomy and case studies that examine populations whose citizenship is in question, see Lawrance and Stevens (2017).

and immigration laws, political elites can choose to not only include or expel groups, but also place certain populations in limbo. The term "limbo" denotes being caught at a border; it is apt for referring to populations who are suspended in the boundary zone of the citizen/alien binary. In the Christian tradition, the theological meaning of the term "limbo" refers to a state of being barred from heaven but not sent to hell – a condition structured by the suspension of any final resolution. The secular meaning of the term likewise refers to "an uncertain period of awaiting a decision or resolution; an intermediate state or condition."[16] Adapting this concept to citizenship outcomes, I argue that populations inhabit a limbo legal status when they reside in a territory for a protracted period without accruing citizenship rights. In such cases, the outcome of national incorporation is neither inclusion nor expulsion – it is instead suspended for a protracted period.

The UAE is an important case for the study of contemporary migration and citizenship politics and it was selected for two key reasons. First, the country has a high value on the outcome of interest – limbo statuses – making it a suitable choice for a most-likely case study research design.[17] The overwhelming majority of the UAE's population comprises people who are on temporary and renewable work visas. Today "guest workers" make up over 88.5 percent of the UAE's total population (National Bureau of Statistics 2011). Guest workers are on short-term residency permits that are constantly renewed over protracted periods, at times over generations, but this permanent residency never translates into an ability to accrue permanent rights. As a result of restrictive citizenship policies, noncitizens now far outnumber Emirati citizens, making the UAE the country with the highest number of foreign nationals in the world (United Nations Department of Economics and Social Affairs, Population Division 2017). Second, in addition to creating limbo statuses informally by renewing "temporary" residency permits, the UAE government has found a way to formalize limbo statuses. The invention of offshore citizens may seem like a puzzling deviation from global trends in citizenship policies, but it more accurately represents an extreme articulation of contemporary trends rather than a deviation away from them.

It is worth explaining what this book does and does not do in order to further the study of limbo statuses, especially when it comes to the

---

[16] *Oxford Living Dictionaries*, "limbo, N," accessed April 2, 2019, https://en .oxforddictionaries.com/definition/limbo.
[17] For more on "most-likely" case study designs see Eckstein (1975); Levy (2008).

question of generalizability beyond the UAE case. This book presents a fine-grained account of one case study involving different actors within the UAE (including different rulers across the federation and the British authorities), the Union of the Comoros, private sector actors, nongovernmental organizations (NGOs), and a variety of individuals and communities who are waiting for citizenship in the UAE. The book's main outcome of interest is explaining how and why the outsourcing of citizenship occurred. When answering this question, I situate this case of outsourcing and explain how and why it is a codified limbo status. The book's secondary outcome of interest is to explain how the individuals and communities who inhabit limbo statuses navigate being neither fully incorporated nor expelled from the UAE for a protracted time period. The book draws on a combination of interviews, archival analysis, and anonymized information from clinical work on ongoing legal cases.

When it comes to generalizing beyond this case, I argue that while the outsourcing of citizenship is unique to the UAE, it was a solution that was explicitly designed to fit the *kafāla* guest worker system. In that regard, the UAE is similarly situated to the other migrant-receiving states of the Gulf; they all share a common regulatory framework for migration and exclusionary citizenship policies, especially since the discovery of oil. These commonalities allow me to carefully generalize some aspects of this argument to the Gulf region. In so doing, this study contributes to the literature on rentier citizenship. The dominant explanations of authoritarianism in the oil-rich Gulf tend to depict rentier citizenship as a social contract between a regime and an acquiescent population.[18] The rentier literature has largely elided the question of citizenship policies, but Bearce and Hutnick (2011) argue that the "resource curse" is actually an "immigration curse" because when controlling for immigration, the standard resource variables lose significance in a democratization model. The authors somewhat spuriously explain this relationship between energy production and immigration by stating that many resource-rich countries "also tend to be labor-poor" (691). Rather than seeing the correlation between high numbers of foreign residents and oil wealth as being

---

[18] While this relationship between rentier regimes and their citizens is often assumed or imputed, recent work by Jones (2015; 2017) has shown that autocrats partake in active policies of social engineering that do not conform to the expectations of rentier theory. Indeed, instead of attempting to "buy off" citizens with oil wealth, ruling elites can attempt to shape new "liberal" citizens as part of their development and modernization initiatives, even if these efforts have downstream unintended consequences that could challenge their own political survival.

coincidental (or purely determined by preexisting demographic inputs), this book shows that the high concentration of noncitizens in the Gulf is an outcome of active policies that constructed existing residents and new migrants as being "alien" to these new nation-states, just as oil wealth began trickling into the region. In other words, rather than assuming a direct relationship between a regime and its population that ignores the legal status of residents, this study focuses on the legal statuses that determine who is able to gain access to resources in rentier states – and who is barred from doing so. Studies that take the national unit and boundaries of a citizenry as a given tend to overlook the competition over resources preceding the consolidation of resource-reliant states. Doing so effectively omits the most contentious dimension of the politics of resource wealth and redistribution – the struggle to define the boundaries of the in-group. Instead of focusing on how citizens feel about a regime, this study seeks to understand how the population is segmented by examining who can get access to ID documents, which ID documents translate into economic privileges and permanent residency, and how those ID documents are distributed – or withheld. This approach reorients the understanding of rentier citizenship from the level of political psychology to the level of documentation and practices – examining the administrative structures, legal maneuvers, and enforcement patterns that allow for authoritarian resilience in resource-rich states.

Beyond the Gulf, this case study acts as a plausibility probe that begins the path of theory-building when it comes to explaining how and why states adopt limbo legal statuses. In this vein, the book's larger underlying question is: why and how do states create limbo legal statuses that enable groups to reside in the territory but remain outside of the nation? My review of the literature in Chapter 1 demonstrates that there are incidences of these types of limbo statuses across regime types and world regions. This analysis places the state and state formation at the center of the narrative, linking temporary statuses to the national dilemma and the exclusion of certain populations from the nation. This allows me to contribute to the literature on state formation, nationalism, and citizenship by demonstrating how states create buffer zones around their demographic boundaries. For these in-between populations the question of national incorporation is evaded in the short run through the creation of temporary legal statuses and effectively suspended in the long run.

While the UAE case is in many ways unique due to its demographic composition and its outsourcing of citizenship cases, the adoption of limbo statuses to suspend the question of national incorporation is a much wider state practice that extends far beyond this case. Not all states fully incorporate or expel migrants and minority populations; many states create temporary and circumscribed legal statuses that authorize residency rights for certain groups while simultaneously foreclosing their access to citizenship. Moreover, this practice is not limited to the boundary-enforcement strategies of authoritarian states; democratic states – especially the large migrant-receiving states – have developed a plethora of short-term accommodations to postpone the larger issue of national incorporation for certain groups who reside within their territories.

How does the UAE compare to a larger universe of cases of major migrant-receiving states? Few have attempted to systematically compare the immigration and citizenship policies of the Gulf with those of migrant-receiving states outside of the region, but Joppke's (2017) recent comparative study provides a helpful point of departure for this discussion.[19] He argues that while Western migrant-receiving states may have variations among them, they are all essentially "inclusive," while the autocratic Gulf states are ultimately "exclusive." This inclusive/exclusive dichotomy emerges because "in a liberal-democratic constellation the natural tilt is toward more inclusiveness. Liberal democracy requires the 'congruence' between the subjects and the objects of rule (Dahl), and it shuns the existence of 'second-class' citizens (Walzer)" (Joppke 2017: 387).

Grafting an inclusive/exclusive binary onto a regime-type difference is intuitive at face value. After all, as Joppke rightly points out, none of the Gulf states can be considered democratic and they all systematically foreclose citizenship from the vast majority of their foreign residents, regardless of the length of residency. Moreover, all of the oil-rich Gulf states have created criteria that link citizenship to those who can trace their lineage to a "cut-off" date prior to the discovery of oil, in an effort to limit the group of beneficiaries who may profit from the rents of this resource. But this practice of foreclosing access to citizenship by creating

---

[19] Milanovic (2016) deals with immigration to the Gulf minimally, but he places it in comparative perspective by suggesting that the dual strategy of decreasing barriers to immigration while increasing barriers to citizenship should serve as a model for the West and could decrease global levels of inequality. Meanwhile Ruhs (2013) integrates the Gulf into his comparative study, but he does not address how the *kafāla* system differs from other immigration systems because he argues that the Gulf states and their Western migrant-receiving counterparts (such as the United States, EU, Canada, and Australia) should all be considered as part of the same category of high income migrant–receiving states.

legal statuses that allow certain groups to reside in a country without ever being eligible for naturalization is not limited to autocratic states, rentier states, or the Gulf region. Indeed, the strategy of tempering the criteria of citizenship to exclude certain groups of residents is a practice that long precedes state formation in the region.

An inclusive/exclusive democratic/autocratic binary only makes sense if we focus on liberal values rather than the actual practices of liberal states. Scholarship on liberal states has often reaffirmed the importance of liberal values in undergirding laws even when inclusionary values have coexisted with the empirical contractions of the exclusionary practices of those same states. Labeling democratic migrant-receiving states as inclusive would require ignoring a robust literature that has shown how democracies have almost always been simultaneously inclusive and exclusive, depending on the group in question. The same states that are heralded as beacons of democracy have long histories of creating gradations of citizenship that allowed certain populations to reside in the territory without enjoying the full rights associated with citizenship. This includes slaves, labor migrants, women, and racial minorities – all populations who were either excluded from the very definition of who is eligible for citizenship or allowed to exercise only partial citizenship rights in liberal democracies (e.g., citizenship status but without full political enfranchisement).[20]

For example, the United States not only scores highly on almost every metric of democracy but it is also a prime example of a traditional immigration state. And yet for the vast majority of its history as a nation – from 1790 to 1952 – the ability for immigrants to naturalize was restricted to those who came from a racially defined group (white), and denied to all others, even if they were allowed to reside in the territory.[21] The institution of citizenship, since its earliest manifestations, has critically depended upon the labor of those who are outside the body politic while remaining inside that polity's territory and playing an integral role in its economy. Kasimis (2013) shows that the Athenian democracy was based on a political economy supported by not only slavery, but also a large class of resident aliens – the *metics* (*metoikoi*) – a free immigrant population

---

[20] For a discussion of the racialization of citizenship across democratic contexts see Fitzgerald (2017), Hesse (2004), and Mehta (1997). On how British citizenship in particular was redefined to create and exclude different categories of British subjects see Paul (1997).

[21] Fitzgerald (2017: 131). For the impact of these policies on different communities of Asian Americans see Ngai (2004).

that was assimilated but disenfranchised, on the basis of blood, generation after generation. It may be tempting to dismiss the exclusive dimensions of citizenship as a bygone relic of earlier periods of imperialism but there is evidence that (after a period of liberalization in the twentieth century) liberal democracies are actually becoming more exclusionary rather than more inclusive.[22] If citizenship is a liberal institution that calls for congruence among members of the in-group, then it has simultaneously also functioned as what Mehta calls a "liberal strategy of exclusion" (1997). The institution of citizenship and the sovereign prerogative to define the boundaries of the citizenry have enabled liberal states to use legal (not extralegal) mechanisms for legitimating exclusion. Those who are deemed unworthy of full enfranchisement are "aliens" who are not party to the laws or due processes that make democracies democratic.

Cohen argues that instead of a clear demarcation between full citizens and outsiders, democratic states produce "semi-citizens" – a spectrum of in-between categories with different combinations of rights. The literature on democratic citizenship has overwhelmingly focused on normative conceptions of what citizenship "should" be (i.e., equality), and not what citizenship actually is (unevenly granted rights). "Rather than representing mistakes or bias, semi-citizenships are the institutional embodiments of compromises between conflicting logics of membership" (Cohen 2009: 96). Conflicts over who should be included in politics, to what degree, on what grounds, and under which conditions, systematically produce "semi-citizenships," or partially enfranchised individuals with different combinations of rights. When different factions of a polity cannot agree on the inclusion or exclusion of a particular population, it is more politically convenient for political elites to invent new forms of legal statuses that document people without extending full citizenship rights.[23]

---

[22] Even prior to the current backlash against asylum seekers in Europe, the literature has shown a trend of retrenchment of citizenship laws across Europe due to a variety of factors, including growing resentment against foreign workers, attempts to curtail citizenship laws that previously included former colonial subjects, and the rise of populist movements of the extreme right (Goodman 2014; Paul 1997; Tichenor 2002; Schain, Zolberg, and Hossay 2002).

[23] In T. H. Marshall's (1950) classic formulation, modern citizenship comprises multiple dimensions of rights that can be divided into three distinct arenas – civil, political, and social rights. By civil rights, Marshall refers to all of the rights necessary for individual freedom – including freedom of speech, thought, faith, the liberty of the person, the right to own property, the right to conclude contracts, and the right to justice. Political rights refer to the right to participate in the exercise of power "as a member of a body invested with political authority or as an elector of the members of such a body" (Marshall 1950: 11). Finally, social rights refer to a whole range of social welfare and security: "from the

Rather than treating regimes as either inclusive or exclusive, it is more apt to consider citizenship regimes as existing on an inclusive/exclusive spectrum. This spectrum would account for how citizenship policies can undergo both liberalizations and retrenchments over time; it also accounts for the fact that the same state can have quite different responses toward different resident groups.[24] This perspective moves away from the assumption that there are preexisting national citizenries that clearly delineate insiders from outsiders. The distinction of whether someone is a citizen or not is not a depoliticized empirical determination based on whether an individual meets the stable criteria of a state's citizenship policies, but rather a shifting political determination based on a government's changing political prerogatives. An attention to the use of limbo statuses shows that states across regime types can be inclusive toward some groups, exclusionary toward others, and place yet another subset of the population in limbo at the cusp of entry or exit for protracted periods.

If the importance of these ambiguous citizenship statuses is measured purely quantitatively, then the problem appears to be limited and exceptional; numbers of ambiguously situated individuals tend to be small in each country. However, a review of the literature shows that we can draw connections between groups who are related not through their common geographic concentration in one part of the globe, but rather through their common relationship vis-à-vis state authorities. Taken collectively, a much wider population of "in-between" and ambiguous statuses emerge. This research demonstrates the importance of treating the interstitial space between citizens and aliens as its own discrete citizenship outcome. In the next chapter I introduce the concept of

right to a modicum of economic welfare and security to the right to share to the full in the social heritage and to live the life of a civilised being according to the standards prevailing in the society" (11).

[24] This approach builds upon the literature on citizenship outcomes that has focused on differentiated forms of citizenship – asking why some groups have only partial access to citizenship rights. One branch of the scholarship has focused on differentiated citizenship from the perspective of why foreign residents have gained a range of citizenship rights (including political rights) without having the formal juridical status of a legal citizen (Chung 2006; Gurowitz 1999; Soysal 1995). Meanwhile, others have approached citizenship hierarchies from the perspective of why some groups who are formally citizens still do not enjoy the same rights as other groups of citizens. In these works, authors have documented how liberalizations have been simultaneously accompanied by retrenchments to create differentiated rights and hierarchies within citizenries (Hancock 2004; Holston 2008).

precarious citizenship to refer to people who are unable to gain access to secure citizenship rights and instead inhabit limbo statuses for protracted periods.

CHAPTER SUMMARIES

The way that political actors use time is critical to claims of legitimacy when it comes to constructing and policing national boundaries. Time is important to nation-making both in terms of the temporal boundaries that delimit who becomes "native" in the founding of a new state and also in terms of the way that political actors deploy increments of time to police national boundaries. These two dimensions of the temporal politics of national boundary-making are situated within the literature in Chapter 1, and expanded upon empirically in Chapters 2–6.

Chapter 1, "Limbo Statuses and Precarious Citizenship," explores the way that time is suspended for different groups of individuals who inhabit legal categories that do not lead to citizenship.[25] The chapter examines four categories of people who are unable to gain a secure citizenship status over a protracted period: (1) individuals who cannot obtain national identity documents and become stateless; (2) individuals who may have one state's identity documents but who lack legal status in their place of residence and become "illegal"; and a spectrum of groups with temporary statuses that are neither stateless nor fully unauthorized, including (3) those with temporary humanitarian protection or (4) those with temporary work authorization. While the majority of this book focuses on a part of the globe where the stakes of formal citizenship are particularly high, resource-rich states are not the only states that make people wait for citizenship. Temporary and conditional statuses are created because they represent a strategic government response to avoid resolving dilemmas about citizenship, especially when it comes to the incorporation of minorities, refugees, or labor. Meanwhile global boundary-enforcement processes (biometric ID management, ID regularization, and deportation drives) are drawing more and more people into the documentary power of the state system without providing them with a secure place within it.

Chapter 2, "Making the Nation: Citizens, 'Guests,' and Ambiguous Legal Statuses," then proceeds to the empirical study of the UAE case. The

---

[25] This chapter draws from and builds upon a previous publication on "Statelessness, 'In-Between' Statuses, and Precarious Citizenship" for *The Oxford Handbook on Citizenship* (Lori 2017).

chapter provides the historical context for the creation of Emirati citizens, guest workers, and a gray zone of people who did not clearly fit into the new state's citizen/alien binary. It focuses on the period immediately preceding the state formation of the UAE, highlighting the importance of temporal boundaries in the creation and definition of the new national citizenry. Time and ethnicity become intertwined when the citizenship law requires UAE citizens to trace their lineage to 1925, a temporal deadline that circumscribes the "insiders" to the Arab tribes documented by the British census. There is a temporal gap between this imagined homogeneous community of 1925 – Abu Dhabi's image of the citizenry – and the much more heterogeneous demographic reality of the federation across all of the emirates in 1971. The chapter documents the key role that Persians, East Africans, and South Asians played in the political economies of Dubai and the remaining emirates, which led the rulers of these emirates to count these minorities as citizens. Meanwhile, Abu Dhabi's rulers had a much more restrictive understanding of citizenship that was tied to Arab lineage, and (as in the case of Iranians) it even required certain minority groups visiting or living in other emirates to apply for visas. The codification of the citizenship law thus ignited a national dilemma between Abu Dhabi and the remaining emirates over who should be counted as a citizen. This chapter illustrates how this unresolved contestation between the different rulers laid the path to the creation of liminal populations who inhabit the UAE's territory but are not part of the nation.

While Chapter 2 focuses on national boundary formation, Chapter 3 illustrates how the new federal state's national boundary was subsequently securitized and policed as the UAE matured as a union. Chapter 3 examines how migration and security come to be interlinked in the UAE, illustrating why it becomes increasingly difficult to inhabit an ambiguous legal status over time. It begins by examining how migration flows came to be associated with national security threats, even prior to the formation of the UAE. Political interests shaped the pattern of migration flows into the region away from Arab migrants; both the British authorities and Trucial State rulers were invested in suppressing labor strikes, Arab nationalism, and insurrectionary threats. In response to the increasing number of migrants entering the Trucial coastline, the British authorities and Trucial State rulers began building an infrastructure for migration enforcement. This meant not only policing the shoreline, but also developing domestic identity checks to police the interior. This mobilization of resources toward migration enforcement restricted access to Emirati citizenship – delaying the cases of pre-1971 domestic minorities on the one hand, and foreclosing the very possibility of citizenship for post-1971 migrants on the other. It may have been the national dilemma (contestations over who is a citizen) that led to the creation of a gray zone of people, but it is the security dilemma (the mobilization of resources toward documenting the entire population and checking legal statuses at all times), that makes precarious citizenship real. As a vast network of private and public institutions that check identity documents in the UAE was built over time, it has become increasingly difficult for anyone with an ambiguous citizenship status to continue living and working in the state.

Time, or duration of residency, is typically a way of accruing membership rights in a political community; states can withhold rights by refusing to recognize the time spent of particular individuals or groups. Chapter 4, "Permanently Deportable: The Formal and Informal Institutions of the *Kafāla* System," examines the temporal politics of the *kafāla* guest worker program. The chapter focuses on the formal and informal institutions of the guest worker program to show that even though guest workers are officially temporary, they exhibit many features associated with permanent settlement.[26] The way that the UAE and other Gulf states enforce temporary residency is by externalizing the costs of migration enforcement to individual national sponsors in the private sector; but social practices and economic ties often lead these sponsors to extend the residency of the foreign residents that they sponsor. Thus while the authorities can prevent migrants from gaining access to citizenship, they have much less control over permanent settlement. Foreign residents can fall into a limbo state when their short-term residency permits are constantly renewed, even over generations, but this residency never translates into a secure path to citizenship.

Returning to temporal politics as a recurring theme of the book, Chapter 5, "*Ta 'āl Bachir* (Come Tomorrow): The Politics of Waiting for Identity Papers," illustrates the importance of bureaucratic delays as a means of policing national boundaries. This chapter demonstrates that another way people fall into limbo statuses is when they have citizenship cases that are never denied but are instead constantly postponed. It examines what it means to wait for citizenship for a protracted time period from the perspective of those undergoing the process. The chapter documents the MOI's tactic of constantly prolonging the duration of

---

[26] Some of the dynamics that allow temporary statuses to become permanent were discussed in a previous publication (Lori 2012). These initial findings have been updated with interviews and new demographic data to reflect the most recent publicly available figures.

residency required for citizenship.[27] If a UAE resident cannot trace their paternal lineage to the Arab tribes of 1925, then they must undergo a naturalization process, even if they were born in the country and can trace their family's settlement over generations. The written law states that this process takes seven years, meanwhile in interviews civil servants acknowledge that the minimum is actually thirty years of residency in the same emirate, and yet interviews with those undergoing the process make it clear that many have transgressed this thirty-year threshold and continued to wait for citizenship. The postponement of cases in the naturalization process illustrates how bureaucrats deploy temporal obstacles that place people in a limbo status; this at once entangles these individuals into the web of the state, while also effectively excluding them from the national body politic.

Chapter 6, "Identity Regularization and Passport Outsourcing: Turning Minorities into Foreigners," builds upon the discussions of time in the making and policing of national boundaries by explaining how the UAE and Union of the Comoros developed a codified legal status that renders people permanently "temporary." It shows how upgrades in ID documents can create critical junctures for authorities to expand or contract the boundaries of the citizenry using the depoliticized language of identity management. I show how the MOI in Abu Dhabi used the transition from paper identity documents to a digital national ID system in 2008 to consolidate the exclusion of domestic minorities. By adopting the strategy of offshoring, elites in Abu Dhabi were able to circumvent the citizenship decisions of Dubai and the Northern Emirates, effectively turning some of their previously incorporated citizens into "guest workers." This chapter addresses alternative explanations (inclusion and expulsion) for the outsourcing of citizenship in a more detailed manner, drawing on evidence from interviews to explain how and why these passports have codified a new limbo status of permanent temporariness.

In the Conclusion, I return to the importance of limbo statuses as a citizenship outcome and summarize the key ways that temporal politics are critical to the codification of citizenship regimes and national boundaries. There are two key ways that political entities use time to construct and police national boundaries. First, when it comes to constructing

---

[27] Some sections in Chapters 3 and 5 on the role of the Ministry of Interior in citizenship cases draw on earlier insights from a previous publication (Lori 2011). These initial findings have since been deepened with a historical analysis of the British archives and updated with interviews.

national boundaries, countdown deadlines freeze a particular point in time to legally codify a population as the "native" population – after which everyone else becomes foreign or alien. Second, states also deploy time – and its miscounting – to police national boundaries. Political entities do this by developing legal maneuvers that separate the chronological advancement of the clock from the counting of time under the mantle of the law. What matters is not how much time a person has *actually* resided in a territory, but rather how that time is counted by the state. By pegging rights to a specific legal status, and counting the time of different statuses differently, states can suspend, slow down, or speed up chronological time in order to exclude, delay, or (conversely) hasten the inclusion of particular noncitizen residents. Temporary legal statuses allow states to delay or suspend the time of undesirable migrants while citizenship-by-investment schemes speeds up time for desirable (wealthy) migrants. This chapter returns to some of the comparative implications of limbo statuses, and identifies avenues for future research, arguing that this study of limbo statuses is relevant to contemporary debates about citizenship and migration across political contexts.

Finally the book includes a methodological appendix to provide additional information on the interview and archival research conducted for this book, as well as introduce readers to the legal advocacy that has accompanied this book to support some of the interviewees. To examine an ambiguously situated population of individuals who are neither foreign workers nor secure citizens, this work is based on extensive qualitative research in the UAE, drawing from 180 semi-structured in-depth interviews (2009–2011; 2012–2016) and over 3,200 archival documents. The interviews yielded rich ethnographic material that does not appear in this manuscript. The methodological appendix explains the reasons for this, expanding upon the changing political environment and calculation of risks to informants. As a result, when possible information from interviews was supplanted or replaced with information gathered from archival sources throughout the manuscript.

I

Limbo Statuses and Precarious Citizenship

The "offshore citizens" deal between the UAE and the Union of the Comoros is in many ways unique. The arrangement allows the UAE government to outsource national identity documents and formally create a permanently "temporary" class of noncitizens. The passport recipients are caught in a legal limbo between the official population categories of citizens and guests. But to what extent is this arrangement an example of a larger trend toward the adoption of legal statuses that suspend the question of national incorporation for certain groups? This chapter places the offshore citizens arrangement in comparative perspective by providing an overview of other categories of populations who are caught in a demographic boundary zone in between citizens and aliens.

I draw from recent studies on citizenship and migration in other regions to argue that the maturation of the nation-state system has – in addition to creating citizens and aliens – also systematically created demographic boundary zones of limbo populations. As states have monopolized the authority over legitimate interstate movement by building identity management infrastructures, they have also generated a proliferation of new visa categories and legal statuses that circumscribe and delimit access to citizenship. Since documentation is easier to resolve than larger questions of inclusion, the increasingly global drive toward identity regularization has (often inadvertently) produced a margin of people who lack access to permanent and secure citizenship rights. I use the concept of precarious citizenship to refer to people who are unable to gain access to secure citizenship rights and instead inhabit limbo statuses for protracted periods. Precarious citizenship is primarily experienced by two groups of people: (1) migrants who cannot accrue citizenship rights even after a protracted period of residency, and (2) internal "others" who are not recognized by the states in which they reside. People caught in this margin may hold ad hoc and temporary identity documents or they may lack any formal legal status; in either case they are unable to use documentation to "prove" their right to belong to a community and access citizenship rights in the long term. The type of identity documents individuals carry significantly impacts livelihood outcomes, because identity management infrastructures increasingly link travel documents to employment, education, housing, healthcare, and other public services.

Why do states produce ad hoc and temporary legal categories instead of either fully incorporating or expelling certain groups? Not all of those who experience precarious citizenship experience it because of a targeted policy of exclusion; limbo statuses can also emerge as an unintended consequence of identity regularization drives. Whether such statuses are produced to account for ethnic minorities, refugees, or labor migrants, in each case they represent short-term fixes for larger national dilemmas. Ad hoc and temporary statuses allow governments to address the immediate imperatives of identity management faster than they can resolve dilemmas about the boundaries of the national body politic. Limbo statuses allow decision-makers to circumvent constraints and placate competing factions that seek to expel or incorporate certain groups by evading rather than resolving the issue.

One characteristic that is common to all of the limbo statuses discussed in this chapter is the presence of constraints on a regime or executive branch's ability to fully expel a particular group. At times the source of these constraints may stem from international laws and norms, such as the norm of non-refoulement in the case of people fleeing conflict zones.[1] In the case of stateless or internally displaced populations, the constraint against full expulsion may come from the fact that the state lacks the infrastructural capacity to expel people, or quite simply that there is no clear place to deport people to. Constraints on decision-makers also often emerge from the domestic arena, such as competing stances on citizenship between political parties or elite factions (as in the UAE case), or as a result of challenges from a different branch of the state (such as the courts), or even from the local community (including immigration activists and civil

---

[1] Non-refoulement refers to the customary international norm of prohibiting states from expelling aliens who risk persecution if forced to return to their place of origin.

rights groups). In all of these scenarios, the regime or executive branch's desire to permanently exclude a population cannot be fully realized, and it is instead manifested in the creation of ad hoc and temporary statuses that are often renewed, but can also be revoked at any moment. The state's deployment of time in this way renders populations expendable, allowing authorities to respond to a specific group in flexible and contradictory ways.

This chapter begins by defining precarious citizenship as an outcome of limbo statuses. It then parses precarious citizenship into subtypes based on the documentary profiles of the individuals in each group – that is, what documents they have and how those documents align (or misalign) with the state's authorization of secure and permanent residency. This documentary lens is necessary because citizenship status must be proven through evidence. People who do not hold the right documents can be expelled from the territory even if they meet the legal conditions of citizenship in practice.[2] Secure access to citizenship means having all of the necessary identity documents to be able to benefit from citizenship rights domestically and to travel internationally. The four subtypes examined below include: (1) individuals who cannot gain national identity documents and become stateless; (2) individuals who may have one state's identity documents but who lack legal status in the state of their residence and thus become "illegal"; and a spectrum of groups with temporary statuses who are neither stateless nor fully unauthorized. Such groups include (3) individuals with temporary humanitarian protected statuses, and (4) temporary guest workers. Rather than being denied the authority to live in a state, these groups have temporary and circumscribed residency authorization.

1.1 PRECARIOUS CITIZENSHIP

I employ the overarching concept of precarious citizenship to refer to the structured uncertainty of inhabiting a limbo status and being unable to secure permanent access to citizenship rights.[3] The concept of precariousness has gained prominence in recent years, but the term dates back to at least the 1600s, and its early usages refer to a sense of

---

[2] For example, on the deportation of US citizens, see Stevens (2011).
[3] "Precarious citizenship" is used interchangeably with "precariousness" and "precarity" as synonyms for the outcome of inhabiting a limbo legal status.

insecurity related to bodily harm or the means of one's subsistence.[4] The term is now most commonly used to denote economic insecurity. Precariousness is used to describe the erosion of social protections and labor rights, including drops in average job tenure, increases in long-term unemployment, outsourced and temporary work, unsafe work, and the reduction of pensions and insurance (Waite 2011). Somers (2008) connects this form of precariousness to the concept of citizenship by arguing that marketization and neoliberal reforms have led to a growing number of people who are formally citizens being stripped of the social protections associated with citizenship, rendering them socially excluded and "internally stateless." While Somers focuses on the recent erosion of rights for certain groups who already have citizenship due to marketization processes, I deploy the concept of precariousness to focus on the challenges people face when trying to gain formal access to citizenship from the dimension of legal status. Taken from this view, precarious citizenship is not an outcome of recent neoliberal policy reforms, but rather a consequence of longer historical contestations over the boundaries of the national body politic. This status-centric approach to the study of citizenship privileges an examination of how legal rights are mitigated by the rules that surround who should have access to them.

Citizenship status is critical because "precarious legal status ... goes hand-in-hand with precarious employment and livelihood" (Paret and Gleeson 2016). In other words, uncertain legal statuses compound the effects of economic exigencies by rendering certain populations more likely to experience insecurity and uncertainty. The lived experience of having a precarious legal status can impact almost every aspect of an individual's life and can lead to, among other costs: psychological trauma; increased illness and loss of access to medical services; the inability to obtain gainful employment; the loss of secure, stable, and affordable housing; the loss of educational opportunities; the increased incidence of domestic violence; and significantly higher risks of being trafficked (as forced labor and, especially for women and children, in the sex industry). Because of the systematic impact of citizenship status on economic uncertainty, Paret and Gleeson argue that migration provides the best lens through which to understand economic inequality and how it is maintained in the global capitalist system. This focus on migration also

[4] "Precariousness," *Oxford English Dictionary*, 3rd edition (New York: Oxford University Press, 2007).

emerges in the definition of precarious legal status promulgated by the Upper Tribunal of the United Kingdom in its interpretation of section 117B of the 2002 Nationality, Immigration and Asylum Act.[5] The Tribunal's definition of "precarious" encompasses any legal status that is temporary and revocable, even when such status is valid and lawfully obtained.

While these definitions link precariousness to migrant deportability in general, this chapter focuses on precarious citizenship as an outcome of both migration and internal exclusion to account for the large number of people who fall into limbo statuses without ever crossing an international border. By grouping together both migrants and internal minorities, this definition of precarious citizenship is determined by the type of legal status an individual has vis-à-vis a state authority rather than whether or not one has migrated. The focus on the state's authorization of residency (or lack thereof), rather than the act of migration, is important for excluding some migrant groups from the definition of precarious citizenship.

Migrants are not all equally vulnerable. Precarious citizenship is experienced by migrants who cease to be migrants in the proper sense, i.e., they become long-term, de facto settled residents without accruing long-term rights (as opposed to, for example, seasonal migrants). These more settled groups of noncitizens can be usefully compared to the *bidūn* and other stateless minorities – while truly short-term economic migrants are a less relevant comparison group to whom the big questions and concerns of this book do not really apply. For example, many Western migrants who are commonly referred to as "expatriates" in the Gulf live and work in the region for relatively short periods of time, earning tax-free income and returning to their countries of origin (or a third country) without falling into a limbo status. Their experiences are closer to what scholars have labeled as mobility rather than migration (Bauböck 2017; Mau et al. 2015). In contrast to migration, mobility refers to the creation of expedited tracks for travel and residency for particular categories of desirable noncitizens. These arrangements are usually based on international treaties as in the case of European citizens living within the European Union (EU), and Gulf citizens within the Gulf Cooperation Council (GCC).[6] Falling

---

[5] *AM (S 117B) Malawi* [2015] UKUT 260 (IAC), at para. 4, headnote ("A person's immigration status is 'precarious' if their continued presence in the United Kingdom will be dependent upon their obtaining a further grant of leave").

[6] The Gulf Cooperation Council is a security pact between six member states: Bahrain, Kuwait, Oman, Qatar, Saudi Arabia, and the United Arab Emirates. The agreement allows for legal residency and work authorization for any citizens of these states across the region.

"in between" legal categories can be a marker of privilege if an individual is not clearly a citizen or an alien because they carry multiple citizenships and have the economic means to capitalize on citizenship-by-investment schemes (Shachar 2017). Contemporary border enforcement is thus shaped by a double movement of policies that use sophisticated legal tools to selectively restrict undesirable populations while accelerating the entry of desirable populations.

While it may be tempting to suggest that all wealthy or Western migrants are privileged and exempt from experiencing precarity, the key distinction between those who experience precarious citizenship and those who do not is not national origin, but rather an individual's status vis-à-vis a particular political authority. For example, Western migrants in the Gulf can experience precarity when their residency is protracted. Even at higher income levels, long-term residency with short-term rights creates its own set of challenges – such as when migrants are unable to own their own property and businesses and are forced to depend on local sponsors, who may capitalize on this dependency.[7] Ambiguous legal statuses are even more likely when there are multiple political authorities operating in the same space. For example, Simola (2018) finds that even the "mobile citizens" of the EU can experience precarious citizenship due to the mounting backlash and national policies that restrict intra-EU migration. In the absence of straightforward EU legislation and explicit government policies, administrative actors use their discretion to draw indeterminate boundaries enforcing conditionality and temporariness of status for EU citizens in precarious work arrangements, often increasing the pressure on them to take further precarious jobs.

This discussion undergirds the importance of time in the policing of national boundaries. What matters is not how much time a person has

---

At the time of publication, however, the political split between Qatar, on the one hand, and the UAE, Saudi Arabia, and Bahrain on the other has made travel and residency of GCC citizens more challenging (but not fully restricted).

[7] The need for *kafils* (national sponsors) has generated a parallel market for Gulf nationals who can earn an income by charging noncitizens for sponsorship affiliations while being silent partners on business ventures or property. In 2018, the UAE cabinet announced that it would abolish this restriction on foreign ownership and that noncitizens would soon be able to own their own property. It remains to be seen whether these restrictions will be lifted and whether all noncitizens will be able to own their own property. The UAE had already loosened some of these restrictions on high-income noncitizens/foreign investors by establishing "free zones" that allow for foreign ownership of property. Outside of such zones, all property and businesses must be at least 51 percent owned by a national sponsor (an Emirati citizen or majority Emirati–owned company).

resided in a state for but rather how that time is counted. In theory, migrants are assumed to experience a transition from being temporary to becoming permanent over time – migration is an act that should recede into the backdrop as time of residency progresses. However, in reality this act (migration) becomes a noun (migrant) that can cling to an individual over time and even over generations. In other words, in practice the transition from temporary to permanent must occur not only through the register of time as duration, but also on the level of changing legal statuses and requisite rights. The disjuncture between these registers of time means that for most migrants "in practice not only are the transitions often far from smooth, but also many people find themselves in prolonged liminal statuses" (Anderson 2018: 1). When duration loses its meaning, because one's time spent residing in a state is not counted toward accruing rights in that state, then the individual – whether a migrant or internal minority – is in a limbo legal status. At its core, precarious citizenship is thus an outcome of the fact that political entities routinely refuse to count the "time spent" of some their residents, creating "asynchronicities between subjective experiences of time and administrative requirements" (Anderson 2018: 13). A common thread across all of the categories of precarious citizenship presented below is the way that asynchronicities of time structure everyday life; limbo legal status is experienced as a protracted waiting – waiting for documents, waiting for resettlement, or waiting for authorization to be able to access the tools of a secure life, especially legal employment and residency.

1.2 THE RISE OF LIMBO STATUSES AND "IN-BETWEEN" POPULATIONS

What accounts for the proliferation of precarious citizenship statuses? This section provides an overview of why and how precarious citizenship is experienced by two groups of people: (1) migrants (including both migration "forced" by political conflict or natural disaster, and the argu-ably "chosen" path of clandestine economic migration); and (2) internal "others" who are not recognized as citizens in the state in which they reside. The literature identifies a range of variables that condition the experience of precarious citizenship – the structural, institutional, and individual factors that make insecure citizenship status (and the intensity of the risks associated with it) more or less likely.

The most common route to precarious citizenship is "unauthorized" movement or residency; that is, entering a state without the proper government authorization or overstaying the duration of one's authoriza-tion. Despite the risks associated with unauthorized entry and residency, millions of people migrate without authorization – often because they are forced to. While the speed and reach of human mobility have certainly increased over the past two centuries, this mobility is hardly "new"; what is relatively new is the criminalization of movement. By the end of the nineteenth and into the twentieth centuries, modern states monopolized the authority over legitimate movement into and out of their territories, aiming to settle mobile populations (Scott 1999; Tilly 1989; Torpey 2000). Whether driven by climate change, political conflict, or economic pressures, unauthorized migration – or more accurately state responses to unauthorized migration – challenges the ideal of a globally inclusive citizenship system. When displaced populations are unable to access dur-able solutions (repatriation, local integration, or third-country resettle-ment), they may face criminalization, becoming "illegal" immigrants or stateless persons. Instead of being formally incorporated, these popula-tions persist – sometimes over generations – with precarious citizenship statuses. The outcome is a vicious cycle: displacement creates illegality and in some cases statelessness, and those who experience protracted periods of precarity as illegal aliens or stateless persons are often forced to migrate for survival, creating even more displaced populations.

People can also be excluded from permanent and secure access to citizenship in the absence of migration if they are unrecognized by the states in which they reside. The current distribution of populations does not neatly align with the current configuration of the imagined national communities of sovereign states, and most (if not all) states encompass populations that do not fit into the dominant national narrative. While more scholarly attention has been paid to how and why states choose to incorporate or expel minority populations, for much of the twentieth century states have also been able to ignore their internal "others," thereby creating pockets of populations invisible in the state's legal self-image. Unlike the physically displaced, these populations disappear from their place of residence de jure, without crossing a border or leaving their place of birth. Examples include the Rohingya in Myanmar/Burma, Kenyan Nubians, and Dominicans of Haitian descent.

When states fortify their boundaries – by adopting biometric ID cards, diffusing internal identity checks, and strengthening border control – these minority populations become the object of intensive regularization. Identity regularization is a multifaceted process that for some can mean the issuance of an identity document, but for others can mean the loss of residence, bank accounts, and assets, and expulsion from the state. The global rise in boundary enforcement is itself part of the process that is exposing a growing number of people to the risks of precarious citizenship.

The UAE case illustrates how identity regularization drives can lead to statelessness. Individuals who were born in the UAE (without family books marking them as citizens) could reside in Dubai, Ras al Khaimah, Sharjah, and other emirates and gain access to state services during earlier periods of state-building (in the 1970s and 1980s) using birth certificates and other forms of ID. But by the time the identity regularization drive of the mid-2000s began, all of those who did not carry family books were eventually targeted by the federal government and registered as "stateless" *bidūn*. The UAE's "statelessness problem" was thus not due to an external exigency or crisis, but rather due to the federal state's own attempts to exhaustively count and categorize all residents in the country without expanding the boundaries of the citizenry.

To a great extent, structural pressures beyond the control of individuals account for the proliferation of statelessness and in-between statuses. Imperial breakdown, state formation, and restructuring can lead certain populations to be excluded from new political arrangements, thus generating precarious legal statuses and statelessness through the very processes of state-building (Štiks and Shaw 2013; Shevel 2011; Zolberg 1983). The expansion of the global labor force, rising levels of income inequality, and climate change are all examples of structural factors that stimulate migration and with it, precariousness. People are forced to move for a wide range of reasons, but the international legal framework on forced displacement only legitimates a small proportion of them through its focus on persecution. Under the 1951 Convention Relating to the Status of Refugees, a refugee is a person who has been targeted on account of their race, religion, nationality, membership in a particular social group, or political opinion. To meet this definition, an individual must be able to show that they were individually targeted for persecution because of their identity. The emphasis on individual persecution not only excludes many push factors of forced migration, such as generalized violence, it also requires a high burden of proof that can be difficult to meet, especially when people flee without identity documents. In response to the political and procedural challenges of asylum, states have developed a range of ad hoc legal statuses to fill the gap between the 1951 Convention on Refugees and the reality of contemporary forced migration.

The challenges of unauthorized travel and residence can be relatively manageable or unsustainably precarious, depending not only on individual resources but also on the strength of the host state's identity infrastructure and its incentives for enforcing legal status. Indeed, the very concept of "unauthorized" only makes sense vis-à-vis a political authority that has the capacity to check identity documents domestically as well as at national borders. The strength of an identity management infrastructure depends not only on a state's level of economic development but also on the robustness of its security apparatus and the role of public institutions in domestic migration control. Policing and monitoring occur not only at borders but also through schools, hospitals, and employers.

Global trends in international security, biometric technology adoption, and deportations have heightened state efforts to enforce citizen/noncitizen distinctions, increasing the risks of precarious citizenship. The heightened securitization of travel and domestic ID checks, particularly after the turn of the twenty-first century, has meant that deportations are reaching record highs in almost every world region (De Genova and Peutz 2010). As non-state actors eclipse interstate conflict as a major threat to international security, governments – particularly in the developing world – are facing mounting pressures to document their populations accurately and strengthen the infrastructure of their identity management systems. Development institutions like the World Bank promote the adoption of electronic identity management systems, and the first decade of the twenty-first century witnessed a proliferation of new population identification technologies. By 2010 there were 160 cases where biometric identification was adopted in developing countries for economic, political, or social purposes (Gelb and Clark 2013). This ubiquitous adoption of biometric identification coincides with unprecedented levels of mass displacement. The heightened security imperative to accurately categorize people thus comes at a time when more and more people do not neatly fit into preexisting national categories. With the new global security trends in identity management and the increasing dependence on digital governance, these irregular cases are brought to the fore to create a proliferation of statelessness globally.

Precarious citizenship is produced as an intended and unintended consequence of boundary-enforcement processes. In the next sections, I examine four groups of people who can be described as having precarious citizenship; for each, I show how state-building and regularization processes have worked to formalize, rather than alleviate or eradicate, the precarious legal statuses of these groups. The risks associated with precarious access to citizenship apply to all documentary profiles discussed in this chapter (stateless populations, unauthorized residents, or temporarily authorized residents), but there is variation across these statuses as some are more precarious than others. Individuals with temporary and circumscribed authorization experience precarity when they fall out of status and cannot gain access to permanent residency and citizenship for protracted periods. Stateless populations, on the other hand, find themselves in a permanent state of precarity – they have no authorization to either reside in their current location or travel. "Illegal" immigrants experience precarity only when they travel without authorization or overstay their visas, but the likelihood of being forced into this status is unevenly concentrated cross-nationally due to the hierarchies of the global visa regime. All of these groups experience precarious citizenship as an indeterminate waiting for citizenship that creates a generalized state of insecurity.

1.3 NO NATIONAL IDENTITY DOCUMENTS: STATELESS POPULATIONS

Those who are most at risk of precarious citizenship are the individuals denied national identity documents in their country of birth. This document may be a passport, or a different ID as states often use passports for the purposes of international identification and have separate systems for domestic identification. Stateless populations are often not "undocumented" – they can carry local documents (birth certificates, local IDs, or ration cards) but are considered stateless if those documents are not recognized by the ruling government as establishing citizenship. Statelessness is caused both by exogenous shocks like conflicts and imperial breakdowns, and by much slower boundary-enforcement processes like state-building and identity regularization.

It is not surprising that much of the early scholarship on statelessness focused on its association with the refugee cycle, interstate conflict, and state formation (Jenkins and Schmeidl 1995; Zolberg 1983). Zolberg develops "political persecution" as an analytic category and argues that mass displacement "arises most prominently as a by-product of the secular transformation of empires into nation-states" (Zolberg 1983: 24). By being denied access to national identity documents, stateless persons are deprived of the "right to have rights" (Arendt 1976: 296). Arendt, who coined this phrase, was particularly interested in how stripping people of citizenship rights served as a prelude to persecution –

paving the path to genocide. In the aftermath of World War II an international human rights framework emerged to protect people targeted for persecution because of their identity. Conflict, persecution, and forced displacement often result in statelessness, particularly when refugees are not integrated and cannot obtain identity documents either in their host country or in their state of origin. The current challenges that displaced Syrians face in registering their children born in Lebanon, Jordan, Egypt, Turkey, and Iraq provide a case in point (Dunmore 2014). Statelessness also occurs in the absence of state formation, conflict, or displacement. Perhaps counterintuitively, the stateless are not free-floating individuals; "the primary injustice of the stateless experience," writes Gibney, "is not that they cannot find a state to grant them citizenship but that the state which should grant them citizenship will, for various reasons, not do so" (2009: 50).

A key reason for the emergence of statelessness in the absence of displacement is the variation among citizenship regimes. Failures to show parentage or place of birth and conflicting state citizenship laws can put people in the position of being unrecognized by any state. In the Middle East, a key path to statelessness is the predominance of patrilineal citizenship. By making it so that only fathers can confer nationality to their children, patrilineal citizenship regimes often create statelessness, as, for instance, in cases where the father is a refugee, from an unrecognized minority, or absent.

More recent scholarship on statelessness has focused on how state-building and political restructuring can effectively strip minorities of nationality rights, expanding research to include situations of de facto statelessness. De jure statelessness is explicitly treated in the 1954 Convention Relating to the Status of Stateless People and the 1961 Convention on the Reduction of Statelessness. By contrast, de facto statelessness is a term developed in the literature to refer to individuals who were (at least at some point) formally documented by a state but continue to be systematically excluded from state protection and assistance. De facto statelessness lacks an international legal framework because states frame these exclusions as part of the sovereign prerogative to define the national body. De facto statelessness is often not produced by forced migration, but rather through the institutionalization of new nationality laws or the revocation of residency rights. For example, the cases of Slovenia, Kosovo, and other states of former Yugoslavia, demonstrate that political restructuring creates liminal and stateless populations (Blitz 2006; Štiks and Shaw 2013. Štiks (2010) illustrates how some groups of former Yugoslav citizens became post-Yugoslav aliens who had to go through a process of naturalization. In Slovenia, the young state's attempts to establish itself in opposition to Yugoslavia led to a campaign of national homogenization that created thousands of stateless persons. In the process of this campaign, "more than 18,000 former Yugoslav citizens were deleted from the Slovenian State register in 1992 and subsequently became known as 'erased persons'" (Blitz 2006: 2). These individuals were then deemed to be "illegal aliens" and had their residency revoked.

De facto stateless persons are not always actively targeted by the state for denaturalization; individuals can also become effectively stateless over time as they experience delays or refusals when attempting to renew identity documents. This becomes especially important when the infrastructure of the state develops to integrate identity checks into the provision of public services, so that individuals who could previously access education, healthcare, or public housing are no longer able to do so. While statelessness through displacement may occur rapidly, de facto statelessness through state-building is more incremental. As the discussion on Asian-Ugandan refugees in Chapter 5 illustrates, experiencing crisis-driven statelessness in one context does not immunize one from experiencing de facto statelessness in another – quite the contrary. Those who are in the "margins" do not cleanly fit into any state and their precarity is often compounded over time, across multiple legal contexts, and over generations. Where the concept of statelessness is not recognized, the de facto stateless can easily become "illegal immigrants." The colloquial reference to "illegal immigrants" presumes the bearer of the label to be a newcomer or foreigner, but locally born minorities can also fall into a state of illegality.[8] For example, the UAE's identity regularization drive in 2008 registered some individuals as stateless and others as "illegal infiltrators" who were subject to deportation. The boundaries between the stateless and those deemed to be "illegal" are fluid and based on the state's categorization of an individual at a given time rather than any fixed characteristic about individuals themselves. That is one defining characteristic of precarity; one's citizenship status is not secure, but fluctuates, and often not is a way that is controllable by the individual inhabiting these legal statuses.

---

[8] As a case in point, the *bidūn* in Kuwait are referred to by the government as "illegal residents." See, for example, Human Rights Watch (2015):3.

1.4 NO AUTHORIZATION: "ILLEGAL" IMMIGRATION

Individuals become "illegal" under the law of a state when they enter into or reside in a country without the proper authorization in the form of a valid passport and visa. Unauthorized migrants inhabit a precarious position when they are unable to draw upon any state's protections. They can face challenges procuring local IDs or national identity documents, registering births, and accessing social security benefits. Illegality only makes sense in reference to a state authority; people become "illegal" through an active process when the state criminalizes their presence in the territory. Studies have demonstrated how unauthorized immigrants can achieve various forms of social and civic integration despite being formally excluded. Irregular migrants are often integrated at the local level – in schools, churches, community groups, art collectives, and political associations (Chavez 1991; Coutin 2000; Holston 1998; Van Der Leun 2003). Moreover, instead of juxtaposing formal exclusion on the one hand with informal incorporation on the other, the dynamic of exclusion and incorporation "does not always pit formal law against informal practices or social resistance, but is often located within law itself" (Chauvin and Garcés-Mascareñas 2012: 243). Irregular migrants can be integrated into different parts of a state's formal institutions despite being otherwise "illegal" (Coutin 2000; Laubenthal 2011; Lewis and Ramakrishnan 2007; Menjivar 2006; Varsanyi 2010).

The term "illegal" is highly problematic when used to refer to people instead of actions, as the Associate Press noted when it excluded "illegal immigrant" from its vocabulary in 2013. Scholarship has moved away from the "illegal immigrant" as a reified category to pay attention to an analysis of "illegality" as a juridical status and sociopolitical condition (Andonova 2004; Coutin 2000; Heyman 2004; Ngai 2004; Willen 2007). Andersson (2014) examines the whole illegality "industry," including those who partake in policing and patrolling (border guards), caring and rescuing (aid workers), and observing and knowing (media and academia). This attention to the actors and processes that create conditions of illegality is key for showing that "becoming illegal" requires an active process of targeting on behalf of state authorities (often with the complicity and assistance of the private sector, NGOs, and intergovernmental bodies like the International Organization for Migration). In her work on the experiences of West African and Filipino migrants in Tel Aviv, Willen shows how a massive regularization campaign of arrest and deportation transformed these migrants from benign "others" into wanted "criminals" (Willen 2010).

While domestic security concerns often motivate such campaigns, foreign relations and external pressures can also lead states to regularize migrant populations and target "unlawful" residents. For example, Spain's entry into the European Union enabled the Spanish-nationality inhabitants of Ceuta and Melilla to become full citizens of the EU, while thousands of their ethnic Moroccan counterparts who had been living in those enclaves for decades became targeted as "illegals" subject to deportation (Barbero 2012).

While irregular migrants are often treated like criminals in these regularization drives, unlawful presence does not always take on the form of criminalization. This legal distinction is important for shaping how migrants are able to respond to such deportation campaigns. In the in United States, for example, unlawful presence (whether via unauthorized entry or visa violation) has been treated as an administrative violation. The fact that unauthorized migration is not formally criminalized has led US courts to conclude that deportation is not tantamount to punishment in the criminal context; this has thereby insulated the government from being constitutionally required to offer due process protections (e.g., appointment of counsel) in deportation proceedings.

One of the paradigmatic experiences of precarious citizenship is the lack of certainty; those who are deemed to be "illegal" face the danger of arrest on a daily basis once they have been targeted by the state. The next two categories of those with precarious access to citizenship also experience daily uncertainties, but they often oscillate from being authorized to being criminalized as "illegal." This is due to the fact that they have circumscribed and temporary authorization to reside in the state, and yet tend to inhabit these temporary statuses for protracted periods.

1.5 TEMPORARY AND CIRCUMSCRIBED HUMANITARIAN AUTHORIZATION: AD HOC PROTECTED STATUSES

The precarious status holders covered in this section are neither stateless nor "illegal"; they have temporary and circumscribed authorization to reside in the host country for humanitarian purposes. States have developed a plethora of temporary and ad hoc statuses to accommodate the large gap between those who are displaced, and those who meet the stringent criteria required for refugee resettlement. These ad hoc statuses highlight the long-standing tension between a state's right to control the makeup of its population, and the customary international norm of non-refoulement.

Many states have developed temporary statuses in response to the fact that most displaced people find themselves in "refugee-like" situations but are not eligible for refugee status as defined under international law. Examples of temporary statuses include exceptions made for rejected asylum seekers or reprieve from deportation because of unstable conditions in one's country of origin. At times these practices of temporary protection are codified, such as temporary protected status (TPS) in the United States, which Congress passed in 1990 (Frelick and Kohnen 1995). Temporary protection is also offered in Germany and Turkey, and, at least on paper, could be triggered in the European Union.

At other times these temporary statuses emerge informally, in the ad hoc practices of deferring deportation and exempting passports that cannot be renewed because of conflicts. The UAE, for example, is not officially a refugee-receiving state, but the rulers of Dubai and Abu Dhabi have sporadically and informally granted refuge for those fleeing humanitarian crises. This was especially the case during earlier periods of the UAE's state formation (the late 1960s and early 1970s) before the federation was fully consolidated. As such, the rulers of Dubai and Abu Dhabi granted refuge for those fleeing the Zanzibar Revolution in 1964 and Idi Amin's expulsion of South Asians from Uganda in 1972. From the outset, these groups did not have an official refugee status in the country, but were provided ad hoc and temporary documents that were continually renewed to allow these communities to gain access to services and settle in the country. (This policy continued until 2008, when these former refugees were grouped together with the *bidūn* and other minorities and issued Comoros Islands passports under the offshore citizens arrangement.) The UAE is not alone in creating informal mechanisms of temporarily accommodating those fleeing humanitarian crises. More recently, for example, all of the Gulf states created informal accommodations for Syrian refugees. The largest population of Syrians in the Gulf is in Saudi Arabia, which is also not officially a refugee-receiving state. The Saudi Arabian government has in some cases diluted the restrictions of the *kafāla* system to allow Syrian residents to bring their families to join them and renew their work permits despite being unable to renew their Syrian passports. Saudi Arabia therefore accepts fewer refugees than other host states in the region, but it also provides them with a status that allows for their legal employment, while most host states prohibit refugees from working.[9]

---

[9] For an analysis of how many Syrians were accepted by Saudi Arabia and other GCC members states, see De Bel-Air (2015). According to the Saudi Foreign Ministry, Saudi

While ad hoc and temporary humanitarian protections emerge out of humanitarian and political concerns, they often have the unintended consequence of placing individuals in a position of structural ambiguity for a protracted period. The research demonstrates how people with temporary protection often oscillate from being authorized to becoming "illegal" – both in cases of formally codified and informal protected statuses. For example, in cases of informal temporary protection, individuals are often forced between living as a "refugee" inside a refugee camp (protected from arrest and deportation but without the freedom to work or move) or as an "illegal" immigrant outside the camps (able to move and work in the informal sector but vulnerable to exploitation as well as arrest and deportation) (Frelick 2014). At times forced migrants can also gain the right to legally reside as temporary workers in the host state. Frelick explains that refugees can work legally in Thailand if they choose *not* to claim refugee status and instead present themselves as migrant workers to the Thai Ministry of Labor. This can lead to the acquisition of a temporary work visa and permit (valid for two years) that can be renewed once (Frelick 2014). For migrants who cannot return home claiming asylum can lead to a rejected application and deportation, but being strategically silent can allow for temporary reprieve from deportation.

The existing research demonstrates that individuals can also face this structural uncertainty even in contexts where temporary protection is formally recognized. For example, in her research on Central American migrants under TPS in the United States, Menjivar argues that they are neither documented nor undocumented but rather fall into a gray area in between legal statuses (Menjivar 2006). TPS is not asylum because it is explicitly designed to not be an avenue for permanent residency.[10] Rather, it is a stopgap measure to protect designated nationalities from being deported during times of armed conflict, natural disasters, or "temporary and extraordinary" conditions. While asylum is individually determined, TPS is granted to all nationals of a designated country, as a "blanket"

Arabia has hosted more than 2.5 million Syrians from 2011 to 2015. However, as De Bel-Air notes, because none of the Gulf states systematically release demographic data on the national origin of noncitizens in each country, it is very challenging to actually verify government claims about how large the Syrian population is (or disentangle how many of those Syrians were already present in the Gulf before the crisis began).

[10] The law explicitly precludes TPS holders from adjusting to lawful permanent residence (LPR) status: Immigration and Naturalization Act, § 244(h). Individuals who are on TPS may qualify for asylum – but by law one may apply for asylum only within the individual's first year in the United States. Because asylum processing is lengthy and cumbersome, immigration judges and applicants alike often opt for TPS despite its limitations.

form of relief for people who face reasonable threats but are not individually persecuted. Though TPS was set up as a temporary measure, TPS designations have become increasingly protracted since it was established. Because TPS is not meant as path to permanent settlement, each extension of TPS works to lock beneficiaries in "a 'legal limbo,' rendering them unable to fully integrate into life in the United States" (Bergeron 2014: 22). Menjivar argues that a state of "liminal legality shapes different spheres of life" for these migrants, not just constraining livelihood outcomes but also shaping social networks and family, the place of religious institutions, and artistic expression (Menjivar 2006). They are neither "legal" nor "illegal" because they are neither fully recognized as economic migrants nor political refugees; at times they are treated as refugees and granted temporary relief from deportation, and at other times their permits are not renewed and they fall into being "illegal" migrants again.[11]

1.6 TEMPORARY AND CIRCUMSCRIBED EMPLOYMENT AUTHORIZATION: "GUEST" WORKERS

Another form of temporary and circumscribed authorization that may lead to precarious citizenship exists in the sphere of transnational labor mobility. In many other cases, guest workers comprise only one subset of inward migration flows, but in the UAE (and remainder of the GCC states), temporary employment is the main (and only) official way that noncitizens can reside in the country. Work visa categories are designed with the host state's labor market needs in mind, rather than the needs of the migrant. Low income temporary visa workers are more vulnerable to exploitation of their labor, and rarely have recourse to legal mechanisms for adjusting their status to permanent residency. In such situations, and where migrants have spent the bulk of their lives outside of the state of their citizenship, formal citizenship may lose its function as a guarantee of political and legal belonging or source of protection against rights violations.

---

[11] As a case in point, this oscillation between amnesty and illegality has been recently illustrated by the case of El Salvadorans in the United States. President Trump's administration has terminated El Salvador from the TPS list (effective September 2019) for the first time since it was placed on the list of protected countries in 2001. This move renders members of this community illegal and subject to deportation – including people who have resided in the United States for 18 years (over three times the duration of what is formally needed for acquiring citizenship if they were counted as legal permanent residents).

Guest worker programs are designed to increase the supply of labor without increasing the number of permanent residents. As expanded upon in Chapter 4, this design rarely maintains coherence in reality because migration that begins as temporary quickly takes on a more permanent quality as governments struggle to control settlement once workers have entered the country. As one migration scholar put it, "there is nothing more permanent than temporary foreign workers" (Martin 2001: 1).

When it comes to the vulnerability of those with temporary work authorization, regime-type differences are important because the presence of liberal democratic institutions, particularly courts and civil rights organizations, can allow individuals with insecure status to leverage different resources within the state to gain legal status. This is exemplified in the way "temporary" workers in Europe were able to gain permanent residency and citizenship rights, while such formal inclusion is foreclosed for long-term "temporary" workers in the Gulf. In the case of postwar migration to Western Europe, migrants were able to move from temporary work authorization to more permanent residency statuses and gain political rights at the local level (Hammar 1990). These reforms occurred despite what were often heated and racialized political battles about the growing number of foreigners, especially postcolonial minorities, in places like the United Kingdom, and France (Feldblum 1997; Paul 1997).

In contrast, the lack of checks and balances in authoritarian states allows them to seal off naturalization policies from scrutiny as a realm of national security. The large oil producers in the Gulf all have citizenship policies that entitle citizens to redistributed wealth but make it nearly impossible for "guest" workers to obtain citizenship. Foreign residents are treated as "temporary" workers regardless of the duration of their residency. Instead of becoming legal permanent residents after long periods of residing in a state, migrants in the Gulf become permanently deportable – their authorization for remaining in the country is always conditional and circumscribed.

Vora's (2013) work on Indians in Dubai demonstrates that the disenfranchisement of Indian residents is produced both by the policies of the autocratic UAE and the democratic state of India, which does not extend NRI (nonresident Indian) statuses to Gulf populations in the way it does to the Indian diaspora in the West. Vora shows that while Indians are legally temporary "guests," the Indian community has existed in Dubai for over a century and its members are into their second, third, and in some cases even fourth generation. Moreover, she demonstrates that the day-to-day management of migrants habitually falls to elite foreign employers and managers (who recruit employees through migration chains from India). Elite noncitizens frequently act as proxies for their citizen business partners, who often exist on paper only. Vora refers to this practice as "substantive citizenship," since in governing other migrants Indian elites legitimize the state and perform a responsibility delegated to Emirati citizens. This informal – yet systematic – dependence upon noncitizen *kafīls* (national sponsors) in the governance of other noncitizens is critical to the longevity of the guest worker program as a whole. It shows that certain noncitizens enforce the very citizen-noncitizen divide that excludes them, effectively becoming "part of the production of the state's authority" (Vora 2013: 113).

It may be tempting to limit the political importance of foreign residents to major migrant-receiving countries like the UAE or assume that the regularized exclusion of certain laboring bodies is tied to the "exclusionary" practices of authoritarian states. However, a review of the literature demonstrates that limbo statuses are found across regime types and world regions. When these current practices of conditional inclusion and limbo statuses are considered alongside the plethora of studies showing how democracies have systematically withheld citizenship from domestic populations (especially native populations, slaves, and racial minorities), it becomes clear that migrant incorporation is contentious because at stake is power itself. Incorporation changes the distribution of power in a society (whether that power is voting rights and electoral distributions or the right to assets and services and a distribution of material well-being).

1.7 CONCLUDING REMARKS

The notion of precarious citizenship offers one approach to systematizing the experiences of the large number of people across the globe who cannot gain access to secure and permanent citizenship statuses. This chapter identifies four forms of precarious citizenship, arguing that in each case, precarious citizenship is produced as an intended and unintended consequence of boundary-enforcement processes. Ambiguous and temporary statuses are growing because they represent a strategic government response to avoid resolving dilemmas about citizenship (especially questions about the incorporation of minorities, refugees, or labor) by postponing those decisions, perhaps indefinitely. Moreover, the very processes of boundary enforcement (biometric ID management, ID regularization, and deportation drives) have pulled more and more people into the documentary power of the state system without providing them a secure place within it.

To what extent does precarious citizenship emerge because of intentional state strategies to conditionally include certain populations versus being an unintended outcome of overlapping policies and prerogatives that are not consciously aligned? This chapter illustrates that limbo statuses are both an outcome of conscious political strategies and an unintended consequence of boundary-enforcement processes. It brings together recent scholarship on a wide range of groups who are unable to gain access to citizenship as a legal status; individuals in these groups are stateless or inhabit a liminal position "in between" legal statuses. For these individuals, exclusion from the national body politic occurs not just through crisis-driven forced expulsion, but also through the gradual institutional forces of state-building, standardization, and centralization.

Though larger global pressures drive migration, people fall into precarious statuses because of state policies – not depoliticized economic forces. Ad hoc and temporary statuses are proliferating because they provide political elites with a means of avoiding larger dilemmas about the boundaries of the nation. Drawing from across world regions and regime types, this chapter shows that by holding people in a pending status for protracted periods, states often create the very ambiguity in legal status that challenges a government's ability to have a comprehensive registry of the entire population and place everyone into a discrete category. Precarious citizenship is thus a direct result of boundary enforcement: the drive to strengthen boundary enforcement may be motivated by a desire to eliminate undocumented or uncertain legal statuses, but it often achieves the opposite, reifying uncertainty in the legal status of migrant and minority populations. This uncertainty has gradually crystallized as a constitutive ambiguity in the legal status of an increasing number of people across the globe.

2

Making the Nation: Citizens, "Guests," and Ambiguous Legal Statuses

2.1 THE MAKING OF AMBIGUOUS CITIZENSHIP STATUSES

This chapter provides the historical context for the creation of Emirati citizens, guest workers, and a gray zone of people who do not clearly fit into the state's official citizen/alien binary. This historical analysis is used to illustrate how – in addition to creating citizens and noncitizens – national foundings and state formation processes also produce demographic boundary zones of ambiguously and conditionally included individuals. Using the British records to examine the creation of a common immigration and citizenship policy in the UAE, this chapter shows that ambiguous citizenship statuses emerged historically because of a disjuncture between the more restrictive incorporation practices of Abu Dhabi on the one hand, and the more expansive incorporation practices of the remaining emirates on the other. As Abu Dhabi has slowly monopolized its power over the federation, its more restrictive understanding of citizenship has been adopted as the national policy, creating gaps in the coverage of citizenship laws for minorities who were incorporated by the remaining emirates.

In the early state-building period, seven ruling tribes united under the leadership of Sheikh Zayed Al Nahyan, the ruler of Abu Dhabi. A state form was imposed on a set of political kinship structures, which immediately produced disputes over territory and border, citizen and noncitizen, allegiance and treason, and state nationalism and heterodox nationalisms. While the founding pact of the union granted the rulers of each emirate the authority to determine who is and is not a citizen, the Ministry of Interior (MOI) in Abu Dhabi now effectively controls this domain. Abu Dhabi constructed this hegemony over time at the federal level through oil, luck, leadership, wealth, and good initial starting conditions that only became useful at later and different conditions. The official primordial nationalism seen today with its procedural emphasis on bloodline and allegiance can be traced to this period of intense struggles over categorization. Strategic primordialism is a mechanism of political competition, along with the notion of purity that inevitably comes out of such processes. The process of codifying and institutionalizing tribal allegiances produced and formalized the new state's "citizens" and "noncitizens." Grafting this state form, a square peg, onto the round hole of Gulf networks of merchant capital with its diasporic, eclectic, non-territorial logics led to the creation of a demographic boundary zone of ambiguous legal statuses.

In 1971 the UAE was founded on a federal bargain, and all units but Abu Dhabi created a formal rule for incorporation, while Abu Dhabi adopted an informal practice of withholding citizenship and keeping cases pending. This delaying tactic was adopted due to the fact that Abu Dhabi's vision of the citizenry was more ethnically homogenous than that of Dubai or the Northern Emirates. I argue that the stances of the different rulers on who should be nationally incorporated was largely determined by two key economic factors: (1) the economic activities of each of the emirates (referred to as Trucial States prior to 1971) and (2) the sources of income to the rulers. When economic development is based on mobile assets and trade (as they are in Dubai), ruling elites are likely to adopt expansive incorporation practices that encourage the mobility of capital and labor. In the case of Dubai, this included abolishing visas for key trading partners and issuing passports to facilitate the travel of merchants. When, on the other hand, economic development is based on a fixed asset like oil (as in Abu Dhabi), ruling elites are likely to adopt more restrictive incorporation practices, including greater barriers to citizenship and migration controls. In the case of Abu Dhabi, this meant restricting citizenship only those Arab tribes who could trace their lineage in the territories to 1925, before oil was discovered. This gap between the different approaches to national incorporation produced a gray zone of people who were locally incorporated but excluded from the national citizenry.

This chapter is primarily based on the archives of the *Records of the Emirates* (hereafter BRE; see the methodological appendix) from 1938 to 1971, with most of the analysis based on the records from 1961

onward, when oil revenues increased the stakes of citizenship and immigration policies.[1] The multiple volumes of this collection, published in
1990, 1992, 1997, and 2002, collate all of the British records of the
Emirates from all of the respective branches of the British government,
particularly from the Foreign Office in London, the political residency of
the Gulf (first located in Bushire and then in Bahrain), and the political
agencies in the Emirates (first in Dubai only, and then in Dubai and Abu
Dhabi after 1966).[2] Since all of the archival materials in this chapter are
culled from one broad source (the British authorities), it does not aim to
provide an exhaustive history on the state formation of the United Arab
Emirates. But since the British agency had jurisdiction over foreigners,
this source is appropriate for illustrating how the current migration
system was erected and how resident "foreigners" were carved out and
distinguished from the "citizens" of the new state. For the sake of
coherence and legibility, the in-text parenthetical citations refer to
the year and page number of the BRE collection.

2.2 THE DEMOGRAPHIC COMPOSITION OF THE EMIRATES

The United Arab Emirates occupies the southeast corner of the Arabian
Peninsula. It borders the Persian Gulf waters to the north and northwest,
Oman to the east and southeast, Saudi Arabia to the west and southwest,
and Qatar to the northwest. The federation stretches from Abu Dhabi, its
capital in the west, to Fujairah in the east. Formed in 1971, the union
comprises seven administrative political units: Abu Dhabi, Dubai,
Sharjah, Ajman, Fujairah, Umm Al Quwain, and Ras Al Khaimah
(which acceded to the union in 1972). Until the eighteenth century these
territories were a part of Greater Oman, which extended from south
Qatar to the Indian Ocean, comprising the Sultanate of Oman and the
Emirates. While European colonial powers could never penetrate the
territories' arid and inhospitable desert interiors, the Gulf shores enticed
colonial powers as a key waterway for trade between Europe and Asia. In
the early sixteenth century (shortly after Vasco da Gama discovered the
trade route to India) the Portuguese sent their armies to seize control of the

---

[1] Petroleum was first discovered in the UAE in 1958 in the Umm Shaif field of Abu Dhabi.
[2] Within the British administration, the Trucial States were first under the jurisdiction of the
government of India, before the Foreign Office took over following the demise of the India
Office with Indian partition and independence. On April 1, 1948, the Foreign Office
assumed all responsibility for the residency and agencies in the Gulf (BRE 1946–1948).

coasts, setting up military forts and crushing rebellions for the following 100 years. By the early seventeenth century, the British fought with and eclipsed the Portuguese to dominate the region, especially after the establishment of the East India Company in 1600.

In the early nineteenth century, British dominance was temporarily weakened by the coordinated efforts of the Arab tribes on the southern shores of the Gulf. There were two major tribal coalitions that fought the British, the Qawasim, a maritime power that controlled the territories of today's Sharjah and Ras al Khaimah, and the Bani Yas federation, which controlled the territories of today's Dubai and Abu Dhabi. After protracted battles, the British naval forces succeeded in quelling the rebellions, and forced the tribal chiefs (*shaykh* pl. *shuyūkh*) to adopt a maritime treaty called the General Treaty of Peace in 1821 (Al-Muhairi 1996). The series of treaties that followed culminated in a maritime truce in 1853, after which the territories of today's UAE came to be known (in British sources) as the "Trucial States," "Trucial Coast," or "Trucial Oman."[3]

From the early nineteenth century until 1971, the tribes of the Gulf shoreline lost their independence to the British forces. The British policed the area and controlled its foreign relations, while granting the tribal *shuyūkh* internal autonomy in dealing with their own populations. The Trucial agreements were brokered between the British and five Trucial States in 1853, which only became seven in 1866 after the Qasimi sheikhdom broke down into Sharjah, Ras al Khaimah, and Fujairah. This division of political authority between the British and tribal *shuyūkh* was formalized in the Trucial States Order in Council of 1946.

Despite centuries of external intervention and trade, official nationalist narratives paint the UAE as an ethnically homogenous space prior the discovery of oil. In the official discourse the UAE is, above all, an "Arab" nation, and this is promulgated in article 6 of the federal

---

[3] Some British sources treat these truces as paternalistic agreements that the British adopted to "protect" the region's inhabitants from piracy (Kelly 1968; Lorimer 1915). This tendency depicts the Arabs along the Gulf shores, especially the Qawasim, as being engaged in violent looting that aimed to disrupt international trade in the Gulf, Red Sea, Arabian Sea, and Indian Ocean from the end of the eighteenth century into the first two decades of the nineteenth century. This view fits into a larger discourse equating Arab tribes with a proclivity for violence and blood lust. This historical narrative is challenged by others who have pointed to the seizing of assets as the rightful resistance to the encroachments of colonial powers (Al-Qasimi 1986).

constitution: "the UAE is a part of the greater Arab nation to which the UAE is linked by the ties of religion, language, history and common destiny. The people of the UAE are one people, and a part of the Arab nation" (Federal National Council 2010: 6). Much of the media coverage and scholarly literature about the UAE's demography has tended to take such nationalist claims of "Arab purity" at face value, attributing its current cosmopolitanism to the rapid demographic inflows that accompanied the country's post-oil economic development since the 1970s. The dominant historiography paints the UAE as a "rags-to-riches" story of an impoverished desert prior to the discovery of oil; the main characters of the UAE's formation are the Arab tribes and the British, with only passing references to the ethnic minorities who were integral to the UAE's pre-oil economy and demography (Al-Fahim 1995; Davidson 2005; Heard-Bey 1982). More recently, historians and anthropologists of the Indian Ocean have excavated the historical networks of travel and trade between the Persian Gulf, South Asia, and East Africa to show that the Gulf shoreline was an ethnically heterogeneous and polyglot space for centuries prior to the discovery of oil (Ahmad 2012; Allen 1981; Al-Sayegh 1998; Bishara 2012; Bose 2006; Das Gupta 2004; Ho 2004, 2006; Onley 2007). In the following subsections I examine the largest minority groups who were present in the UAE prior to the influx of guest workers postindependence: the Persians; East Africans; and Indians, Pakistanis, and Baluchis.

2.2.1 Persians

Of all of the minority groups present on the Trucial Coast, perhaps none is more intertwined, or contentious, than the Persians. Concerns about ethnic purity and the dilution of bloodlines through Arab and Persian miscegenation precedes state formation in the Gulf, but the rise of modern nationalism and ever-deepening political rifts between the Iranian and Arab states have hardened these boundaries. Nonetheless, Arab and Persian populations have intermingled for centuries. The Gulf waters (still bitterly contested as "Persian" or "Arabian") separate the southern shores of Iran and the northern shores of the UAE by only 120 kilometers (75 miles) (see Figure 2.1).

This is a distance very easily traversed by boat. Indeed, prior to the erection of stronger border controls in the late twentieth century, merchants and laborers could easily make the round-trip journey from one

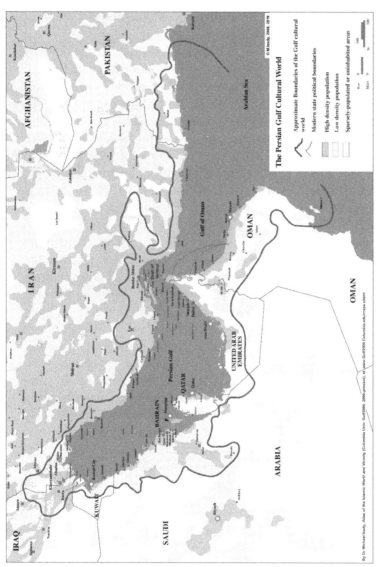

FIGURE 2.1 Gulf littoral cultural world[4]

4 Source: Dr. Michael Izady at http://gulf2ooo.columbia.edu/maps.shtml. This particular map was created by Izady to depict the Gulf littoral zone as a civilizational unit and is also used in Potter's *The Persian Gulf in History* (2009). Potter calls for a holistic approach to Persian Gulf history that incorporates both sides of the shoreline, demonstrating the imbrications between Arab and Persian populations.

side of the Gulf to the other on the same evening.[5] This has led to interlinked kinship ties across the shores of the Gulf (Najdmabadi 2010).

Maritime historians like Pearson (2006) have argued that while histories often draw the boundaries of communities on the national scale, "shore folk have more in common with the other shore folk thousands of kilometers away on some other shore of the ocean than they do with their immediate hinterland" (353–354). The lack of an infrastructure of roads connecting the southern shoreline to the interior of Iran meant that, prior to the twentieth century, there was greater trade across the Gulf than with other districts inside Iran. As Najdmabadi explains, "communications and commerce between the Iranian coastal settlements and their Arab neighbors were often more effective and frequent than with the Iranian interior. For example, it was easier to import foodstuffs into Gavbandi from across the Persian Gulf than from the centre of Iran. In exchange, the Iranians exported meat and dried fruits to the Arab coast" (2010: 22). It is thus perhaps not surprising that in Najdmabadi's research on southern Iranian migration to the Arab Gulf states, she finds that "given the historical entanglement of the two regions, these migrants actually feel less marginalised in Arab countries than when travelling to places in the interior of Iran" (2010: 21). Prior to the heightening of border controls with the national formation of the Arab states in the 1970s and the Iranian Revolution in 1979, the Gulf shorelines were intertwined economically, culturally, and even politically.

Between the middle of the eighteenth century (during the Zand dynasty) and the rise of Reza Shah in the 1920s, Arab tribes controlled the Iranian coastal region in service of the Iranian government. The central government in Tehran did not have the infrastructure to effectively project its power to its southern territories, and after being further weakened by internal conflicts, it entered into contractual security agreements with Arab tribes like the Qawasim (descendants from the ruling families of today's Sharjah and Ras al Khaimah) to police the southern shores (Hawley 1970; Najdmabadi 2009, 2010). There was a mutual

---

[5] As Potter explains: "in his autobiography, Essa Saleh Al-Gurg, an Arab from Lingeh whose family moved to Dubai after World War I (where he became a leading businessman and diplomat), relates a family tradition of family dinners when relatives from Sharjah and Ras al Khaimah would cross the Gulf in time for the evening prayer and, after dinner, return to the Arabian shore, arriving around midnight. Today, Iranian smugglers from Bandar Abbas who sell sheep and goats in Khasab, on the Musandam peninsula of Oman, and bring back cigarettes to Bandar Abbas can make the trip in as little as 45 minutes in a fast boat" (Potter 2009: 5).

dependency between the Iranian government and the chiefs of Arab *shuyūkh*. In exchange for providing security, the *shuyūkh* "had the right to levy taxes on all revenue sources of the local population: agricultural products, livestock and goods imported into the harbours" (Najdmabadi 2010: 22). This arrangement was halted by the rise of Reza Shah in 1924–1925. While a few districts of south Iran are still heavily economically dependent upon the Arab Gulf states, the consolidation of Iranian nationalism in the 1920s and 1930s marked the beginning of the erection of modern boundaries between the northern and southern shores of the Gulf.[6] This triggered successive waves of migrations from south Iran to the UAE and other Arab territories.

The first major migratory wave occurred from 1930 to 1935, when Reza Shah's government ended the agreements with Arab tribes and monopolized levies and trade tolls. These political and economic pressures led Arab families (including large merchant families) to move back to the Arab side of the Gulf, contributing to an economic decline in the shoreline districts of southern Iran. Other political changes during this time, including mandatory conscription and regulations revoking Islamic clothing, were also push factors for emigration from Iran to the Arab side of the Gulf. A second migratory wave occurred in the 1970s after the oil boom led to an increase in labor demand in the Arab Gulf states. Finally, a third wave occurred in the wake of the Islamic Revolution of 1979, when Sunni Iranians in particular emigrated to the Arab (Sunni) states (Najdmabadi 2010).

The position of Persians in the Arab Gulf became increasingly precarious as political tensions with Iran heightened. National identities and the myth of purity on both sides became more seductive in the wake of greater political insecurities. For the Arab Gulf states these perceived security threats included not only Iranian nationalism under the Shah, but also the specter of Arab nationalism and Marxist revolution in Oman (1962–1969), the Iranian Revolution (1978–1979), the Iran-

---

[6] The dependency of the southern areas of Iran on the Arabian side of the Gulf is documented by Najdmabadi who finds that the district Gavbandi (in the province of Hormuzgan) is still deeply connected to the Arab states of the Gulf: "Until 2000 almost 80 percent of Gavbandi's population profited from the remittances provided by migrants who had emigrated with their immediate family members in order to establish a new life in the Arab countries but who still felt responsible for relatives and villages left behind" (2010: 19). These remittances went beyond supplementing the income of families in Iran; they also funded the district's infrastructural development, leading to the construction of cisterns, mosques, hospitals, and school facilities.

Iraq War (1980–1988), the first Gulf War (1990–1991), and Iran's territorial claims over Bahrain and UAE territories (the Tunb Islands and Abu Musa). Political impasses between central governments have ripple effects on their populations across the shores, even after generations of settlement.

On the Arab side of the Gulf, these political pressures have led to the erasure of Persian cultural and linguistic roots and the Arabization of Persian populations. This goes beyond the exclusion of Persian populations from the national museums or the renaming of Persian architectural spaces as "Arabian" or "Islamic" – it also impacts how populations are externally identified and self-identify. For example, historian Ahmed Al Dailami examines the construction of the population category of the "Hawala" – a category that encompasses many of the large and entrenched merchant families in the UAE (especially Dubai) as well as Bahrain, Qatar, and Kuwait. As a category, the term means "literally, 'the wanderers' or 'those who transform'" and it refers to "a category of identification whose spoken root lies in an act of transference from Arabia to Iran and back" (Al Dailami 2014: 300). In other words, this group is yoked together by a common narrative of departure to Persia and then of return to Arabia. Instead of treating this group as a primordial and stable community of people, Al Dailami argues that it should be understood as *a claim to authenticity*, to being Arab as opposed to Persian, necessitated by, and increasingly encoded within, the postcolonial state-building projects of the Gulf at particular historical watersheds" (Al Dailami 2014: 301, emphasis in original).

Importantly, while there are families who have this particular lineage – Arabs who settled in south Iran and then returned to the Arab side of the Gulf – the category has now swelled to include the much larger population of Persians settled in the Arab Gulf who have adopted this identity to create a space for themselves within a national imaginary that views the only legitimate citizens as ethnic Arabs. As Al Dailami explains, assimilation meant the erasure of heterogeneity and "impurity." As colonialism and nationalism made it increasingly undesirable to be of Persian descent in the Arab side of the Gulf:

the result was that another category of people, far more numerous than the historic or "real" Arab Hawala, began to speak of themselves as such. They were the large community of Sunni Persian speakers from the south of Iran, who until then had been satisfied to speak of themselves as *Ajam*, the generic term in the Gulf for Persians or Persian speakers. (Al Dailami 2014: 311–312)

The Hawala category was especially convenient for the large numbers of Sunni Iranians from the south who, after 1979, found themselves as part of the "'wrong' sect in Iran and the 'wrong' ethnicity in Arabia" (Al Dailami 2014: 314). The ability of these families to narrate themselves out of this precarious position has much to do with how they are eventually externally identified and documented by the state. While some families successfully gain citizenship in the UAE and other Gulf states, others come to be at the center of heated contestations about how the national body will be defined – contestations that have even higher stakes once formal citizenship becomes connected to the distribution of oil rents.

2.2.2 East Africans

Africans, especially East Africans, comprise another large population of non-Arabs with significant roots in the Gulf. With the notable exception of Bilkhair's (2006) article on Afro-Emiratis, Africans have been made largely invisible in the Arab-centric histories of the UAE, despite the fact that records suggest that Africans accounted for 28 percent of the Trucial Coast's population in 1905 – the largest in the Gulf at the time (Lorimer 1915: 1437, reprinted in Hopper 2015: 9).[7] The extensive trade between East Africa, the Persian Gulf, and South Asia meant that large numbers of Africans moved to the Gulf shores, many of them as slaves in a trade that survived well into the twentieth century. Enslaved Africans in the Gulf tended to come from coastal East Africa and the islands of Zanzibar and Pemba, and their ethnic origins are from Tanzania, northern Mozambique, Malawi, and eastern Congo (Hopper 2015). While the dominant historical narrative about Indian Ocean slavery is that the British Royal Navy eliminated the trade in the aftermath of the slave trade treaties of 1873 (Clarence-Smith 1989), more recent research has challenged this narrative to show that the slave trade continued to thrive for almost a century after its formal abolition by the British (Hopper 2015; Mathew 2012). Slavery was still a documented problem in the UAE in the 1960s, as evidenced by the fact that the Trucial States

---

[7] The UAE (at that time Trucial Coast) hosted the largest African population in the Gulf at the turn of the twentieth century. Africans comprised 11 percent of Kuwait's population, 22 percent of Qatar's population, 11 percent of Bahrain's population, and 25 percent of Muscat and neighboring Mutrah's populations (Oman) (Hopper 2015: 9). See Lorimer 1915: 238–241, 489–490, 1058–1077, 1382–1451.

Council issued a joint decree calling for the abolition of slavery in the Trucial States in 1963.

This slave trade continued to survive past its formal abolition for several reasons. Mathew argues that the "abolitionist efforts neglected the smuggling traffic, condoned those slave transactions which resembled kinship transactions and privileged British businesses in transactions of 'free' labour" (2012: 140). He explains that the British experiences with transatlantic slavery meant that they fundamentally misrecognized the slave traffic in the Indian Ocean, expecting large slave markets and shackled cargo. The British navy thus often disregarded the broker-centered traffic that was how most labor transactions were made, over-looking the fact that slaves were often the free-moving crews on the dhows they were being transported in.[8] The substantial traffic in women and children continued to grow throughout the abolition treaties, and their trade was often legalized through adoptions and marriages. In addition to the challenges associated with the enforcement of the abolition treaties, slave labor was also inextricably linked to the Gulf's export production and the region's position within the global capitalist system.

Far from being an impoverished and underdeveloped space prior to the discovery of oil, the Gulf region's economy expanded significantly in the nineteenth century to meet the global demand for pearls and dates. Ironically, "some of the same countries that pushed for the abolition of slavery were also the largest consumers of the commodities produced by slave labor" (Hopper 2015: 9). Between the 1860s and 1920s, both the date and pearling industries expanded, and slaves from East Africa comprised a critical part of the labor force behind both commodities (Hopper 2015; Ricks 1989). The United States became the Gulf's largest foreign consumer of dates, and the US demand was met by importing greater numbers of slaves from East Africa to do the work of watering, tending, harvesting, and packing dates. Africans also formed the backbone of the pearling economy, with slaves accounting for half of the Gulf's diving population. Slave labor was in even greater demand in the nineteenth century as pearls found new markets in Europe and the United States (in addition to the more established markets of India and the Middle East) (Hopper 2015).

Japan's introduction of cultured pearls, in combination with a global recession, led to a decrease in the African slave trade in the Gulf by the 1930s (although cases of slavery continued to be reported into the 1950s

---

[8] Dhows are wooden lateen-rigged sailboats used in the Gulf and Indian Ocean.

and 1960s). While subsequent waves of African migrations did occur (such as after the Zanzibar Revolution in 1964), these flows were relatively small. The discovery of oil in the late 1960s and the development plans of the 1970s led to a spike in demand for labor, South Asians eclipsed Africans as the main labor source.[9] The existing African populations were largely assimilated into the Gulf states, carrying the names of the Arab tribes they were held by, and identifying as ethnic Arabs (Bilkhair 2006; Hopper 2015).

2.2.3 Indians, Pakistanis, and Baluchis

While much of the attention on South Asian migration to the Gulf focuses the vast numbers of laborers who have moved to the region since the discovery of oil, mobility between the Indian subcontinent and the Gulf shoreline extends back for centuries. Migration from Greater India occurred through preexisting networks of trade and commerce, and instead of being disrupted by the British imperial presence, it expanded under the British Raj and its Arabian frontier. The British encouraged Indian migration by privileging the movement of British subjects within its sphere of influence (Kumar 2012; Onley 2007, 2017). Migration from the Indian subcontinent preceded the partition of Greater India, and prior to the mid-twentieth century migrants were not categorized by national origin but by their ethnicity, geographic region, or religion. Thus national origin categories like "Indian" and "Pakistani" are ahistorical for examining the roots of migration flows from the Indian subcontinent to the Gulf. For example, when taking stock of the population of the Trucial Coast shoreline in 1905, Lorimer uses ethnic and religious categorizations to provide a census breakdown, listing the number of Baluchis, Hindus, Khojahs, Muhammadans (i.e., Muslims), and Persians (Arabized or not).[10] However, for the purposes of categorization, I loosely divide these groups into Indians (Hindus and a wide variety of religious, linguistic, and ethnic groups from provinces that become part of the Republic of India post-partition), Pakistanis (largely Muslims who come from

---

[9] See the next chapter for an explanation of why there is a preference for South Asian migrants over Arab migrants.
[10] "Besides the foregoing there are about 1,400 Baluchis at Dibai Town, Ghallah and Ras-al -Khaimah; 1944 Hindus at Abu Dhabi, Dibai, Umm Al Quwain and Sharjah Towns; 214 Khojahs or other Indian / Muhammadans at Dibai, Ras-al-Khaimah and Sharjah Towns; and Persians, some Arabicised and some not, about 2,400 at Abu Dhabi and Dibai Towns, Khor Fakkan and Ghallah" (Lorimer 1915: 1436–1437).

provinces that are later part of Pakistan), and Baluchis (who are some-times referred to in the historical records as a distinct ethnicity, and at other times categorized as Pakistanis, or Persians, or even Arabs). The migratory patterns of these groups to the Gulf differed both prior to and with the British presence. These distinctions are important because how migrants are categorized and identified in the records and census data shapes whose legal jurisdiction they fall under, what rights and protec-tions they may claim, as well as their eventual citizenship status.

There are a variety of reasons behind Indian migration and settlement in the Gulf. In examining migration flows from 1820 to 1947, Kumar (2012) finds that Indians moved to the region for three main reasons: as merchants and traders, labor migrants, or hajj pilgrims. Merchant dia-sporas of Gujaratis, Parsis, Sindhis, Bohras, Lohanas, Bhatias, and Khojas were already well entrenched in almost all of the port cities of the Gulf shoreline by the 1830s (Pearson 1998). During the late nineteenth and early twentieth centuries, Indian merchants were especially concentrated in Dubai and Sharjah. After the Persians, they comprised the second largest merchant community in Dubai and the northern shoreline of the Trucial States with stakes in the pearl trade, gold, and the banking sector (Kumar 2012; Ray 1995).

The presence of Indian merchants also led to inflows of Indians laborers through interethnic and kinship ties. Vora's work (2013) explores how elite and middle-class Indians have been critically involved in the recruit-ment, settlement, and repatriation of other Indian migrants. Through these informal networks, generations of families have settled in the UAE, especially in Dubai. Indeed, as readers familiar with Dubai will recognize, there are spaces of the city that are culturally much more Indian than Emirati, so much so that one of Vora's book's recurring themes is that while Indian foreign residents disavow formal citizenship in the Emirates, they simultaneously also stake claims on Dubai as "an extended city of India" (2013: 71).

In addition to the trade connections between India and the Gulf, the British imperial presence also encouraged Indian migration to flourish. As Onley (2007) and Kumar (2012) document, the British employed large numbers of Indians in their Gulf protectorates and conferred upon them the special status of being a "British subject," "British citizen," or "British protected person."[11] Indian merchants (mainly Bani Yas and Khojas)

---

[11] Changes in British laws in the metropole have a ripple effect on those under British jurisdictions in its colonial holdings. The distinctions between these categories of

were employed as native agents in service of the British Empire. And many other Indians were brought in as laborers to support the Gulf residency structure and maintain British hegemony, doing the work of soldiers, cooks, houseboys, water-carriers, sailors, sweepers, and gardeners, among other jobs (Kumar 2012: 60–61; Onley 2007: 53). The British political controls created economic and political advantages for Indian merchants over Persians and Arab merchants and shielded them from the jurisdiction of the Trucial State rulers:

> As British protected persons, Indians were entitled to the same treaty privileges that British merchants enjoyed in the Gulf ... The benefits of British protection included exception from search of private property, exemption from local taxes, right of full discharge from creditors if declared bankrupt, British assistance in recovering debts, British official representation in any local trial and exemption from direct interference by local authorities. (Kumar 2012: 61)

As oil prospecting began on the Arabian side of the Gulf in the mid- to late twentieth century, increasingly larger flows of Indians migrated to the region and filled clerical, skilled, and semi-skilled manual occupations (Birks and Sinclair 1980; Seccombe and Lawless 1986). The British actively promoted the employment of Indians as British subjects over Persian, Ottoman, and Arab migrants for fear of challenges to their sovereignty over the Gulf. The British desire to maintain hegemony in the Gulf led to the establishment of nationality controls on migrant flows, with much emphasis placed on ensuring that the labor imports of oil companies were mostly from India.

The religious pilgrimage of hajj provided another reason behind the large flows of migrants from the Indian subcontinent to the Arabian Peninsula, specifically to Mecca and Medina. While religiously motivated, the pilgrimage is an immense commercial as well as a religious enterprise that generated lucrative business ventures for those who facilitated the movement of migrants and provided goods and services to migrants along the routes. This trade also flourished inside Mecca and Medina, and many pilgrims used their religious passage to establish a more permanent presence in Saudi Arabia, catering to new flows of hajj pilgrims from the Indian subcontinent. The advent of the steamship had a decisive impact on

British citizens, subjects, and protected persons are really only solidified in the late twentieth century, especially after the British Nationality Law of 1981. See the government's definition of these distinctions at www.gov.uk/types-of-british-nationality/british-protected-person. For an explanation of how the British nationality laws in the postwar period led to retrenchments in citizenship, see Paul (1997).

the pilgrimage from British India. With maritime travel being no longer dependent upon the monsoon cycle, pilgrim traffic increased exponentially. As Kumar explains, "while previous generations of pilgrims were confined mainly to elite officials, wealthy merchants and the *ulama*, after the introduction of the steamship the hajj also became accessible to ordinary Indian Muslims of modest means" (Kumar 2012: 66). The significantly lower cost of travel thus changed the demographics of the pilgrims, making the route accessible to larger swaths of the society.

In addition to migrating to the Gulf as merchants, laborers, and religious pilgrims, a third group from south and central Asia – the Baluchis (or Baloch) – have also had a long and intertwined history with the Gulf shores due to their roles as mercenaries and their involvement in Indian Ocean slave networks. It is difficult to quantify the Baluchis by either their common ethnos or a common language; "based on available statistics, the total number of Balochi speakers may amount to around 10 million. Possibly just as many regard themselves as Baloch by ethnic descent but do not speak Balochi" (Janahi 2014: 5). The largest number of Baluchi speakers is found in Pakistan (6–7 million), and there are also approximately 1.5 million Baluchis in Iran. The greater geographic area of Baluchistan stretches across Pakistan, Iran, and Afghanistan. In the late nineteenth century Baluchistan was divided between Persia, Afghanistan, and British India. Political and economic interests – rather than cultural composition – shaped the resulting break-up of this territory, and the new borders aligned with the Goldsmid Line (1872) and the Durand Line (1893). The Goldsmid Line separating Persia and British India was particularly important for the British interests in protecting the British telegraph line, which had reached the port city of Gwadar in 1863 (Janahi 2014: 20). In addition to this concentration of Baluchis across three countries in South and Central Asia, estimates suggest that close to 2 million Baluchis live outside of this area in Oman, Turkmenistan, the UAE, Bahrain, Kuwait, India, and parts of East Africa (Janahi 2014: 5).

There are competing narratives about whether Baluchis are "originally" Persian, Desi, or Arab; these disagreements illustrate how ethnic identification is driven by the politicization of identities rather than the unveiling of a primordial "truth" about the origins of a community. As Janahi explains, in the official discourse of Iran, Baluchis are narrated as "Aryan/Iranian," with the argument that Baluchi is a dialect of Persian. On the other hand, "there is a strong inclination among the Baloch across the Persian Gulf to identify as Arabs and to 'return to their original Arabic language'" (Janahi 2014: 7). Meanwhile, after the partition of India, Baluchis came to be associated with Pakistan, due to the fact that "Baluchistan" is now one of the four provinces of Pakistan and the country hosts the largest number of Baluchi speakers.[12]

There are several reasons for the migration of Baluchis into the Arab Gulf states. First, Baluchis were historically recruited as soldiers in the region, especially as part of the Omani Empire, and this trend has continued with their recruitment into the military forces of the Arab Gulf states (Al Ameeri 2004; Nicolini 2007; Peterson 2013). Baluchi mercenaries were an integral part of Bu Sa'id's military force when the Omani Empire extended its control from the Gulf of Oman toward the east coast of Africa in the first half of the nineteenth century (Suzuki 2013). This martial role continued over centuries. As Peterson explains:

> Baluch mercenaries have served as soldiers and armed retainers in the service of more than one Gulf ruler, but especially the rulers of Oman, where their presence has been recorded with the Ya'rubi imams in the sixteenth and seventeenth centuries. Recruitment directly from Baluchistan continued well into the twentieth century in Oman and Bahrain. (2013: 232)

This recruitment of Baluchis by the Omani forces was partially facilitated by the historical connection between the port city of Gwadar and Oman, since Gwadar was under Omani control from the 1792 until becoming part of Pakistan in 1958 (Al Ameeri 2004; Peterson 2013). Oman's first modern organized army unit – the Muscat Levy Corps – was entirely Baluch in composition when it was formed in 1921. Indeed, "because of the preponderance of Baluch, the language of command was Urdu and remained so until the unit was absorbed into the SAF [Sultan's Armed Forces] in 1958" (Peterson 2013: 236). Baluchis came to be associated with military prowess, and were actively recruited to help the Omani Empire's expansion to East Africa, and later fill the ranks of the military and police forces across the modern Gulf, especially in Oman, Bahrain, the UAE, and Kuwait.

While this martial role is well documented in the historiography of the Gulf, less studied is the role that the Baluchis have played in the slave trade, as both slave brokers and slaves. Suzuki (2013) examines the British records from 1829 to 1951, finding that 23.4 percent of the slave

---

[12] Indeed, in several of my interviews with civil servants in the UAE, Pakistani and Baluchi were used interchangeably. The *bidūn* were explained away as "Pakistani Baluchis" who entered into the country illegally, rather than viewed as an older minority who had been in the Gulf prior to the formation of the modern UAE or Pakistan.

statements in the archive involve Baluchi slaves. In his analysis of the network of cases, Dubai emerges as a central node in this trade. This is because "it was through Dubai that the Baluchis passed most frequently during their enslavement. Around 15.1 percent of passages went through Dubai – probably owing to Dubai's location: close to a number of pearl banks, it had already begun to be a regional hub, and no British representatives were stationed there" (Suzuki 2013: 216–217). Instead of studying the Baluchis through a preset geographic frame, he uses these slave narratives to show how this diaspora is threaded through every port of the Indian Ocean, linking South Asia and East Africa with the Persian Gulf and Arabian Peninsula.

This overview of three minority groups illustrates that the Trucial coastline hosted a diverse population prior to the discovery of oil. These groups were not transient visitors but rather settled communities who were deeply intertwined with the region's economy.

2.3 PROTO-STATES ON THE COASTLINE: MULTIPLE AUTHORITIES AND JURISDICTIONS

If the Trucial States were home to a multiplicity of ethnic groups prior to national formation, then there was also a multiplicity of actors who had the jurisdiction and political control over these groups and determined their rights. These rights included which laws applied to individuals, which courts had jurisdiction over them, who issued their travel documents (and whether they were subject to mobility controls), property rights and inheritance laws, as well as which levies and taxes they had to pay. Today, there are only two official population categories of residents in the UAE: citizens and "guest workers." Instead of assuming that all the "guests" arrived as temporary workers after national formation, in this section I show how the legal categories of "citizen" and "foreign resident" were carved out of the existing populations based on which jurisdiction a particular group fell under. Far from being mutually exclusive categories, there were often overlapping and competing claims to jurisdiction that led to the creation of gray zones of belonging.

2.3.1 Precursor to "Citizens" versus "Guests": The Order in Council

In broad strokes, the populations who became UAE "nationals" were those who fell under the jurisdiction of the different Arab tribes in the division of power with the British, while those who fell under British jurisdiction, regardless of their duration in the country, became "guests" when the nation-state was formed. The British government and the Arab tribal chiefs (*shuyūkh*) of the Gulf coastline adopted a series of maritime truces from 1821 to 1853. These agreements gave the British authorities jurisdiction over the "external affairs" of the *shuyūkh*, including jurisdiction over those who were considered to be "foreigners" in their territories. While it is tempting to view the Arab tribes in a monolithic manner with the emergence of Emirati nationalism, the records reveal that there were significant differences and competition between the tribes. Lorimer's Gazetteer illustrates a complex panoply of the important political actors in these territories, showing that at the early twentieth century "the people of Trucial 'Oman belong to numerous distinct tribes; indeed, the country is tribally one of the most composite and perplexing in the Persian Gulf" (Lorimer 1915: 1431). Lorimer goes on to provide a census of 44 distinct tribes in 1905. And while these tribes were externally grouped together by British sources, referred to as the Trucial States or Trucial Oman, they were externally united only through their relationship with the British and did not necessarily self-identify as one unit. Indeed, at the turn of the twentieth century these territories did not have a general name in Arabic: "the region in question consists of the actual possession of the Shaikhs of 'Ajman, Abu Dhabi, Dibai, Umm-al-Qaiwain and Sharjah and of the territories of the tribes who, in fact or in theory, are directly subject to their influence; but in Arabic it has no general name" (Lorimer 1915: 1427). The fact that the British authorities had to develop separate agreements with the ruling tribes illustrates that, prior to the discovery of oil, there was no singular political authority that could adequately consolidate its power over the entire territory. Populations shifted between competing tribes for political and economic gains.

While the division of jurisdiction began as an informal practice with the establishment of the maritime truces, oil prospecting heightened the need to codify the realms of influence over resident populations in the territories of the Trucial States. As oil companies began prospecting for oil from the 1930s onward, the British became increasingly concerned with codifying their role over foreigners entering the country. British authority over migration flows was connected to control over economic penetration (and power) in the Trucial States. As early as 1938, in anticipation of new inflows of British and "non-Moslem foreign subjects" with the oil prospectors, the British India Office in London began instructing the Political Resident of the Persian Gulf (then based in Bahrain) to codify British jurisdiction over foreigners. "Even at present the Shaikhs seem to recognise in some rather vague manner that we have a shadowy jurisdiction over British subjects, and we could make use of this later to approach them in the blandest possible manner with a view to 'putting the matter on a more definite basis'" (BRE 1938: 168). This tactic of codifying jurisdiction in the "blandest possible manner" worked well, and by 1945, a series of letters were exchanged between the British Political Resident in Bahrain, the rulers of Dubai, Abu Dhabi, Ras al Khaimah, Ajman, Sharjah, Umm Al Quwain, and the regent of Kalba to set the basis for the codification of split jurisdiction.[13] The British framed this move as a mere formalization of their jurisdiction over foreigners that had been "a custom since olden times" (BRE 1945: 158). All of the rulers formally consented to "maintaining this custom" and by 1946 the division of jurisdiction was codified in the Trucial States Order in Council.

The Trucial States Order in Council defined the key political actors with jurisdiction and political authority over the different populations residing on the Trucial Coast. This document identified seven legitimate Arab tribal rulers and codified British jurisdiction over four different subsets of the resident population. The first was "British subjects," defined as such in the British Nationality and Status of Aliens Act of 1914.[14] The second category included "British Protected persons," defined as any person who is not a British subject but is deemed to have his majesty's projection in the Trucial States. The third category includes any corporation incorporated under the law of any part of his majesty's dominions, protectorates, protected states, or mandated territories. Finally, the Order in Council granted the British jurisdiction over all "foreigners," defined as any person, or corporation, who is not a British or Trucial States subject (BRE 1946: 170).

The Order in Council specified that local rulers could not permit the residence of any foreign agent without British consent, and could not grant any oil concession without British approval. The British used nationality controls to try to prevent the Americans from gaining a commercial and political foothold in the region. As oil prospecting began in earnest in the 1930–1940s, companies recruited foreign workers

---

[13] Kalba was a Trucial State from 1936 to 1951 before being incorporated into Sharjah. Kalba lies just south of Fujairah, which is currently an emirate of the UAE but was missing from the Trucial States in the Order in Council. Fujairah is the only emirate that has no coastline along the Persian Gulf (only on the Gulf of Oman) and it established treaty relations with the British (joining the other "Trucial States") in 1952.

[14] Or in the case of those born prior to 1914, any person who is a British subject under the common law and acts that preceded the Nationality act.

to bring in skills that the local population did not have. The British used the Order in Council to shape the composition of the immigrant workforce through the terms of the oil concessions. With the exception of Al-Hasa (eastern Saudi Arabia), the British monopolized the commercial contracts of the entire Arabian side of the Persian Gulf. The British authorities claimed jurisdiction over all foreigners who entered into the territories. As a result, the migrant workers recruited by British oil companies were largely sourced from other British holdings, particularly the Indian subcontinent, while in Saudi Arabia the American oil companies recruited labor from a broader array of locales, including the Italian settlements in Eritrea (Seccombe and Lawless 1986).[15]

The Order in Council was designed to allow the British to prevent opposition to their hegemony in the Trucial State territories. In addition to codifying British jurisdiction over all foreigners, the Order in Council provided a foundation and legal basis for deporting any foreigners who wrote, sold, or otherwise circulated any written materials that were considered seditious against the British or Trucial State rulers.[16] This document reveals a pattern of associating migration with an economic and political threat. The assumption that migration inherently poses a security threat appears as a continuous thread in the British records of the colonial era; this assumption also continued to drive the UAE's policing strategies after national independence.

With the codification of the Order in Council, two types of disputes over jurisdiction emerged. The first type of disputes involved cases of conflicting claims between the Trucial State rulers and the British about whether particular groups of residents should be considered Trucial State subjects or "foreigners" who fell under British jurisdiction. The binary division of the population that was codified on paper was much more difficult to enforce on the ground, especially when it came to Persians and other Muslim minorities. The second type of disputes involved cases of Arab tribes with unclear allegiance to various Trucial State rulers, with contestations arising between rulers about whether or

---

[15] To the disappointment of the British authorities, the American oil companies also gained oil concessions in Bahrain and (in partnership with a British company) in Kuwait. For a history of the American role in oil prospecting in the region see Vitalis (2009).

[16] Any materials "calculated to excite tumult or disorder, or to excite enmity between persons subject to this Order and the Trucial Sheikhs or their subjects, or between different classes of person subject to this Order, or between the Trucial Sheikhs or their subjects, shall be deemed to be seditious matter within the meaning of this Article" (BRE 1946: 180).

not a particular tribe belonged on their roster. If oil prospecting heightened the need to codify the realms of authority of the British and Trucial State rulers, it also created an imperative to clearly define the jurisdictional boundaries of each of the Trucial State rulers over their constitutive populations. The concessionary agreements with oil companies dictated that the usage of a particular area by a certain tribe was translated into territorial possession for the ruler that tribe recognized. Unsurprisingly, the development of the oil industry thus led to a series of heated disputes between the Trucial States over which tribes constituted their subjects.

2.3.2 Precursor to Ambiguous Legal Statuses: Disputes over Trucial State Subjects versus British Subjects

While the Order in Council carved out the political jurisdiction over the "foreigners" and "natives" residing in the Trucial States, census categories are political and social rather than natural classifications. In practice, different authorities could (and did) claim jurisdiction over the same people, and individuals could (and did) claim to belong to competing authorities for strategic purposes. The category an individual fell into had a direct impact on their legal rights. If an individual was a "foreigner" who fell under the jurisdiction of the British, then they could refuse to appear in the rulers' courts or accept their judgment. British subjects could opt to appear in the rulers' courts in civil matters, but were explicitly prohibited from appearing in local courts on criminal matters.

The potential for disputes over the definition of who was a foreigner appears in the initial discussions between the different factions of the British bureaucracy in preparation for the Order in Council. In a telegram to three British officials (in London, New Delhi, and Bahrain), the Political Resident in Bushire admitted that "it would be impossible to persuade shaikhs to cede jurisdiction over Moslem foreigners" (BRE 1939: 135). He calculated that the Trucial State rulers would likely concede jurisdiction over British subjects and non-Muslim foreigners, and would hand over any "enemies" from these groups to the British. However, he rightly predicted that, despite British claims to jurisdiction over the Persians and other Muslim migrants, the Trucial State rulers would challenge the British and consider these populations as Trucial State subjects and not foreigners. The British nonetheless claimed jurisdiction over Muslims from other countries until 1959, when the concession was officially made to acknowledge the jurisdiction of Trucial State rulers over all other Arabs and Muslims.

The question of jurisdiction over Persians was more complicated. Dubai and some of the northern Trucial States had large numbers of resident Persians, including wealthy merchant families, and they had a strategic interest in counting this population as Trucial State subjects. The question of the status of Persians on the coast is exemplified in a 1946 exchange between the Political Resident of the Persian Gulf in Bahrain, Geoffrey Prior, and Political Agent in Bahrain, A. C. Galloway. The Political Resident explained that while the British would like to claim jurisdiction over all residents who are not Trucial State subjects, "there are, however, numbers of Persians domiciled in the Trucial Coast and it is possible that, as at Kuwait, the Rulers regard them as Trucial subjects. Please report if in fact this is the case and, if so, whether the number involved is large" (BRE 1946: 165). In response, the Political Agent Galloway reported that there was a significant resident population of Persians in the Trucial States: "it is estimated that Persians form 40 per cent of the total population in Dubai, 25 per cent in Sharjah and Kalba, 10 per cent in Abu Dhabi, and about 5 per cent in other Trucial States. The majority of these have been born on the Trucial Coast and are regarded by the Rulers as Trucial subjects" (BRE 1946: 166). A significant number of these Persians were born on the coast, regarded themselves as Trucial State subjects, and carried Trucial State passports. Another group of Persians (not included in the above census breakdown) received Trucial State passports from some of the rulers, after fourteen years of residency, to facilitate their travel to India. According to Galloway, in 1946 this latter group of "Persians do not regard them-selves as Trucial subjects and are not so regarded by the Trucial Shaikhs. Only 82 of these passports have been issued so far" (BRE 1946: 166). Galloway ends the correspondence by suggesting that the nationality law not be addressed yet, and that the British should treat all Persians not born on the coast as foreigners from now on: "this will automatically bring them within the jurisdiction of the Order-in-Council" (BRE 1946: 166). There were thus different tiers of Persians in the Trucial States: some of them were Trucial subjects, some of them carried Trucial State identity documents but were not considered subjects, and yet others were considered foreigners who fell under British jurisdiction. By 1946, this population thus straddled the native/foreigner divide, an ambiguity that later became instantiated in the nationality and citizenship laws that separate the UAE's citizens from its "guests."

In addition to the challenge posed by Persians, clearly delineating jurisdiction became difficult when it came to the status of Pakistanis and other populations from South Asia after the partition of Greater India. As a British official in the Chief Court in Bahrain asserted in a letter to the British Political Agent in Abu Dhabi, "I do not really see how we can avoid insisting that all Pakistanis etc. are under our jurisdiction and so long as they remain so they have the right to expect our protection" (BRE 1969: 336). The real issue was whether a subject could provide the necessary identification to prove which legal category they fell under:

As most of the Pakistanis in Abu Dhabi are, I imagine, illegal immigrants, they are unable to prove easily that they are Pakistanis and if, in fact, they are Baluchis they could, I suppose, have Iranian nationality. We have at the moment a very difficult case on our hands in Dubai in which a Baluch was convicted of murder by the Ruler's Court some years ago and is now claiming to be a Pakistani. In fact he probably is, but he will have the greatest difficulty in proving it .... I do not of course mean that a Pakistani loses his rights simply because he is an illegal immigrant, but if we claim jurisdiction and are challenged, we have to be able to prove the nationality. (BRE 1969: 336–337)

The presence of these kinds of cases in the records points to the fact that – even before this division of jurisdiction was translated into the current categories of citizens and guest workers – the boundary between native and foreign populations was often nebulous, contested, and politically charged. Rather than the "true" origin of an individual, the key factor that determines whether one will gain access to a particular set of rights is ultimately how an individual is documented and counted by a political authority.

2.3.3 Disputes over Jurisdiction: The Codification of Tribal Allegiance

In addition to disputes over whether or not an individual was a foreigner or a Trucial State subject, disputes emerged between the Trucial State rulers over which tribes constituted their subjects. Oil prospecting heightened the need to clearly define the membership of each of the Trucial States because the concessionary agreements with oil companies dictated that usage of an area by a certain tribe translated into territorial possession for the ruler recognized by that tribe. In addition to the resources the ruler could gain from oil rents, the codification of tribal membership was important because rulers paid subsidies to their tribe members in exchange for allegiance. Without proper documentation individuals could potentially receive subsidies from and declare allegiance to more than one authority.

This redistributive aspect of tribal authority preceded the discovery of oil, but the stakes increased significantly because of this precious resource. As such, by the early 1950s, "tribal allegiance to one Ruler or another – at all times the most important issue in tribal politics – became the subject of a great deal of probing and research" (Heard-Bey 1982: 54). To settle territorial disputes, the concerned parties sought to collect as much evidence as possible on the wandering habits and allegiances of tribes, and on the number, habitat, occupation, tax payments, seasonal movements, and other questions regarding the settled or seminomadic population.

While oil prospecting started in all of the Trucial States, the vast majority of the UAE's oil reserves are found in Abu Dhabi, which controls 85 percent of the UAE's oil output capacity and more than 90 percent of its oil reserves (Butt 2001). Abu Dhabi's fiscal dominance within the union only began to appear in the late 1960s and early 1970s after prospecting attempts in the other Trucial States were primarily unsuccessful. Abu Dhabi's oil rents grew especially after Sheikh Zayed Al Nahyan replaced his brother Sheikh Shakhbut Al Nahyan as ruler of Abu Dhabi in 1966.

As oil wealth trickled in, families from elsewhere in the Trucial States began to migrate and declare allegiance to the ruler of Abu Dhabi. There were increased job opportunities and greater financial benefits associated with belonging to Abu Dhabi, such as stipends and housing allowances. In an illustrative dispute from 1969, the ruler of Ras al Khaimah (RAK), Sheikh Saqr Al Qassimi, sent some of his security forces to intercept vehicles from Dubai and Sharjah that were loading the luggage of 100 people from the Jazirat Al Za'ab area in RAK to relocate to Abu Dhabi. They had heard that every male Abu Dhabi citizen would receive a stipend and house. The ruler of RAK arrested some members of this group for changing their tribal allegiance, and forbade their emigration without proof that they had the agreement of their families and were not leaving any debts. He also announced that they would not be able to return on their own terms and that all who left the territory would have to a letter from Sheikh Zayed announcing that he would accept them into Abu Dhabi (BRE 1969: 379).

Contestations over allegiance were particularly important when it came to counting populations who inhabited border regions between Trucial States or areas with significant water or oil resources. In 1961, Dubai and Abu Dhabi agreed to a British delineation of their common frontier, but by 1962 there was a reemergence of the Abu Dhabi/Dubai border dispute. In 1965, a dispute about the maritime boundary between Dubai and Abu Dhabi became especially heated because the extent of the Continental Oil Company's concession was at stake. Another one of many border disputes also arose at Dibba (a key site of maritime trade historically) between the Trucial States of Sharjah and Fujairah and the Sultanate of Oman. Indeed, contestations between Trucial States over specific tribal groups or territories were so common that by 1964 the British helped set up a central court to deal with cases of mixed Trucial jurisdiction.

The British records give some indication of how rulers responded to the fact that multiple allegiances among tribes created tensions within the nation-state formation process. Once it became clear that the oil holdings were monopolized by the rulers of Abu Dhabi, the question of multiple allegiances no longer created disputes over identifying which ruler should receive the oil rents, but instead generated a new problem of internal migration to Abu Dhabi. Sheikh Zayed appears to have attempted to alleviate these tensions by discouraging the depopulation of any one Trucial State. He encouraged those who moved to Abu Dhabi to leave their families behind and began diverting Abu Dhabi's resources to finance the establishment of security forces and state institutions in the remaining emirates to support economic growth outside of the capital.

In the years leading up to the formation of the union, the rulers were concerned with maintaining state rights and preventing the depopulation of any one Trucial State. For example, in 1967 a dispute emerged between Sheikh Zayed bin Sultan Al Nahyan of Abu Dhabi and Sheikh Rashid bin Saeed Al Maktoum of Dubai because of a number of Dubai families who were transferring their allegiance from Dubai to Abu Dhabi. This prompted Sheikh Rashid of Dubai to complain to the British that Sheikh Zayed was attempting to gain possession of the wells used by those tribes. Sheikh Rashid demanded that Sheikh Zayed return the firearms (rifles) that he had supplied to those families. In a letter to the British Political Resident in Bahrain, the Political Agent in Abu Dhabi reported that Sheikh Zayed's response to the incident was to assert that:

[T]here should be freedom of movement and employment around the Trucial States for the subjects thereof but that he had made it clear to people from elsewhere in the Trucial States who wished to work in Abu Dhabi that he would prefer them to come without their families and leave them in their native Shaikhdom. Shaikh Zaid then went on to restate his belief in "State Rights" and his determination never to permit the depopulation of any one of the Trucial States. (BRE 1967: 409)

Sheikh Zayed explained the demographic flows from Dubai to Abu Dhabi by asserting that many of those families were originally from Abu Dhabi and had simply moved to Dubai for work purposes; they were now naturally returning to their rightful home of tribal allegiance.

When it came to disputes between Trucial States, the strongest rivalry was between Dubai and Abu Dhabi, since Abu Dhabi's oil wealth was shifting the balance of power away from Dubai as the historic commercial center of the coast. In addition to disputes over tribal allegiance and territorial possessions, Sheikh Rashid's closeness to the Al Saud royal family of Saudi Arabia became an additional source of tension with Abu Dhabi, since the Saudis continued to lay claim to large swaths of territory that Sheikh Zayed (and the British) viewed as Abu Dhabi's territory. The tensions were alleviated somewhat when prospectors found oil in Dubai in 1966 and Sheikh Rashid could count on the prospect of an external source of revenue to alleviate his dependence upon the (Indian, Arab, and Persian) merchants and fund subsidies to citizens. Nonetheless, these reserves ended up being modest compared to what was found in Abu Dhabi. With the exception of Dubai's reserves and a much smaller amount of hydrocarbons on an offshore field connected to Sharjah, the oil prospecting in the remaining Trucial States was unsuccessful. Consequently, in the years immediately preceding and succeeding the formation of the federation, there was an exodus of populations out of the remaining Trucial States into Abu Dhabi in particular.

In addition to migration flows and the shifting of tribal allegiances to Abu Dhabi, by 1969 the extent of Abu Dhabi's growing power vis-à-vis the other Trucial States was evident in its position as the financer of early efforts at unionization. Under the leadership of Sheikh Zayed, Abu Dhabi began financing the incipient security apparatuses and government institutions of the Trucial State administrations (other than Dubai). This growing economic influence over the other Trucial States came with political conditions, and the British archives are littered with references to Sheikh Rashid's complaints about Abu Dhabi gaining power over the other states. The British Political Agent in Dubai reported to the British Political Resident in Bahrain that though he "normally den[ies]" that Abu Dhabi is trying to take over the smaller Trucial States, Abu Dhabi's influence in Fujairah "has reached a level that I find disquieting" (BRE 1969: 397). Sheikh Zayed attached conditions to the annual subsidy Abu Dhabi provided Fujairah, and by 1969 Abu Dhabi had appointed and paid for key members of Fujairah's political and security apparatus. The British

Political Agent in Dubai had received intelligence that Naji Awad – the Abu Dhabi-appointed Iraqi advisor to Fujairah – was receiving direct instructions from the Abu Dhabi delegation about how Fujairah should vote in the UAE meeting in Doha. Moreover, the Fujairah police were now being paid for and trained by Abu Dhabi, and several police officers clad in Abu Dhabi police uniforms were in charge of the police forces.

Abu Dhabi's monopolization over the security forces and legitimate means of violence posed a larger challenge to the sovereign authority of Trucial State rulers. The Political Agent responded to the presence of Abu Dhabi policemen in Fujairah by advising:

that Shaikh Muhammed had better not bring his Abu Dhabi policemen to Dubai with him next time he comes over. I added that so long as the policemen remained in Fujairah on the present basis they constituted an instrument by which Zaid could get rid of Muhammed at any time, thus involving HMG in an extremely difficult situation. They also made a laughing stock of Shaikh Muhammed in his own capital, and provided ammunition to Rashid and others who suspected Zaid of aiming at an empire of the Trucial States. I hope that the Abu Dhabi police party could either be converted into a proper training mission, or given local uniforms like the two or three in Umm al Qaiwain. (BRE 1969: 397)

This example helps illustrate that there was autonomy and competition between various Trucial State rulers. Each ruler was considered sovereign and Abu Dhabi's dominance over the union was not taken for granted, even though it was already taking a leadership role in the infrastructural and institutional development of the other Trucial States.

As populations moved between Trucial States, the British kept records about which tribes recognized which rulers as a matter of jurisdiction. In reference to the flows of families from Dubai to Abu Dhabi, the British Commandant of Police in Dubai wrote to the Commandant of Police in Abu Dhabi that:

in view of the natural inclinations of the bedu to apparently maintain allegiance to more than one Ruler and thereby derive the additional benefits from this deception, Shaikh Zaid may wish to provide a list of the names of these bedu who have changed their allegiance in his favour. (BRE 1967: 402)

The distribution of welfare funds as a new citizenship right in Abu Dhabi required the authorities to design and build an identity management infrastructure across the Trucial States. Though tribal allegiance was historically fluid, the codification of allegiance on paper during this early stage of state-building would later shape national citizenship – and who could gain access to it – in what was to become the UAE federation. Arab Tribes who inhabited resource-rich regions were documented closely. Meanwhile the ethnic minorities who comprised the majority of the labor force in the Trucial States were largely left out of the documentation of tribal allegiances. This would prove to later have significant consequences after the formation of the UAE, when federal authorities began requiring individuals to prove their UAE citizenship through family books that document tribal ancestry and allegiance.

2.4 STATE FORMATION AND CHALLENGES TO A COMMON CITIZENSHIP AND IMMIGRATION POLICY

This section illustrates how citizenship and migration policies were erected at the formation of the UAE as a federation, shaping the future boundaries of the Emirati nation. I argue that ambiguous citizenship statuses emerged because of a divergence between the more expansive incorporation practices of individual Trucial States that predates national consolidation, and what became the UAE's more restrictive federal nationality policy under the leadership of Abu Dhabi after the union was formed. This disjuncture between national incorporation and local accommodation created gaps in the coverage of citizenship laws that have in turn produced gray zones of belonging and ambiguous citizenship statuses.

To illustrate how ambiguous citizenship statuses emerged with state formation, this section begins by identifying the key causes behind why the Trucial States formed a union. It then proceeds to examine the main challenges to forming a common citizenship and immigration policy during the founding of the federation. Due to the divergent accommodation practices of the Trucial States, there were two policies at the formation of the union – one for Abu Dhabi and another for the remaining emirates. I argue that the variation in the local incorporation practices of Trucial States is due to the distinct economic activities of each of the Trucial States and the sources of income to their rulers. The preservation or expansion of economic activities led rulers to differentially accommodate the mobility of capital and labor in their territories. These differences in defining who was a citizen and who was a foreigner led to the creation of gray zones of partial incorporation, eventually resulting in groups with ambiguous citizenship statuses.

2.4.1 The Formation of a Union

From 1966 until 1971, the Trucial States were under immense external pressure to form a federation and agree upon a common citizenship and immigration policy. The British defense review of 1966 led to the decision to withdraw the British forces from South Arabia (ending colonial rule in Aden in 1968). This created an exodus of Adenis, Yemenis, and Somalis from Aden into the Trucial States, heightening the pressure on the Trucial State rulers to agree upon a common immigration policy and strengthen security. This pressure to unionize mounted even more by 1968, when the increasing deterioration of Britain's economic situation led the British government to reduce its public expenditure at home and overseas. Consequently, it announced its withdrawal from the Gulf for March 1971.

The British had envisioned handing over their jurisdictional authority (external affairs and security) to a union of nine, encompassing the seven Trucial States, Bahrain, and Qatar. There were two issues that dominated the discussions on the mechanics of the union and delayed its formation: the structure of representation and the location of the capital.

Bahrain had the largest population, and its rulers wanted Manama to be the capital of the union and argued for representation in the union council under permanent construction to be based on a population census. The five smaller Trucial States (Sharjah, RAK, Fujairah, Umm Al Quwain, and Ajman) attacked provisions that would allocate voting power based on census representation because their populations were far less numerous. Dubai and Qatar supported the smaller Trucial States, and Abu Dhabi abstained. Eventually, the larger union of nine failed for several reasons – including Iran's claim to Bahrain and tensions between the Bahraini and Qatari royal families. Bahrain and Qatar strengthened their ties with Saudi Arabia to increase their security in light of the British withdrawal and were able to secure recognition from the UN as independent states.

The remaining Trucial States, however, proceeded with negotiations to form a union.[17] One of the intransigent issues in the negotiations for

---

[17] Abu Dhabi, Dubai, Sharjah, Fujairah, and Umm Al Quwain formalized the union in 1971, and Ras al Khaimah (RAK) only joined one year later in 1972. According to Heard-Bey (1982), there were three key reasons for this delay. First, the ruler of RAK resented the fact that he did not share an equal rank with the four larger states (Abu Dhabi, Dubai, Bahrain, and Qatar) when it came to issues of delegates or voting rights. Second, the ruler had expected to gain oil income from an offshore concession, and delayed entry into the union with the hopes of joining it as an oil-rich state with more power. However, this plan failed because the amount of oil found in RAK's offshore site was deemed insufficient to

a union was the disagreement over a common immigration and citizenship policy. Citizenship and immigration policies were contentious because they would determine the concentration of citizens across political units in the new federation, raising the core issues of political representation and the distribution of resources.

2.4.2 The National Dilemma: Divergent Citizenship and Immigration Policies

One key challenge to forming a common immigration and citizenship policy stemmed from the fact that individual Trucial States had been issuing their own passports based on their assessments of who was considered their subjects since the early 1950s. Individual Trucial States began issuing their own passports after the Saudi Arabian government levied heavy fees on travelers carrying British passports or identity certificates in 1952. These Trucial State passports were only recognized in Saudi Arabia, around the Persian Gulf, and in India and Pakistan. The rulers issued these travel documents so that trade between the Trucial States and Saudi Arabia and Greater India could continue to flow without taxation (BRE 1952: 44). Identity documentation practices are often determined by the accommodation of labor and capital mobility, and in this case the Trucial State rulers (especially Sheikh Rashid Al Maktoum of Dubai) were invested in protecting their local trade and commercial activities.

British attempts to unify the nationality policies of all the Trucial States in the early 1950s failed due to the fact that the territorial boundaries between states were still not fully determined. In addition to the question of territorial boundaries, the matter of nationality was further complicated by the uncertain allegiance of some of the Arab tribes. Moreover, there was no joint agreement to decide under which circumstances non-Arab populations on the Trucial Coast should "be regarded as having acquired local nationality" (BRE 1952: 44). The key question was how the populations who fell under the jurisdiction of each of the Trucial States would be counted in the population census. Who – from the range of

---

justify the cost of production. Finally, RAK was involved in a legal battle with Iran who claimed sovereignty over two Tunb islands; the ruler made it a condition of entry that the UAE would address the question of Iranian occupation of RAK's islands (Heard-Bey 1982: 370).

populations who lived in the Trucial State territories – would be considered a citizen of the new federal state?

The large and entrenched Indian population in Dubai and Sharjah was not considered in these negotiations because South Asians fell under the authority of the British political agency. This status meant that Indians and other South Asians present in the territories at the time were considered foreigners and not counted in the national census figures. Ironically, the privileged status of Indians under the British rule led to their guaranteed exclusion from the new postcolonial nation-state. This pattern of excluding Indians after the British withdrawal was of course not limited to the UAE. Across the disintegrating British Empire, members of the Indian diaspora were excluded from the citizenries of newly minted nation-states for being associated with the former colonial power. In the case of the UAE they were permitted to stay but given no path to citizenship; in other cases they were summarily deported – as with the notable example of Idi Amin's expulsion of South Asians from Uganda in 1972. Meanwhile, the retrenchment of British citizenship laws in the metropole as decolonization spread (especially the 1981 British Nationality Act) also solidified the Indian diaspora's exclusion from the British national citizenry.

Since Indians and other foreigners who fell under British jurisdiction in the Order in Council were not considered for Emirati citizenship, the British had envisioned handing over authority to a federal body in charge of immigration. But by 1971, with only months before the scheduled British withdrawal, the British could no longer afford to wait for a suitable federal entity to be created. It instead handed over this authority to the Abu Dhabi government (BRE 1971: 303). The existing system for regulating the stay of foreigners was based on the use of No Objection Certificates (NOCs). In a brief to the Political Resident in Bahrain, the Political Agent in Abu Dhabi explained how critical NOCs were to migration enforcement:

No Objection Certificate (NOCs). These are the most important documents in the whole machinery for issuing visas. The essential feature of the system is that the applicant for a visa must be recommended to H.M. Political Agent in Dubai or Abu Dhabi by a sponsor, who must already be legally resident in the Trucial States. The sponsor undertakes to pay the cost of repatriating the visitor if so requested, and gives a guarantee of his good behavior. (BRE 1971: 506)

In other words, as an enforcement mechanism, NOCs did two things: (1) they provided a record of every foreigner employed in the territories, and pegged that foreigner to a national sponsor; and in so doing, (2) they privatized the cost of migrant defection by holding individual Trucial State subjects financially and legally responsible for new labor migrants. This NOC system provided the framework for the *kafāla* sponsorship system that currently regulates the residency of foreigners under temporary employment contracts across the Gulf.

In terms of a common policy across Trucial States, the issue of how to regulate those under British jurisdiction or new migrants was much clearer than what do with older minorities. When it came to the region's ethnic minorities – particularly Persians and Baluchis – the determination of whether they were citizens or foreigners was far less clear. A main source of contention was over the Persians: how was the large number of Persians residing on the Trucial Coast to be counted? And would Iranians require visas to enter the UAE? The Persian question is a protracted one; from the early 1950s to the formation of the union in 1971, the question of how to count Persians and what identity documents they should be issued was not resolved.

The Persian question became even more contentious by the 1970s because of the impact of Arab nationalism on identity politics in the region. The strength of Arab nationalism points to the importance of external pressures in defining national identity. For most of the twentieth century, Arab nationalism spread the notion of a distinct "Arab world" that is a "'single homogeneous whole [stretching] from the Atlantic Ocean to the Persian Gulf' and that Arabs constitute 'a single nation bound by the common ties of language, religion and history'" (Karsh and Karsh 1996: 367). Whether under the Hashemite championship of Arab nationalism in the 1930s or under the leadership of Nasser and the other Republican regimes in the 1960s, this external pressure on the Gulf made it increasingly difficult to narrate Persians as being rightful citizens of any of the "Arab" Gulf states. In the UAE the Persian question created a contentious split between the rulers.

Because of disagreements between rulers at the inception of the union in 1971, the UAE did not have a unified immigration policy toward Persian residents and Iranian migrants. Dubai and some of the northern Trucial States had large Persian populations, who they counted as subjects and issued passports to. They also depended on trade with south Iran, and therefore had a strategic interest in keeping mobility flowing without the imposition of visas. Dubai and the northern Trucial States exempted Iranians from landing fees or visas; their policy toward Iranians was to encompass them within the visa-free access given to "people of the Gulf." For example, in a 1952 discussion of naturalization and nationality, the British political agency's minutes of the Trucial Council meeting reflected

Sheikh Rashid of Dubai's position on what constituted "Trucial Nationality":

The Ruler of Dubai instanced his subjects of Persian origin and said that those who settled in Dubai permanently, and those who were born there, and those who after a protracted period of residence voluntarily applied to become his subjects were to be considered his subjects. (BRE 1952: 293)

Abu Dhabi, on the other hand, required Iranians to apply for visas and considered Persian residents to be foreigners not Trucial State subjects. The distance between the Persian and Arab sides of the Gulf shores is much shorter than the distance between south Iran and Tehran in the north. As such, for Iranians living far away from Tehran it was extremely inconvenient to attain visas to Abu Dhabi. Iranians also knew that, in practice, they didn't really need a visa as they could enter the territories through Dubai and then make their way to Abu Dhabi quasi-illegally (BRE 1968: 421).

In addition to the challenge posed by the large number of Persians on the coast, some of the northern Trucial States had issued passports to Baluchis (from Oman, East Africa, and South Asia) and Adenis (from Southern Yemen). The British authorities were wary of this practice because other rulers in the Gulf, especially the Saudi Arabian and Kuwaiti ruling elites, did not accept that Baluchis, Persians, and Adenis should be considered Trucial State subjects. The British also did not accept these ethnic minorities as Trucial State subjects and attempted to persuade the Trucial State rulers not to issue travel documents to people of non-Arab origin. In a meeting of the Trucial Council in 1953, the political officer dubbed the claim that these populations were Trucial State subjects as "false": "there had been several cases recently of Persians, Baluchis, Adenis and other nationals obtaining documents in which they were falsely described as subjects of one of the Trucial States" (BRE 1953: 305). When external entities, such as the British or Saudi Arabian authorities, have a different understanding of who constitutes a citizen of a nation-state, they can refuse to recognize travel documents or consider those documents to be "false."

These external pressures led to passport cancellations and the retrenchment of citizenship boundaries. In addition to facing external pressure not to recognize non-Arab minorities as citizens, the Trucial State rulers were also accused of selling passports to supplement their revenue. While at first the records show that all the Trucial State rulers rejected this accusation and insisted that these non-Arab populations were indeed their subjects, the rulers of Dubai, Sharjah, and Ras al Khaimah (RAK) eventually took initiatives to cancel all existing passports. They then required their populations to apply for new ones that were reissued under stricter control. By 1965 the rulers informed the British that this process was complete and that their subjects carried new passports (BRE 1965: 47–100). By the mid-1960s there was thus a concerted effort to make citizenship more stringent than it had previously been, planting the seed for the creation of a partially incorporated population with ambiguous legal statuses.

Because of the differences in incorporation patterns and passport issuing–practices, the Trucial States could not agree upon a common citizenship and immigration policy in time for national independence and the formation of the union. While the negotiations for the union almost failed at times, by 1971 the five smaller Trucial States (all but Abu Dhabi) conceded on some of their demands and an agreement was reached. This was due, in no small part, to the efforts of Sheikh Zayed Al Nahyan of Abu Dhabi, who committed to allocating Abu Dhabi's oil wealth to finance the development of the smaller Trucial States. The leverage of the five smaller Trucial States was also weakened when the British government announced in 1971 that it would not recognize them in the absence of a union. To meet the deadline for unionization the federal nationality law was left nebulous. The outcome of these negotiations is that the UAE's current naturalization process has multiple levels; citizenship must be conferred at the emirate level before an individual can attain federal nationality. This dual process emerged out of the compromises that were made to preserve state rights. The federal nationality law of 1972 aimed to forge a new unified citizenry that would continue to recognize preexisting identities and the sovereignty of each emirate.[18]

2.4.3 Divergent Economic Trajectories and Patterns of Incorporation

The Trucial State rulers had different approaches toward the national incorporation of non-Arab minorities on a local level, leading to gaps in the inclusion of minorities on a national scale and the eventual creation of ambiguous citizenship statuses. What accounts for these divergent approaches toward national incorporation? There are three plausible alternative explanations for the local variation in national incorporation

---

[18] Federal Law No. 17 for 1972 Concerning Nationality, Passports and Amendments Thereof.

policies: a British policy of divide and conquer, divergent cultural out-looks of the leaders and local society in each Trucial State, and divergent economic development trajectories of each Trucial State.

Jamal (2015) argues that the fragmentation and "tiering" of citizen-ship rights in the UAE is a legacy of a conscious divide-and-conquer policy by British officials. British interests, rather than the interests of the rulers, determined the contours of citizenship in the UAE: "the construction of citizenship in the UAE was intimately connected to the political objectives of the British protectorate, even when its goals diverged from those of Trucial State leaders ... to facilitate control of these territories, British authorities implemented divide-and-rule policies including the authorization of each emirate to issue its own passports" (Jamal 2015: 611). The consolidation of the federal gov-ernment under Abu Dhabi has meant that those who were previously incorporated with passports now find themselves in a precarious and ambiguous legal status:

> [P]revious citizens find themselves in a new precarious gray zone. Whereas previously, possession of a passport implied citizenship and resulted in citizenship rights, now passport holders are no longer full citizens of the UAE ... policies to streamline UAE citizenship, including the introduction of the Emirati ID, are resulting in the reversal of citizenship and permanent residency status, regardless of what passport possession previously meant. (Jamal 2015: 606)

While this explanation similarly emphasizes the emergence of ambiguous citizenship as an outcome of the development of institutions over time, Jamal elevates the role of the British to ignore competition between the rulers of the emirates themselves. In particular, the interpretation of emirate-level passport issuances as a divide-and-rule tactic ahistorically assumes that the Trucial coastline was a unitary political unit and that it was British designs that led to its fragmentation. This narrative takes the national boundaries of the modern UAE as a given, even though the different ruling families and emirates had distinct political and historical trajectories that were only made into one with British involvement. Indeed, the Trucial State coastline had no single name in Arabic prior to the formation of the Emirati state and the territory only became one unit because of British pressures to unionize ahead of decolonization. While official nationalist discourses take the UAE nation-state as a natural entity that has existed from time immemorial, it is problematic to retroactively read this federation as "one" entity and blame citizenship hierarchies on British designs.

A second plausible explanation for the divergent incorporation patterns and resulting hierarchies in citizenship is cultural; the rulers and local societies of different Trucial States have divergent cultural attitudes toward minorities. There is support for this explanation in the British records. For example, the differences in Dubai and Abu Dhabi's approaches to national incorporation were captured in a 1967 brief by the Political Agent D. Roberts, who argued that Dubai was unique because in it:

[O]ne finds a mixed community living in apparent harmony whilst in the rest of the Gulf, and particularly in Abu Dhabi and Qatar, there are all the signs of xenophobia which seems to be such a common trait of the nationalistic Arabs, perhaps of nationalism generally ... Abu Dhabi nationals exhibit none of the tolerance towards foreigners which is so characteristic of Dubai. (BRE 1967: 129)

For Roberts, despite the physical proximity between the two city-states, there was a discernable difference in Dubai and Abu Dhabi's approaches to cultural accommodation. This comparison between Abu Dhabi and Dubai is useful for determining whether the ultimate origin of these attitudes toward multicultural societies is indeed deeply cultural in nature. This difference in outlooks cannot be attributed to any preexisting cultural, tribal, or religious differences between Dubai and Abu Dhabi: the ruling and prominent families in Dubai share the same religious school (*Maliki*), come from the same tribal confederation (*Hinawi*), and even stem from the same specific tribal group (*Bani Yas*), as the ruling family in Abu Dhabi. By controlling for primordial tribal or religious differences between the ruling elites in Dubai and Abu Dhabi, I argue that the root of their divergent outlooks and approaches to ethnic heterogeneity is largely driven by economic factors.

The Trucial States developed cultural attitudes toward the incorporation of minorities that supported their own individual economic development trajectories. The ruling elites of each of the Trucial States managed their own economic development path, and this autonomy was preserved with article 23 of the provisional constitution, which ensured that each ruler had the right to independently manage his own hydrocarbon industry (Davidson 2008: 220).[19] These distinct economic development

---

[19] Article 23 of the UAE Constitution states: "The natural resources and wealth in each Emirate are deemed the public property of that Emirate. The community shall preserve and utilize in a good way those resources and wealth for the interest of the national economy" (United Arab Emirates Constitution: 11. www.wipo.int/edocs/lexdocs/laws/en/ae/ae031en.pdf).

trajectories shaped the incorporation preferences and accommodation practices of ruling elites, leading to different patterns of local incorporation. The stances of different rulers on who should be nationally incorporated was determined by two factors: (1) the economic activities of each Trucial State and (2) the sources of income to the rulers.

When economic development is based on mobile assets and trade, ruling elites are likely to adopt expansive incorporation practices that encourage the mobility of capital and labor. This is exemplified by Dubai's approach and policies of abolishing visas for key trading partners or issuing passports to facilitate the travel of merchants. When, on the other hand, economic development is based on a fixed asset like oil, ruling elites are likely to adopt more restrictive incorporation practices, including greater barriers to citizenship and migration controls. This is exemplified by Abu Dhabi's push for citizenship retrenchments (including the cancellation of passports and their reissuance in more stringent terms) and in its erection of procedural obstacles to naturalization (such as the practice of postponing naturalization cases).

Dubai's cosmopolitan character ultimately stemmed from the city-state's extensive trading activities and maritime economy. As Roberts explained:

> My opinion about the reason for this difference in the temperament of the members of the Dubai community and others in the Gulf is that it stems from the interdependence of the various racial and religious groups vis a vis their trading and smuggling activities. The Arab gold smuggler of Dubai needs the Pakistani seaman and the Indian currency exchange dealer. The immense trade, legal and illegal, with Iran calls for close co-operation and understanding between the Arab and the Irani. (BRE 1967: 129)

Sheikh Rashid Al Maktoum of Dubai was dependent upon revenues generated by mobile populations who came from an array of different ethnic groups. Continuing the entrepreneurial vision of his father, Sheikh Mohammed bin Rashid Al Maktoum has continued to develop Dubai as a haven for people from any background while diversifying the state's portfolio of income-generating activities away from oil.[20]

The rulers of Dubai have had a historical preference for laissez-faire policies, and actively invested in an infrastructure for trade and commerce. Dubai hosted an entrenched merchant community and its economy was based on a long history of maritime trade with Iran, India, East

---

[20] By 2008 ninety percent of Dubai's GDP came from non-oil income (Davidson 2008).

Africa, and the Arab world that has thrived despite (or perhaps because of) the conflicts in the region. In the 1890s, Dubai's ruler Sheikh Rashid bin Maktoum Al Maktoum attempted to attract merchants from Persia to lure them to relocate their businesses in Dubai; he "offered these immigrant merchants personal protection and provided them with prime plots of land close to the creek, in order for them to build houses and settle their families" (Davidson 2008: 73).[21] Some of these plots of land continue to survive today, and until recently were known as the old Bastakiya quarter in Dubai (named after the province of Bastak in Iran), before being renamed "al-Fahidiya" in an attempt to Arabize the historical district. Sheikh Rashid's successor, Sheikh Maktoum, also created a policy of welcoming newcomers to his *majlis* to learn what they would need from Dubai for their businesses to flourish.

More recently, Dubai has earned a reputation for being adept at earning an income by being open to capital and businesspeople during moments of larger political or economic upheaval in the region. For example, in addition to benefiting from the influx of Iranian capital, Dubai has acted as a haven for different waves of Arab migrants:

[T]he number of Iraqis moving their businesses to Dubai increased dramatically after Abdul Salam Arif's 1958 Arab nationalist revolution in Baghdad – an influx that remained high following the worsening conditions during the Iran-Iraq war of the 1980s, and the 2003 Anglo-American invasion of Iraq and subsequent civil war. Similarly, throughout the latter quarter of the century Dubai became home to many Lebanese and Kuwaiti merchants, as a result of the protracted Lebanese civil war and the 1990s Iraqi invasion of Kuwait. (Davidson 2008: 88)

Subsequent generations of rulers of Dubai have positioned the city-state to capture the capital flight that accompanies political crises. Dubai has played a key role in absorbing businesses from conflict zones and has provided support for rebuilding war-torn economies through remittances. Because of the various rulers' laissez-faire approach to economic development in Dubai, inward migratory flows were often viewed as an opportunity for development rather than a "problem" that needed to be solved. As Davidson explains, "When some of Sheikh Rashid bin Saeed al-Maktum's

---

[21] Sheikh Rashid bin Maktoum Al Maktoum was the ruler of Dubai from 1886–1894. He was seceded by his nephew Maktoum Al Maktoum (who was the grandfather of Sheikh Rashid bin Saeed Al Maktoum, the ruler of Dubai during the formation of the UAE). As Davidson explains, some of these families from Sheikh Rashid's time continue to thrive in Dubai today and originally included "Muahmmad Hajji Badri, Abdul Wahid Fikree, Sheikh Mustafa Abdulatif, and Ghulam Abbas, the latter of whom had brought about half of the Al-Ansari family with him" (2008: 73).

advisors questioned him on the subject of these 'illegal' residents he simply replied 'What is the problem, so long as they are paying rent in Dubai?'" (Davidson 2008: 91). Dubai's open policy and accommodation of migrants contrasts with what has historically been Abu Dhabi's approach to the incorporation of foreigners and ethnic minorities.

The main source of Abu Dhabi's economic development since the late 1960s has been oil. If Dubai was intent on keeping borders open as it entered the union, Abu Dhabi had different imperatives; with oil wealth came the threat of labor strikes, the need for a system to prevent welfare fraud, and a greater policing capacity at borders, shorelines, and within the state. To protect its economic interests and oil wealth, Abu Dhabi focused more on security initiatives, the erection of boundaries, and the creation of an identity management infrastructure. Moreover, even prior to the discovery of oil in their territories, the pre-oil income of the Al Nahyan did not come from maritime trade as much as from settlements (in the Liwa Oasis and later Abu Dhabi town) and inter-desert trade, making Abu Dhabi much more ethnically homogenous than Dubai. As Abu Dhabi's oil reserves trickled in as rents to the ruler, the administration in Abu Dhabi became increasingly concerned with maintaining records on all families who were Abu Dhabi subjects. These rosters were important for the redistribution of oil wealth, since by 1967, in an effort to quell migration to Abu Dhabi, the British suggested creating a system of family allowances to redistribute the wealth from oil without increasing income levels (Jamal 2015: 626). The rulers of Abu Dhabi were thus much more stringent in the issuance of passports and in their interpretation of who qualified as a Trucial State subject. The British records demonstrate a recurring concern of the leadership of Abu Dhabi with preventing fraud from being committed by those who felt no allegiance to Abu Dhabi and merely wanted to benefit from its oil wealth. The monopolization of oil wealth, rather than the goal of attracting foreign investors and businesses, drove the leadership of Abu Dhabi to adopt a more stringent definition of the Emirati citizen.

2.5 CODIFYING CITIZENSHIP AND IMMIGRATION: INSTITUTIONALIZING AMBIGUITY

The distinct economic trajectories of Abu Dhabi and Dubai meant that the two largest and most powerful Trucial States had divergent approaches to national incorporation when the union was formed in 1971. The rulers of Abu Dhabi were in favor of a more restrictive immigration and citizenship system that would privilege their security concerns and preserve Abu Dhabi's oil wealth, whereas Dubai was in favor of more expansive immigration and citizenship policies that would remove barriers to entry to attract and retain foreign businesses and capital. The remaining five Trucial States tended to side with Dubai on this issue, having little to no oil wealth of their own and similar aspirations in trade and commerce. The disagreements that emerged between Abu Dhabi and the remaining Trucial State rulers over a common immigration and citizenship policy led to the establishment of a dual system that has, over time, created gaps in the coverage of citizenship laws and produced a limbo population with ambiguous citizenship statuses.

Formally, the Trucial State rulers drafted a common citizenship and immigration policy in 1971 during the Trucial State Council meetings that were held in the immediate aftermath of the UAE's independence. In practice, however, the common policy did not actually apply to Abu Dhabi; administratively, authority over immigration was thus split between Abu Dhabi on the one hand and the remaining Trucial States on the other. Evidence of this split appears in the Trucial Council committee meeting minutes of March 29, 1971, when the council agreed to prepare a single unified immigration law and establish a unified ID card system. During the meeting Abu Dhabi and the remaining Trucial States disagreed about who constituted the "people of the Gulf" who should gain visa-free access to the UAE:

Nationals of Kuwait, Saudi Arabia, Oman, Bahrain and Qatar will continue to be exempt from visa requirements. The question of Iranians who at present need visas for Abu Dhabi but not for the other Trucial States is referred to the Rulers for decision. (BRE 1971: 531)

The Iranian question – including whether resident Persians were Trucial State subjects who should gain Emirati citizenship and whether Iranian visitors should require visas – was one of several issues that separated Abu Dhabi from the rest of the council.

The British Political Agent provided the following reasons for Abu Dhabi's hesitation in having a coordinated immigration and citizenship policy with the remaining states: (1) the 72-hour transit visa proposed for Dubai; (2) the visa exemption for Iranians in Dubai; (3) illegal immigration to the northern Trucial States; and finally (4) Abu Dhabi's "general unwillingness to accept subordination to the Trucial States Council" (BRE 1971: 539). Thus while the new federal state had a unified immigration and citizenship system on paper, in practice, the immigration policies of Abu Dhabi were determined by the Abu Dhabi Committee for the

Transfer of Visas and Immigration, while the policies of the remaining states were determined by the Trucial States Council Committee on the Transfer of Visas and Immigration.

The British Political Agent in Dubai explained this dual system in his letter to the Political Resident in Bahrain about the meeting of the Trucial States Council Committee on Visas and Immigration in April of 1971. During the meeting the committee approved a draft immigration law, a draft decree establishing a central department of immigration, and instructions to the department on visas and residence permits. While all seven rulers issued the draft, its application was restricted to the six northern emirates. In transitioning the responsibility over immigration from the British to the new federal state, a central department of immigration was established with one president and two directors. One of the directors was appointed by Abu Dhabi to be responsible for the immigration affairs of Abu Dhabi, while the other director was appointed by the council to be responsible for the immigration affairs of the remaining emirates.

The Political Agent reported that "some rather bitter feelings" were concealed behind this split system:

The Committee felt strongly that there should be a unified system including Abu Dhabi and failed to understand why Abu Dhabi insisted on being independent. The statements of Hammouda, the Abu Dhabi representative, did not help very much because in a typically Arab way he declared that Abu Dhabi wanted complete unity and did not reveal that he had attended separate meetings in Abu Dhabi, where a policy of administrative separation had been determined. I told the Committee that it was my understanding that Shaikh Zaid himself had decided on this policy and we had therefore better face facts and do what we could in the circumstances. I said that for political reasons it seemed best to preserve the image of unity and thus to adopt the decree described above. They eventually agreed with some grumbles to this, but I doubt if we have heard the last of these arguments and they may well be re-ventilated at the June meeting. (BRE 1971: 542–543)

The Political Agent's notes reveal a key tactic of Abu Dhabi's strategy during its negotiations with the other emirates on citizenship and immigration policies – deferral. Instead of either compromising its stance on immigration and citizenship or outwardly rejecting a compromise with the other Trucial State rulers on these issues, the leadership of Abu Dhabi evaded the dilemma by postponing the question instead. Behind the formal facade of unity, the immigration and citizenship affairs in Abu Dhabi would continue as they were prior to the formation of the union, defined by Abu Dhabi's rulers and civil servants without the input or authority of the Trucial Council's committee.

In addition to creating an informal dual system for immigration policies, the new federation's citizenship policy was also split between Abu Dhabi and the remaining emirates. Specifically, citizenship had to be conferred at the emirate level first, and after the naturalization department in a specific emirate had issued an approval for a candidate's citizenship case, a committee from the MOI in Abu Dhabi had to provide the final approval and conferral of Emirati nationality. While passports were initially issued at the emirate level, passports are an external form of identification and do not denote nationality inside the UAE. Within the UAE, citizenship rights and benefits are tied to the nationality document – the *khulāṣat al-qayd* (or family book), which can only come from the federal authority in Abu Dhabi. Individuals with pending citizenship cases are thus neither guest workers who fall under immigration laws, nor full citizens who can gain access to state benefits, but rather reside in a gray zone between legal categories. As a result, the codification of citizenship laws effectively created distinctions between those with full federal nationality (documented with a *khulāṣat al-qayd*), those with passports but not the nationality document, and those with neither passports nor the nationality document who have effectively become stateless (*bidūn*). Jamal (2015) refers to this outcome of a gray zone of ambiguous citizenship statuses as the "tiering" of citizenship rights in the UAE and the hierarchization of its resident communities.

This ambiguity of the citizenship status of some residents was codified into law due to the way that nationality was defined at the formation of the union. According to Federal Law No. 17 for 1972 Concerning Nationality, Passports and Amendments Thereof, by law a citizen is "an Arab who was residing in a member Emirate in 1925 or before and who continued to reside therein up to the effective date of this law" (Federal Law No. 17 of 1972: article 2). In other words, only Arab males (and their children) who could also trace their tribal lineage to 1925 were conferred with citizenship by law. During the early negotiations on a common citizenship policy (1969), the date of 1925 was chosen as the cut-off for citizenship eligibility because it was before the Trucial States had benefited from oil. This stipulation disenfranchised anyone who came after that date – a common feature of the way most of the citizenship regimes in the oil-rich Gulf have been structured. As a British residency official explained, "No one coming to settle here before then could be said to have come to 'cash in' on the oil income" (BRE 1969, reprinted in Jamal 2015: 622). By 1969, however, individual Trucial States had already issued passports to non-Arab subjects and Arab subjects who could not trace their lineage to 1925. The meeting minutes show that there was already an awareness that this cut-off date would create gaps in the coverage of the citizenship laws, potentially creating a statelessness problem. To prevent statelessness from occurring, articles 2 and 17 of Federal Law No. 17 of 1972 Concerning Nationality, Passports and Amendments Thereof extend citizenship to three other categories of the resident population (children of female citizens with undocumented fathers, anyone born to parents with unknown lineage, anyone born to unknown parents).[22] However, despite being formally included in law, in practice all three of these groups have ambiguous citizenship statuses that have made them effectively stateless. Indeed, these three groups form a core part of the population who received Union of Comoros passports from the UAE since 2008.

In addition to defining the cut-off date for qualifying for Emirati citizenship, the federal nationality law of 1972 also defined who could apply for citizenship from among the resident population. The federal nationality law erected a stringent naturalization policy (over 30 years of residency) that would make it difficult for new migrants to gain citizenship. Article 7 states that:

> UAE citizenship may be granted to any fully competent person if he has been legally and continuously residing in the Emirates since 1940 or before and has maintained his original residence up to the effective date of law, has legal means of living, of good conduct, has not been convicted for a crime that impugns integrity, and is conversant with the Arabic language.[23]

This article does not specify that the resident must be an Arab male, which allows non-Arab minorities living in the territories (including those issued Trucial State passports) to apply for federal nationality. Unlike the first

---

[22] www.refworld.org/pdfid/3fba182do.pdf. Article 2 specifies that the citizenship law also imparts Emirati nationality on:

"C. Anyone born in the country or abroad to a mother who is a citizen by law, whose fatherhood is not substantiated.

D. Anyone born in the country or abroad to a mother who is a citizen by law, whose father is unknown or without nationality.

E. Anyone born in the country to unknown parents. A founding (sic) shall be deemed to have been born in the country unless proved to be otherwise" (Federal Law No. for 1972 Concerning Nationality, Passports and Amendments Thereof: article 2).

[23] Federal Law No. 17 for 1972 Concerning Nationality, Passports and Amendments Thereof: article 7.

category of citizens, these individuals must undergo the naturalization procedure to become "full" Emirati citizens and gain the *khulāṣat al-qayd* nationality document. The cut-off date of 1940 for qualifying was chosen because, based on the same nationality law, individuals are only eligible to be naturalized after thirty years of continuous residence in the same emirate.

In order to be naturalized, applicants have to demonstrate that they have been completely integrated and assimilated into Emirati culture. As examined in the next chapter, naturalization does not hinge on whether an individual has met certain "objective" criteria (such as extended continuous residence). Rather, the single most important factor in determining whether an individual could be a citizen is their allegiance (*walā'*) to the UAE. And for the security forces, that kind of determination is a political one – each individual has to be individually assessed for their loyalty, patriotism, and benefit or threat to the society. Naturalization is essentially an issue of "national security" (*'amn al-dawla*).[24]

In summary, through the promulgation of articles 2 and 7 in the nationality law, a difference is codified between residents who simply *are* citizens when the federation is born, and residents who must apply to *become* citizens. The result is that while some residents are secure in their citizenship status, other residents have been waiting to gain full Emirati nationality since the formation of union. While naturalization cases go through the emirate level first, the ultimate decision on a naturalization case must come from the MOI in Abu Dhabi. Similarly to Abu Dhabi's strategy of deferring a compromise on a common immigration system, in practice it has used the tactic of deferral in the realm of naturalization and citizenship. Instead of compromising on the basis of citizenship that would take into consideration the more expansive policies of the remaining Trucial States (or outwardly rejecting the citizenship determinations of individual Trucial States), Abu Dhabi created a dual system, distinguishing "full citizens" from those who have to undergo a more extensive vetting process by the Abu Dhabi security forces. That vetting process is then continually extended, and instead of ever being told "no," residents are told that their cases are being processed – seemingly indefinitely – for decades, and over generations.

---

[24] Telephone interview with key informant from naturalization department, April 10, 2010.

2.6 CONCLUDING REMARKS

An analysis of the historical records points to the importance of temporal boundaries in the creation and definition of the national citizenry. If territorial boundary zones are articulated in space, then demographic boundary zones are articulated in time – people are left at the cusp of entry or exit for protracted periods without a resolution of their legal statuses. The strategic deployment of time is integral to the construction of national boundaries because temporal deadlines delimit and freeze a population as "native" to a state, creating the legitimacy to exclude all those who came after as being "foreign." Cohen (2018) refers to this use of time in politics as a "countdown deadline." Such legal constructions enable states to deem that those who do not meet a temporal deadline are required to undergo a political process of naturalization before entering the national body politic.

In the case of the UAE, time and ethnicity become intertwined when the citizenship law requires UAE citizens to trace their lineage to 1925, a temporal deadline that circumscribes the "insiders" to the Arab tribes documented by the British census. There is a temporal gap between this imagined homogeneous community of 1925 – Abu Dhabi's vision of the population – and the much more heterogeneous demographic reality of the federation across all of the emirates in 1971 (which includes Persians, East Africans, and South Asians). The codification of the citizenship law thus ignited a national dilemma between Abu Dhabi and the remaining emirates over who should be counted as a citizen. As a result of this historical contestation anywhere between 100,000 and 200,000 people are now caught in limbo in the UAE.

This chapter uses the historical records to show that the emergence of a restrictive citizenship regime in the UAE was not a predetermined outcome, but rather the result of heated contestations over which groups could or could not be part of the new nation-state. In addition to local variation in the incorporation practices toward non-Arab minorities across emirates, the UAE can also be contrasted with the history of citizenship of its neighboring Oman, where non-Arab minorities (including Baluchis, Khojas, Zanzibaris, and others) have been accommodated and included to a much greater degree. Primoridalist or purely materialist accounts would predict citizenship laws to be exclusionary in Oman as well (either due to cultural preferences or the logic that rentier states opt to keep the number of beneficiaries small). But explanations that are purely based on ideas about tribal belonging or oil politics on an aggregate national level cannot account for the oscillations of incorporation outcomes, either across different localities or across different states.

Another key finding from the historical records is that local authorities had much greater discretion over citizenship in earlier rather than later phases of the state formation process, and national consolidation brought with it a loss of local jurisdiction over who would be incorporated and counted as citizens. With Abu Dhabi at the helm of state-building in the 1970s, the consolidation of the UAE as a nation-state led to the retrenchment of citizenship boundaries and the eventual disenfranchisement of those who had benefited from the more expansive incorporation policies of the Trucial States in the 1950s and early 1960s. The boundaries of the UAE's citizenry became increasingly stringent as oil production was converted into revenue in the late 1960s and signals of Abu Dhabi's growing influence began to show. Under pressure from Abu Dhabi and the British prior to the formation of the union, the rulers of the smaller emirates began making their own citizenship requirements more stringent, and cancelled passports, reissuing documents on more restrictive terms. By the time the union was formed in 1971, the constitution inscribed a series of elite safeguards against the expansion of the citizenry, and created legal hurdles that would give Abu Dhabi the ultimate discretion over citizenship cases across the Emirates.

To erect hurdles to citizenship, the ruling elites of Abu Dhabi require anyone without a family book to undergo iterative stages of an extensive security vetting for citizenship. This vetting process has become the obstacle itself, as new requirements are added and citizenship decisions are constantly deferred, placing individuals in limbo. While postponing citizenship cases allows Abu Dhabi's elites to evade political dilemmas, it also poses a challenge for the security forces that must enforce borders and clearly document all members of a resident population. As the next chapter examines, the UAE's rapid economic development after the discovery of oil led to large influxes of migrant workers. As the union matured, the authorities in Abu Dhabi increasingly prioritized national security and migration enforcement. This focus necessitated the building of an identity management infrastructure for enforcing migration policies and identity checks domestically and at border points. This security imperative requires placing all residents in a clear legal category. Such is the double bind of delays: by holding people in a pending status for so long, the national authority created the very ambiguity in legal status that challenges its own ability to have a comprehensive vision of the population.

3

Demographic Growth, Migrant Policing, and Naturalization as a "National Security" Threat

This chapter explains how migration and security come to be interlinked in the UAE, illustrating why it becomes increasingly difficult to inhabit an ambiguous legal status over time. While the precise contours of the citizenry were left unresolved as the UAE became an independent state in 1971, the federal authority's prerogatives quickly shifted after national independence to focus on newer flows of noncitizens – "guest workers." From early on in the UAE's history as an independent state, massive influxes of migrant workers led ruling elites to allocate significant resources toward securitizing national boundaries at the territorial borders and inside the state. It may have been the national dilemma (contestations over who is a citizen) that led to the creation of a gray zone of people, but it is the security dilemma (the mobilization of resources toward documenting the entire population and checking legal statuses at all times) that makes precarious citizenship real. As a vast network of private and public institutions that check identity documents in the UAE was built over time, it has become increasingly difficult for anyone with an ambiguous citizenship status to continue living and working in the state.

This chapter examines how the security forces established and consolidated a robust identity management infrastructure in the UAE as growing numbers of migrant workers began to enter the country after its independence. Today, despite its small size, the UAE is the fifth largest host of international migrants in the world and it currently has one of the highest concentration of foreign residents in the world, with noncitizens comprising 88.5 percent of its total population (Federal Competitiveness and Statistics Authority estimates end of 2006, mid-

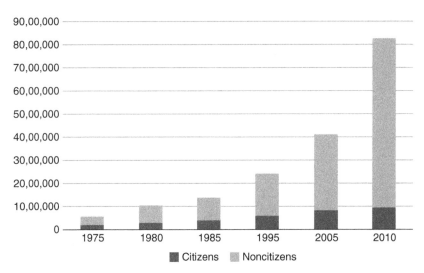

FIGURE 3.1 UAE population by nationality (citizen/noncitizen) (census dates 1975–2005 and 2010 estimate)

2010[1]). This increase in the size of the foreign population vis-à-vis the national population occurred in a concentrated amount of time after independence, especially since the 1990s (see Figure 3.1).[2]

As the new federal state was being consolidated after 1971, the specter of Arab nationalism created a dual pressure on the rulers of the emirates to define the boundaries of citizenry even more narrowly. One pressure came from the focus on "Arabness" in Arab nationalist ideology, which made it increasingly difficult to narrate non-Arabs as Gulf nationals, especially Persians. While there was disagreement among the Trucial State rulers over who should be counted as their subjects from the populations who already resided on the coastline, there was no disagreement about the fact that the new federal state would be an "Arab nation." This is instantiated

[1] Estimates provided by the Gulf Labor Markets, Migration and Population (GLMM) Programme: https://gulfmigration.org/gcc-total-population-and-percentage-of-nationals-and-non-nationals-in-gcc-countries-national-statistics-2017-2018-with-numbers

[2] According to the most recent figures released by the Federal Competitiveness and Statistics Authority (formerly the National Bureau of Statistics), the population in the UAE surged to 8.26 million in 2010, up 65 percent in four years. This growth is due to the influx of foreign workers as the numbers of Emirati nationals grew only from 851,164 in 2006 to 947,997 in the first half of 2010 (Source: Gulf Labor Markets, Migration and Population (GLMM) Programme; https://gulfmigration.org/uae-population-by-nationality-emirati-non-emirati-at-census-dates-1975-2005-and-2010-estimate).

in the constitution and also codified in law as a key determinant of who would become eligible for citizenship in the future. Naturalization is possible – with a multitude of other restrictions and conditions – only for those "of Arab culture" (Federal Law No. 17 for 1972 Concerning Nationality, Passports, and Amendments Thereof, article 2(a)).[3]

If Arab nationalism made it difficult for non-Arab minorities to be recognized as Emirati citizens, it also had the additional effect of making non-Gulf Arabs "undesirable" migrants on the Trucial coastline. By 1967, the British officials in the region routinely referred to other Arab migrants as "undesirables" in the records. The label was generally used to describe Palestinians, but was also applied to Yemenis, especially after the British withdrawal from Aden in 1967 (see, for example, BRE 1967: 145–147). These migrants posed a security threat precisely because they were perceived as being more culturally similar to the local society, and therefore more likely to build linkages and organize labor strikes and political mobilizations against ruling elites. The rulers of the emirates (first alongside the British and arguably even more so later) placed greater scrutiny on Arab migrants in particular and began mobilizing resources to build an identity management infrastructure that would facilitate migration enforcement. The pattern of associating migration with an insurrectionary threat to national security helped to solidify naturalization as a protected realm of national security, making naturalization even more difficult.

This chapter presents the main strategies and institutional developments adopted by the UAE state in its efforts to maintain its guest worker program, while adapting to shifting demographics and national security concerns. It examines the institutional development of the different agencies of the UAE's Ministry of Interior (MOI) in response to the changing demographic makeup of the UAE, especially since the 1990s. It primarily focuses on the security developments in the emirates of Abu Dhabi and Dubai, where the MOI was responding to the highest concentrations of noncitizens. The security agencies of these two emirates have been at the forefront of developing strategies for managing demographic changes, and Abu Dhabi and Dubai continue to have the largest populations in the country. In cities where the surveillance apparatus is highly developed – as it has become in Dubai and Abu Dhabi – identity checks may be

---

[3] This more nebulous characterization of "Arab culture" became more explicitly about ethnicity in the 1975 amendment to article 2 of this law which removed the adjective of culture and referred only to "Arabs."

more robust around strategic locations within the domestic sphere than they are at the territorial boundaries of the state.[4] While territorial closure is generally enforced at the entry points of a territory, domestic closure is enforced through internal identity checks – in interactions with landlords, traffic police, hospital personnel, or school officials. Domestic closure can also be enforced in commercial spaces such as office buildings, hotel lobbies, bars, car rental offices, and malls.

This chapter examines the rise in the internal policing and surveillance of migrant populations that strengthened the internal identity checks in the UAE, making it one of the most heavily securitized countries in the world.[5] This context is important for understanding (1) how naturalization comes to be framed as a national security issue and (2) why it becomes increasingly difficult for those with limbo statuses to reside in the UAE as state institutions develop. This is because in addition to paying attention to the ambiguous legal categories that place people in a liminal zone, it is critical to examine a state's infrastructure for enforcing legal status, which determines the degree to which legal status can come to shape a person's life. When a state's identity management infrastructure is weak, as it is in many parts of the developing world, then the costs of not carrying the "right" national ID are much lower. Individuals with irregular or ambiguous legal statuses can settle, integrate, and even access services or rights reserved for citizens at the local level (Sadiq 2009). However, when an identity management infrastructure is strong, and there are robust identity checks internally across public and private institutions, people become locked out of accessing a wide range of goods and services.

While this chapter focuses on the noncitizen residents who were never considered for citizenship in the UAE, it illustrates how migration policies shape the contours of the citizenry. In the same way that new migrants are regulated through the extant racial hierarchies of a receiving state, racial minorities in large immigrant receiving states are also impacted by inward migrant flows. In this case, the influx of foreign workers renders naturalization an increasingly politicized and protected area of national security, making citizenship even less likely for those caught in limbo as new migrants enter the UAE.

---

[4] To give an example of how the apparatus for identity checks is more robust domestically than at the territorial boundaries, in the UAE GCC citizens are able to enter the territory with their national ID cards, but once inside the territory, they may experience difficulty renting cars or hotel rooms without a valid passport.
[5] Based on the security rankings published by the World Economic Forum (2017), the UAE ranked as the second safest country in the world (after Finland).

3.1 SECURITY IN "UNSETTLED" COMMUNITIES

While the surveillance of migrant populations is increasing globally and much of this technology is introduced through private international companies, cutting-edge technologies can be implemented in the UAE before they are in the United States or the United Kingdom due to Abu Dhabi's large budget, the relatively small size of its geographic area and population, and the lack of a strong civil society or court system to challenge security directives. Moreover, in addition to its domestic calculations of security, the UAE faces a significant amount of international pressure to control the flows of goods and people circulating through its borders. Separating the West from Iran, Afghanistan, and Pakistan, the geopolitical importance of the Gulf to US and European calculations of security cannot be overlooked. In addition to combatting arms, drug, and human trafficking, the UAE's extensive surveillance capabilities and its willingness to share its intelligence with other governments has made it a critical ally of the United States in the "war on terror." While recent developments have heightened this scrutiny, the surveillance of migrant populations and their association with security threats in the Gulf long precedes 9/11.

Even prior to the formation of the UAE in 1971, foreign and domestic political elites in the territories linked its migrant populations to national security threats, arguing that open borders required extensive domestic surveillance. National security, it was argued, must take precedence over individual rights and privacy in high immigration states or "unsettled" societies – a reality that citizens must live with. P. G. Lorimer, the former superintendent of the Dubai police, illustrated this construction of migration as a constant security threat in his report on the security situation in Dubai in 1963. He linked migration into Dubai with the need for constant vigilance and preemptive security measures:

> Although it can not be said that there is an immediate security threat to Dubai, such a threat is constantly with us ... With the changing security situation in the Middle East, caused by the revolution in Yemen and the threat to the Monarchy in Saudi Arabia, which would bring Arab Nationalism to the borders of the Trucial States, we must extend our activities to cover the movements of foreigners in and out of Dubai. (BRE 1963: 629)

Lorimer explicitly linked the movement of populations to the revolutionary threat of Arab nationalism. As new migrants entered the Trucial States in search for work, British officials and the Trucial State rulers became increasingly concerned with controlling the inward flow of Arab migrants in particular. Evading insurrection would require that security forces continue to track the activities of migrant populations even after they entered into the territories and monitor all their collusions with citizens.

In a letter to the Arabian Department of the Foreign Office in London in the same year, the British Political Agent in Dubai elaborated on the rationale of linking migration with the need to privilege security over the protection of individual rights. The British Political Agent had been approached by Sheikh Rashid, the ruler of Dubai, who "was very concerned about the police's habit of searching houses without a warrant" and wanted to know "what was the system in England and to advise what he ought to do in Dubai" (BRE 1963: 631). The Political Agent's response was that the protections in place in England could not be applied to Dubai. The Political Agent explained that in England the police had the right to search and arrest without a warrant only when there was a good reason to believe that a serious offence had been committed, or in pursuit of an individual evading arrest, or when an offence had been committed in the presence of the police officer. However, Sheikh Rashid "should bear in mind that Dubai was not England, that the task of the police here was much more difficult and that it might therefore not be possible to attach *quite so much importance to the rights of the individual* as one did in a settled and orderly community" (BRE 1963: 631, emphasis added). According to the British Political Agent, the United Arab Emirates, and especially Dubai, could not be considered a "settled" community because of the high number of immigrants.

This narrative of privileging national security over privacy because of the security threat posed by immigration is a recurring trope that has endured even after the British departure. In 2010, for example, Dr. Ali Al Khouri, the director of the Emirates Identity Authority (EIDA) (at the time) in Abu Dhabi, exemplified this recurring theme in his keynote lecture on "The Question of Identity in the Gulf" at the University of Exeter.[6] He explained that the Gulf's exceptional demographic growth required governments to develop new instruments of population management – including extensive surveillance and DNA imaging – to preempt the security threats associated with migrant populations. Al Khouri stated that while forensics had typically been used in criminal investigations, they were now being applied to the field of identity management. The

---

[6] The EIDA is now the Federal Authority for Identity and Citizenship (ICA). Dr. Al Khouri is now the advisor to the Arab Economic Unity Council League of Arab States and chairman of the Arab Federation for Digital Economy.

EIDA was spearheading a DNA initiative in "civil biometrics" – the use of forensics to categorize the population into genealogical subgroupings associated with different threat levels. Preempting possible objections from an audience located in the United Kingdom, Al Khouri emphasized that in the Gulf the role of security and the nature of citizenship differed from other regions. According to him, in the United Kingdom this would lead to "the fear of invasion of privacy, but in the GCC states we trust our governments. We can see that they are keeping us safe" (Al Khouri 2010).[7] Although addressing the use of new technologies, Al Khouri's claims about the acquiescence and allegiance of GCC citizens exemplify a common and long-standing narrative about the links between migration and national security in the region. The next section examines the factors that led to the framing of migration as a national security issue even prior to the UAE's state formation.

3.2 THE SECURITY DILEMMA: POLICING MIGRATION PRIOR TO STATE FORMATION

As oil production began in earnest after 1966, the British authorities and Trucial State rulers faced a tension between their rising demand for labor migrants and their simultaneously growing perception of migrants as a national security threat. The need to control the national and ethnic composition of inward migratory flows was both economic and political in nature. The archival record illustrates that, even prior to independence, the British authorities attempted to protect their political and economic interests in the region through the development of nationality clauses in the oil concessions that would force companies to source labor from British holdings. Moreover, with the growth of Arab nationalism from the 1930s onward, the British authorities and the rulers of the Trucial States began associating Arab migrants with subversive threats and consciously attempted to prevent migrants from specific Arab countries from settling in the territories. The attempts to prevent labor strikes and the threat of insurrection led the rulers and British authorities to focus on the development of an expansive domestic security apparatus.

---

[7] These quotes from Al Khouri's keynote speech entitled "The Question of Identity in the Gulf" (which I attended) diverge from the written version of his submitted conference paper "The Challenge of Identity in a Changing World: The Case of GCC countries." The speech was recorded and was previously available for download by conference attendees using the following link: http://socialsciences.exeter.ac.uk/iais_old/all-events/audio/khou ri1.php.

3.2.1 Policing Economic Interests: Nationality Clauses and Oil Exploration

The establishment of political controls on migration flows precedes the UAE's state formation, and the British created policies that would drive migration patterns in their favor. Since the British government had jurisdiction over all foreigners who entered into their protectorates, they used political controls on migrant flows through contractual "nationality clauses" to exclude competing foreign commercial and political interests in the Trucial State coastline. Nationality clauses were first established in the Trucial States in 1937. The nationality clauses required oil companies to grant preference to British and native employees first and foremost and then to other British subjects, particularly from the Indian subcontinent.[8] Any importation of non-British employees was subject to the approval of the British Political Resident in the Persian Gulf. Through these nationality clauses, the British authorities restricted and guided the sourcing of foreign workers at every level of the oil industry, from senior staff to semi- or unskilled labor.

The British authorities were particularly concerned with preventing American companies from gaining political and commercial influence over the Gulf. This fear was exacerbated by the fact that it was two American oil companies, the Gulf Oil Corporation of Pennsylvania (Gulf) and the Standard Oil Company of California (SOCAL), who took the lead with oil concessions in Saudi Arabia and Bahrain. The British feared that the increase in American personnel in Bahrain in particular (where the American Mission hospital and school were already established and actively encouraging American trade) would lead to pressure from the state department to open a US consulate. The nationality clauses were "initially conceived to minimize U.S. penetration [but] these clauses were later invoked to restrict the entry of other foreign nationals, notably

---

[8] The Dubai oil concession states that the oil company has to remain British, changes to the concession cannot be made without the British government's approval, and that the chairman of the company has be a British subject. Moreover, clause 3 in the concession specified that "The employees of the Company in Debai shall at all times be British subjects or subjects of the Sheikh, provided that, with the consent of His Majesty's Government, such persons of other nationality as are required for the efficient carrying on of the undertaking may be employed. Notwithstanding anything contained in the Agreement between the Company and the Sheikh, the importation of foreign native labour shall be subject to the approval of the Political Resident in the Persian Gulf" (BRE 1937: 561). The same clause appears in Sharjah's oil concession (November 12, 1937), Ras al Khaimah's oil concession (March 25, 1938), Abu Dhabi's oil concession (April 11, 1940), and Umm Al Quwain's oil concession (January 29, 1946).

Persians and Iraqis" (Seccombe and Lawless 1986: 554). The British attempts to prevent Arab labor from entering the Persian Gulf became much more explicit in the second half of the twentieth century as the momentum of Arab nationalist movements grew, but political controls on foreign recruitment and employment were in place from the very beginning of the petroleum industry's presence in the Gulf.

It should be noted that the nationality clauses were a largely unwelcome imposition on British oil companies, who often wanted to employ American geologists and experienced drillers. Moreover, from the point of view of these companies, Persians and Arabs provided distinct advantages over Indian workers. First, Persians and Arabs often came at their own expense, and since they did not enter the territory under a formal contract with oil companies they could be easily hired and fired. The recruitment of Indians, on the other hand, was a much more complicated and lengthy process, especially after the 1922 Indian Emigration Act abolished the indentured labor system. This law specified that formal Foreign Service Agreements (FSA) controlled the terms of contracts offered to Indians, and that these agreements had to be authorized by the Protector of Emigrants, a Government of India official (Seccombe and Lawless 1986).

In both American and British oil companies, wages were linked to national origin, so that people of different nationalities received different wages for the same job. In the Gulf, this practice was first implemented in the oil industries during the early twentieth century, and it has since spread to other industries as an increasingly codified practice of the *kafāla* system across the region. Robert Vitalis (2009) refers to this system of paying labor different wages according to national origin as the "racial wage." In his history of the development of the oil industry in eastern Saudi Arabia, he shows how this practice was an inherited and sustained dimension of the way American firms organized labor for over a century prior. He links the American labor practices in the Gulf to the practices of the US mining industry in the American West and Northern Mexico (the Indian territories of Arizona and New Mexico) from the late nineteenth century to World War I, and the American oil industry's expansion into Mexico, Trinidad, Colombia, and Venezuela in the 1920s. In all of these places, including the Persian Gulf after the 1930s, the racial wage was a core issue that pitted laborers against white owners and managers as well as privileged castes of workers. Indeed, as explored in the next section, wage differentials were a critical factor in igniting the first rounds of labor strikes in the oil industry of the Trucial States.

3.2.2 Policing Labor: The Subversive Threat of Arab Migration

This section demonstrates that migration flows were associated with sub-versive threats even prior to the formation of the UAE federation. From the late 1930s onward, the British and Trucial State rulers placed political controls on the national origin of migrant flows. After the 1950s in parti-cular, the more culturally similar Arab migrants were viewed as posing a larger national security threat. Furthermore, in response to the influx of migrants into the territories, intelligence and security officials built new security agencies and adopted a new security approach that would allow for greater surveillance of migrant populations, especially Arabs.

Labor strikes are one of the key reasons that the influx of labor migrants, especially Arab migrants, came to be associated with posing a subversive threat to the British authorities and Trucial State rulers. The first round of labor strikes in the Trucial States occurred in May 1963, when workers interrupted the operations of the oil fields in Jebel Dhanna, Tarif, and Murban in Abu Dhabi and on Das Island (also an Abu Dhabi concession). Across the camps, the strikers had four overarching demands. The first demand was an increase of 50 percent on the existing wages. Secondly, the workers demanded equal pay for equal work. Local employees were particularly resentful of the fact that Indians and northern Arabs (Jordanian and Lebanese employees) were being paid higher wages for the same work. The third demand was that local men should be allowed to do more of the jobs that were currently being given to expatri-ates (such as driving trucks). The fourth demand was that a list of indivi-duals involved in disciplining and managing the labor force (especially the labor officer) should be sacked. In addition to the grievances about the employment of foreigners and low wages, the strikers were also critical of Sheikh Shakhbut Al Nahyan (the ruler of Abu Dhabi at the time) who was beginning to accrue vast incomes from the oil concession without provid-ing more services or redistributing the wealth.

The strikes were largely concentrated among the Arab members of the labor force, and the movement followed shortly after a broadcast on the "*Sawt al-'Arab*" radio about British Petroleum's (BP) wage discrimination.[9]

---

[9] *Sawt al-'Arab* or the "Voice of the Arabs" was a Cairo-based radio station that the former Egyptian president Gamal Abdel Nasser used to broadcast messages of Arab unity and nationalism. It was popular across the Arab world, especially in the 1950s and 1960s. According to the British records, in a 1963 broadcast on BP company oil workers, broad-caster Kamal Abu Talib claimed "that he had in his possession a 'secret' staff list of the British Petroleum Company dated 1st January 1963 showing name, staff member,

Since the demands were virtually identical across all of the camps, the British authorities immediately suspected that the strikes were the result of coordinated outside interference by Arab nationalists – a suspicion that could not be proven. Nonetheless, the association of Arab migrants with a subversive threat to the security of the Trucial States and the operations of oil concessions gained traction, and the British authorities and Trucial State rulers began revamping their security tactics in light of the strikes (BRE 1963: 559–599). This was especially the case because of the spread of Arab nationalist movements that were occurring in other parts of the Arabian Peninsula including Saudi Arabia, Bahrain, Kuwait, North and South Yemen, and Oman (Chalcraft 2010, 2011).

The labor strikes coincided with greater flows of Arab migrants into the Trucial State territories, leading the security forces to develop a "new security approach" that placed Arab migrants under heightened surveillance and scrutiny. This was initiated after cells of Yemeni subversives were found to be operating in Dubai and Sharjah in 1965, with plans to smuggle explosives into Sharjah, start anti-Iranian riots, and assassinate Lorimer, his inspector, and two senior noncommissioned officers. Thirty-five people were deported after these plans were thwarted, but the coincidence of the timing of labor strikes and terrorist plots solidified the idea that Arab migrants posed a subversive threat. In response, the British helped set up new special branches of police forces, including the Dubai Special Branch, the Trucial States Special Branch, a Sharjah police force, and a counter-subversive radio station (*Sawt as-Sahil*) that was run by the Trucial Oman Scouts (TOS).[10] In a correspondence with the Political Resident in Bahrain in 1966, the Political Agent in Abu Dhabi summarized the new security approach and "intelligence task" as being divided into four distinct parts. The first goal was "to keep a watch on Northern Arab circles in Abu Dhabi and Buraimi." The second goal was "to keep a watch on Labour organisations in the oil fields." The third was "to keep a watch for subversive elements among the people of Abu Dhabi, both townsmen and the tribes." And finally, the fourth and arguably most important task was to track any links between the northern Arab circles in Abu Dhabi and labor organizations in the oil fields (BRE 1966: 231).

---

nationality, work, grade and pay. He read out certain entries which, he said, indicated that foreigners (i.e. non-Arabs) were given preferential employment while Arab workers were distrusted and kept a long time on the same low wages" (BRE 1963: 587).

[10] The Trucial Oman Scouts were a paramilitary force in the Trucial State territories that were financed and supported by the British.

In other words, in this "new security approach" the labor strikes in the oil fields were not seen as grievances specifically related to oil industry wage practices, but rather framed as part of a larger subversive threat that was brought in by Arab migrants. Accordingly, while the British had already attempted to encourage the employment of people from the Indian subcontinent over those from Arab countries, the labor strikes made this policy more explicit.

The British authorities' heightened scrutiny of Arab migrants extended beyond the oil fields. There was a sustained effort to increase the surveillance and supervision of Arabs in a wide range of domains – especially in education since many of the teachers came from Egypt or Palestine. The meetings of the Abu Dhabi Local Intelligence Committees involved detailed reports on the exact number of Arab populations entering the territory. In the minutes of one such meeting that was held in 1968, security officials explained that despite their advice to the contrary, Sheikh Zayed Al Nahyan of Abu Dhabi would not refuse entry to Egyptians but allowed them to enter under supervision. Linking Egyptian schoolteachers to a subversive threat, the British security officials also argued that all school textbooks, especially those originating in Egypt, should be scrutinized and vetted for possible subversive influences (BRE 1968: 393). The British intelligence officials consistently cautioned that their "adversaries" – particularly the Egyptians, Iraqis, and Saudis – would use labor migration as a guise for infiltrating the Trucial States through propaganda campaigns, intelligence agents, and terrorism (BRE 1966: 219–223).

In the annual review of 1970, the Political Agent in Dubai expanded upon the British view of Arab migrants as subversive agents:

I am not being sarcastic when I say that some of my best friends are Palestinians, but I hate to see the northern Arabs invading the Trucial States with their bigotry, nepotism and greed ... Yet it seems impossible to keep these people out. They percolate nimbly through the loopholes in our visa system, and once established they send for their nephews and cousins ... Some bring talents that are needed here, just as they are in Kuwait and throughout the area of the Palestinian diaspora, but others are natural material for NDFLOAG [National Democratic Front for the Liberation of Oman and the Arabian Gulf] and its polysyllabic sister organisations. Indeed these may well be their agents. (BRE 1970: 5)

One of the challenges of controlling the influx of Arab migrants was the fact that, though the British technically had jurisdiction over all foreigners, there was little they could do if the Trucial State rulers authorized the entry of Arabs and employed them. The British could refuse the visa of a particular individual, but if a ruler sent a letter of invitation, that letter would be presented to immigration officials upon entry and could not be refused by those officials. The erection of a system of split jurisdiction under the Order in Council thus multiplied the visa loopholes that individuals could use to enter into the territories of the Trucial States.

3.2.3 Policing the Shoreline: The Challenge of "Illegal" Immigration

As the British authorities and Trucial State rulers became increasingly concerned with the spread of Arab nationalism and subversive elements among the migrant population, they developed new security agencies and increased the funding allocated to security forces. The British established the Trucial Oman Levies (TOL) in 1951 for the purposes of defense cooperation across the Trucial coastline. This force was initially raised to maintain interstate security and protect oil survey parties. The TOL headquarters were in Sharjah and led by a British major with officers and ranks from the Jordanian Arab legion. By 1957, this force grew from its initial size of 35 men to over 500 men, and it was renamed the Trucial Oman Scouts (TOS) (Khalifa 1979: 25). The TOS acted as a peacekeeping force throughout the territories of the Trucial States and Oman, and became particularly involved in territorial disputes that emerged due to competition between rulers over oil concessions. It was also mandated to obtain the political and security intelligence necessary for deterring armed infiltration into the Trucial States, and maintain a prison for persons subject to the British jurisdiction (BRE 1961: 187–189). The TOS was the precursor to the federal army and it became the Union Defense Force (UDF) in 1972 when it was handed over to the new federal authorities of the UAE. By the time it was handed over, the TOS had over 1,700 men.

In addition to the TOS, which was a regional force, migration enforcement was increasingly becoming one of the main focuses of local police forces, especially the Dubai police. Because of its status as a port city, the police force in Dubai was "a model of its kind in the Gulf" (BRE 1963: 619). At the time of the union's formation the Dubai police force was by far the strongest in the Trucial States – much stronger than that of Abu Dhabi – despite the fact that Abu Dhabi's population was one quarter of Dubai's and its police force was three times as big. The British paid for the Dubai police force initially, and it was (according to the British Political Resident in Bahrain) the most efficiently run. From 1960 to 1963, the population of Dubai grew by 50 percent from 40,000 to 60,000 people while the budget of the security forces only allowed an increase of twenty men (BRE 1963: 620). By 1962–1963, the Dubai police force began cooperating with the antecedent to Interpol (the International Criminal Police Organization, ICPO) on arms and narcotic trafficking. The Dubai police force also regularly provided valuable intelligence to the TOS and the political residency in Bahrain about Omani rebel activities and commercial sabotage of British vessels, and had the most robust searches of passengers and ships.

However, as the Political Resident in Bahrain explained to the Foreign Office in London, even in Dubai, "the only effectively policed state on the coast, there may be at this moment, according to the Commandant of Police, about 15,000 persons who have entered the state illegally. There is no control whatsoever on immigrants into any of the other states either and no significant control at all on the movement by land between them" (BRE 1966: 224). By the late 1960s, the only identity checks on incoming population flows were in the ports of Dubai, Sharjah, and Ras al Khaimah. There was little the authorities could do to stop people from entering the country outside of these checkpoints. The pressing need to strengthen the Abu Dhabi police force in particular became especially clear when the police provided little help in quelling the labor strikes of 1963. After Sheikh Zayed Al Nahyan took control over Abu Dhabi (deposing Sheikh Shakhbut Al Nahyan in 1966), he began using the oil revenues to finance the building of institutions. He commenced by increasing the wages and training of the Abu Dhabi police force (and subsequently the police forces of the remaining Trucial States).

The police forces in the Trucial States were mercenary forces, following the general pattern of all the police forces in the Gulf. As the British head of the Dubai police explained in a secret note to the Political Agent in Dubai in 1966, "there are a number of so-called Dubai subjects in the Force but these are either Beduin or of Iranian or Balouch parentage. The Rulers are all against having their own subjects in the police forces and armies and prefer to rely on mercenaries" (BRE 1966: 520). The British political agencies in Dubai and Abu Dhabi provided a plethora of justifications for why foreign individuals should be recruited for these posts, usually revolving around the familiar tropes of the purported laziness and ineptitude of locals (BRE 1963: 632). The main reason for the use of mercenaries, however, was that British and local officials wanted to ensure that the ranks of the security forces would remain allegiant to the rulers and

British authorities, particularly in responding to revolutionary or Arab nationalist threats. The Dubai police chief explained that he had doubts about how "particularly those from the South Arabian Federation and Yemen, would act if committed to action involving the use of force by the police against persons demonstrating for some Arab Nationalist, or anti-Imperialist cause" (BRE 1966: 520). The historical use of mercenary forces in the British protectorates of the Persian Gulf, which continues today, further demonstrates that foreigners were present in the Trucial States prior to the large-scale migration flows of the early 1970s and played an integral part in forming the state.

In addition to developing new security agencies, by the late 1960s, the Trucial State rulers and British agents began attempting to develop a more coordinated response to "illegal" immigration into the Trucial States territories. There was no common policy for determining who was allowed to enter all of the Trucial States, which made enforcement challenging. Nonetheless, the Trucial State Council agreed to curb immigration, and the security forces (TOS in cooperation with local police and British authorities) were deployed to police the shoreline in particular, aiming to prevent flows of Iraqis, Pakistanis, Indians, Iranians, and Yemenis from trying to enter the country. The national origin of immigrants who were targeted by the authorities as being "illegal" varied each year, but from 1967 to 1971 – the lead-up to the formation of the union – the British were particularly invested in controlling the unregulated flows of (1) Indians, Pakistanis, and Iraqis (who formed the majority of the low-skilled labor force); (2) Adenis, Yemenis, and Somalis (the British records characterize these nationalities as "semi-educated artisan-type workers" who will be easily galvanized and pose a subversive threat if they do not have jobs that occupy them); and finally (3) Omani rebels and northern Arabs coming from Basra, Kuwait, and Saudi Arabia (these nationalities were characterized as the highest-risk group for subversives) (BRE 1967: 162–163).

These enforcement priorities illustrate what became a consistent pattern in the way that migration was framed as a security threat in the UAE – the greater cultural similarities between immigrants and the host society the larger the perceived threat. The fear of Arab migrants as posing greater insurrectionary threats than non-Arabs would later shape the demographic composition of the UAE – and the boundaries of its citizenry.

3.2.4 Policing the Interior: Domestic Identity Checks

By the late 1960s and early 1970s, it became readily apparent to the security forces that effective migration enforcement would require surveillance and identity checks inside the country as well as at the shoreline. The approach to migration enforcement had initially been about deploying security forces to establish identity checks at the borders, but this tactic was proving to be an ineffective way of combatting illegal immigration for several reasons. First, the border control officials could not stop people who entered surreptitiously by boat during the night, and the Trucial States' long shoreline only exacerbated this difficulty. Second, people who entered legally with a visa would often stay past its expiry date and become "illegal"; this situation could not be addressed by simply instituting stricter border controls (BRE 1966: 619–626). The issue was that once immigrants entered the threshold of the territory there was "nothing to make it administratively more difficult for the immigrants to live and obtain work" inside the Trucial States (BRE 1967: 164). Consequently, from 1966 onward, there was a growing attempt to approach migration enforcement through surveillance and "periodic checks inside the state" (BRE 1966: 621).

Several possible systems of internal control were debated, including the requirement that people carry their passports at all times. The problem was that many of the people (especially Persians and Baluchis) who were employed across the Trucial States did not have passports. While some of these individuals did get passports from some of the Trucial States (all but Abu Dhabi), others did not, which meant that passports could not be used as a universal system for conducting identity checks. Large portions of the nomadic Bedouin population also did not have passports, and when it came to identifying them (such as for the purposes of oil surveying) it fell upon a ruler to claim the tribe as his subjects and up to the leader of that tribe to pledge allegiance to that ruler. Moreover, the passport/visa approach was also problematic because "people of the Gulf" – especially Kuwaitis, Bahrainis, Qataris, and Omanis – did not need visas to enter into the Trucial States.

By 1967, a new approach to migration enforcement had emerged in the negotiations between British intelligence officials, the British Political Agents, and the Trucial State Council which comprised all of the Trucial State rulers. This new policy was made up of two parts. First, it was decided that going forth, visas would be checked even prior to passengers landing on the Trucial Coast. The agreement outsourced the responsibility of identity checking to the master of every ship, who would now have to ensure that every passenger carried a valid passport and visa for entry into the Trucial States before delivering them to the coastline. Failure to comply with these regulations would result in heavy fines and jail time.

Secondly, and more importantly, the authorities decided to implement a "No Objection Certificates" (NOCs) system of resident permits and labor contracts, similar to the system of resident permits that had been in place in Bahrain. This system would tie residency to specific labor contracts, so that (in theory) no one could legally enter or reside in the Trucial States without having a job for which they were specifically recruited. The visa system would be based on local sponsors (individual employers or companies) who would have to obtain No Objection Certificates from the British authorities. The NOC system privatizes migration enforcement by holding individual sponsors responsible for the repatriation of their foreign employees. The idea was that since applications had to be made locally, the NOC system was designed to make it relatively easy for a reputable employer to bring in the necessary labor, while making it difficult for immigrants to "drift in" in search of work (BRE 1971: 508). Critically, all visa applications would have to go through the security authorities, and Arab migrants in particular would have to undergo an additional vetting process through the intelligence department in Abu Dhabi (BRE 1971: 504).

The policy implementation plan consisted of a three-step identity regularization drive that would document all residents on the coastline, providing amnesty and documentation for some residents while targeting others as "illegals." The first step was to establish resident permits for all of those who had been residing in the Trucial States and employed by local authorities for a period of twelve months. The second step was to circulate a notice to private firms informing them that their employees who could prove that they had been employed for at least twelve months would be eligible for work and resident permits. In the third and final stage of the identity regularization drive, a short public amnesty was declared and those who could prove that they have been in the territories for a year would gain work and resident permits. The goal was to keep this amnesty period short enough so that new immigrants could not take advantage of it (BRE 1971: 528).

In order to transfer the jurisdiction and authority over foreign residency permits from the British agency to the new Emirati state after 1971, the Trucial States had to agree upon a common immigration and citizenship policy that would create standardized guidelines for issuing visas and identity documents. As discussed in the previous chapter, this proved to be an exceptionally difficult task. The entrenched disagreements in the domains of immigration and citizenship delayed the formation of the union because at stake was more than simply "illegal" immigration. The way that the population would be divided into "citizens" and "guests" would determine the relative size of the citizenries of each of the Trucial States and, consequently, the distribution of power in the union. The outcome was that at the formation of the UAE as a state, some groups of residents were not "guests" but did not gain full citizenship, falling into an ambiguous limbo status instead. As a result, from 1971 onward, the security forces of the new federal administration had to increase the surveillance and security initiatives targeting migrants, while also negotiating the presence of ambiguously documented populations who did not clearly fit into any legal category. As the new federal state apparatus continued to develop, these ambiguous populations would come to pose a challenge to the security forces' ability to have a synoptic vision or comprehensive registry of the entire population. As migration flows began to increase exponentially after the formation of the UAE, intelligence and security officials responded by establishing new specialized agencies and taskforces and developing new policing strategies that were designed to count, categorize, and monitor all of the UAE's residents.

3.3 SECURITY AND MIGRATION POSTINDEPENDENCE: AN EMERGING "DEMOGRAPHIC IMBALANCE"

The fear of Arab migrants as posing a security threat pushed ruling elites to increasingly source labor from outside of the Arab world, expanding the labor force with people who would never become eligible for citizenship in the new "Arab" nation-state. In the immediate postindependence era, the UAE attracted large numbers of labor migrants who were recruited not only to the oil industry, but across all sectors of the economy.

Even though the British, the Trucial State rulers, and other ruling elites in the Gulf associated Arab migrants (especially those from Egypt, Syria, Yemen, and Palestine) with insurrectionary threats, the rulers also initially sourced administrative and legal support from those same sending countries because of the need for Arabic-language speakers. Arab migrants made up core parts of the legal and educational infrastructures in the UAE and other Gulf states. There is evidence that these earlier flows of Arab migrants were granted citizenship by Sheikh Zayed – especially those involved with setting up the new federal state.[11] As a result, prior to the

---

[11] In a recent magazine article, Al Qassemi (2016) tracks down and documents the lives of several dozen naturalized Arabs who were involved in the earliest phases of the UAE's state formation from Bahrain, Palestine, Jordan, Iraq, Lebanon, Egypt, and Sudan. With

1970s oil boom more than 80 percent of the migrant workers in the Gulf region were Arabs, mainly from Egypt, Syria, Yemen, and Palestine. Migration to the Gulf surged after the 1973 oil price hike, with higher numbers of migrants from poorer Arab nations like Egypt and Yemen rising especially. About 1.3 million migrants were estimated to have been in the Gulf region in 1975 (Rahman 2010). A second price hike in 1979 and the subsequent rise in government revenue led the Gulf states to implement more developmental initiatives and increase the importation of foreign labor. The percentage of Arab migrant workers began declining, primarily due to the inflow of Indians, Pakistanis, Sri Lankans, and other Asian workers. This replacement of Arab expatriates with Asians continued as a dominant demographic trend in the 1990s.

The preference for Southeast Asians over Arab workers became especially apparent following the first Gulf War due to a perception that certain Arab migrants had sided with Iraq in the Gulf War and now posed a security threat. Naturalized Palestinians in Kuwait, Egyptian migrants in Iraq, and Yemenis in Saudi Arabia all became "enemies of the state" virtually overnight for being from the nationality of the opposite camp. Over 3 million legal Arab immigrants were forced to leave the Gulf, regardless of their actual stance on the conflict. This included a mass "return" of Palestinians from the Gulf to Jordan because of the Palestinian Liberation Organization's position on Iraq (Lesch and Lustick 2005; Van Hear 1993, 1995). The Gulf War had massive ramifications not only for migrants in the Gulf but also for the way that Gulf governments perceived their dependence upon labor migrants. As Fargues explains, "political lessons were drawn by states that possess the most strategic resources, but with neither the demography nor the social systems to defend themselves. The war was an occasion for them to reassess their vision of labor and to adopt nationalization policies of their workforce" (Fargues 2011: 279). The Gulf War helped solidify and spread the idea that depending upon migrant labor was a national security threat that made Gulf societies vulnerable. In the war's aftermath, stringent naturalization policies gained popular support as naturalized citizens in the Gulf were depicted as being motivated by the economic benefits of citizenship and not sufficiently allegiant or loyal. Moreover, the economic crisis that followed the Gulf War only served to heighten the growing resentment against migrants.

few exceptions, all the cases discussed are of Arabs who migrated to the UAE from the 1930s to 1970s, either prior to the formation of the state or during the early phases of unionization.

Reconstruction had to be paid for with cheap oil and migrants came to be viewed by citizens as economic competitors. The political developments of the 1990s thus only served to entrench the barriers against migrant incorporation. Though the Ministry of Interior already had regulatory and enforcement power over migration and citizenship policies, the regional conflict and changing demographics led the security forces to take even more active roles by instituting new security initiatives and policing strategies.

The demographic shift away from Arab migrants continued as inward migratory flows increased exponentially with the construction boom of the 1990s. This rapid period of economic development led to incredible demographic changes in the composition and size of the UAE's population at an unprecedented speed. Due primarily to the importation of foreign workers, the population of the country almost doubled in a span of ten years, surging from 1,809,000 in 1990 to 3,033,000 in 2000 (UN Department of Economics and Social Affairs, Population Division 2010). Inward migration has continued to be a key feature of the UAE's economic growth, resulting in noncitizens outnumbering nationals significantly. The construction boom led to two trends in the demographic composition of the UAE. First, along with the rise in the ratio of foreign workers, the influx of construction workers created a rising asymmetry in the male to female ratio. The second trend is that the construction boom led to a shift in recruitment more explicitly away from Arab labor migrants toward labor migrants from Southeast Asia.

The preference for Southeast Asians over Arab workers became even more explicit following the Gulf War, and was partially due to the perception that Palestinians and Yemenis had sided with Iraq during the war (Colton 2010). This demographic shift in the UAE's foreign resident population was the result of an active policy to preempt the political challenge of pan-Arab organizing – a concern that has been present since the earliest flows of workers entered into the oil fields prior to state formation. This trend in the changing national origin of workers was "the result of the policies of the Gulf countries that favored South Asian workers (they were believed to be politically 'safer' than their Arab counterparts)" (Rahman 2010: 10). Fears about the politicization of Arab laborers have driven recruitment and settlement patterns. This general shift away from Arab noncitizens may have also been economically driven by the private sector as the reservation wage of Arab labor migrants is set higher than that of South Asian labor migrants. In short, a combination of factors and the collusion of powerful interests arising in both the private

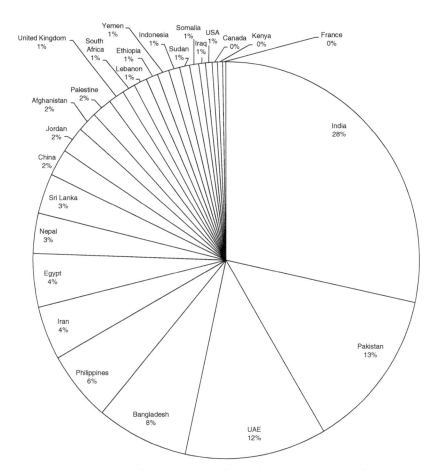

FIGURE 3.2 Estimates of population residing in the UAE by country of citizenship (2014)[12]

and public sectors helped drive this demographic trend. As a result of these policies, South Asians now overwhelmingly outnumber Arabs in the UAE (this skew toward South Asians holds even if one counts all citizens and Arab noncitizens as one group). Based on the most recent estimates approximately 50 percent of the total population of the UAE is South Asian (see Figure 3.2).

[12] Source: Gulf Labor Market and Migration http://gulfmigration.eu/uae-estimates-of-population-residing-in-the-uae-by-country-of-citizenship-selected-countries-2014 This figure draws from a range of different sources for which there was reliable national origin

These demographic changes (especially the non-Arab/Arab ratio) created what has been referred to by Emirati officials and the local media as a "demographic imbalance."[13] By 2010 a new government agency called the Federal Demographic Council (Cabinet Federal Decree No. 3 of 2010) was established for the precise purpose of addressing this problem. The goal of the council was to restore the "demographic balance" in the country, with lawmakers from the Federal National Council calling the imbalance a "threat to national security" (Salama 2010). It is important to underscore that this "demographic imbalance" is the (unintended) consequence of government policies that actively shaped labor flows away from Arab migrants while foreclosing citizenship for non-Arabs, but it is nonetheless construed as a threat to national security. In response, the different agencies of the security apparatus of the UAE grew alongside, and as a means of managing and adapting to, the extensive demographic changes of the 1990s.

3.4 POLICING "IMBALANCE": FAMILY SOCIAL SECURITY AND A NEW POLICING STRATEGY

Despite the fact that the security forces associated Arab migrants with a security threat precisely because of their perceived cultural commonality with the local population, this section shows how the security forces also framed non-Arab migrants as posing a security threat because of their perceived cultural differences. Given the concentration of demographic changes in the emirate of Dubai and the institutional strength of its police force, the Dubai police took an active role in defining the new security challenges associated with the UAE's demographic changes. Since the 1990s the Dubai police department has published a series of studies that define the range of threats associated with having guest workers, the majority of which call upon the MOI to establish specialized task forces (usually under the purview of the Criminal Investigation Division [CID]) to deal with the new challenges of a growing foreign population. These

data, and it is not an exhaustive accounting of all residents in the UAE. While most of the figures are from 2014, they range from 2009 to 2015. This data was originally published in *BQ Magazine* on April 12, 2015. While the UAE government does collect data on the national origin of all migrants it does not publish this data. Instead BQ collected most of the estimates of population percentages by national origin by contacting individual embassies based in the UAE.

[13] The term "demographic imbalance" is used by both government officials and the English news media (see *The National* newspaper [UAE] and *The Peninsula* [Qatar]) and is most frequently applied to the UAE and Qatar. See also Shah (2008).

studies can be broadly grouped into two categories. The first category tends to focus on specific kinds of criminal activities that are associated with open borders, especially drug trafficking. The second category of studies focus on threats that are both criminal and cultural; they probe the impact that the large foreign resident presence might have on the safety and cultural integrity of the citizenry. Together these studies construct the concept of family social security as a new national security realm that emerges as a result of the demographic imbalance. See Table 3.1 for an overview of the studies that the Dubai police published on the realm of family social security between 1990 and 2007.

The studies focusing on family social security demonstrate how the security forces came to associate the presence of noncitizens with threat, how that threat came to be defined, and what measures would have to be taken to manage it. The study "Demographic Indicators and Family Social Security," provides a lens for understanding how the Dubai police forces have created this logical extension migration and security. The study argues that rapid population growth and the higher population density that the UAE has been experiencing requires the MOI to increase its scope and services. It then goes on to link this threat explicitly to the growing presence of foreigners (rather than the "natural" population growth).[14] It argues that, "the problem is not with having foreign workers but it is usually with its percentage to the national residents. The higher the percentage of foreigners especially from the same nationality the higher the risk the national residents are subjected to. Having more than two thirds of the national residents as foreign workers is quit [sic] big" (Fouad 1999: 2).

By specifying that the risk to the national population is greater when the ratio of foreigners increases – especially when migrants are of the same nationality – the study employs a concept of risk that encompasses both criminal and cultural threats. It also provides a description of new population characteristics like unemployment, illiteracy, women's participation in the labor force, and marital status (in this case referring to the decline in married couples, with growing rates of divorce among citizens and unaccompanied bachelors among migrants). It states, "one can notice that the lower the level of the population characteristics the higher the rates of crimes" (1999: 1). In other words, the study argues that the demographic changes associated with having such high concentrations of migrants lead to the dilution of the population and higher rates in crimes. The study also

---

[14] The natural population growth refers to the growth rate that is calculated using the birthrates and deaths of the population not counting migration.

TABLE 3.1 *Dubai police studies related to family social security, 1990s–2007*

Year	Title
1994	• Family and Crime (Arabic) • Social Variables and Their Implications on the Family in the UAE (Arabic) • Strategic Security Planning and Change Management in the Fight Against Terrorism (Arabic) • General Aspects of Organized Crime (Arabic) • Planning to Contain Tensions (Arabic)
1995	• A Look at DNA (Arabic) • Indicators for General Security Panel (Arabic) • Juvenile Delinquency in the UAE from an Islamic Perspective (Arabic) • Indicators on Juvenile Delinquency and Efforts to Confront (Arabic) • Planning Time Element in Security Operations Critical (Arabic) • Community Policing Indicators Cohesion [sic] (Arabic) • Security Satellite (Arabic)
1996	• Juvenile Delinquency Indicators (English)
1997	• Child Security from an Islamic Perspective (Arabic) • Security CCTV (Arabic)
1998	• Rights of the Child in the Emirati Law (Arabic) • Police Planning in Light of the Current Security Challenges (Arabic)
1999	• Population Component in Planning Police Patrol (Arabic) • Demographic Indicators and Family Social Security (English)
2000	• Challenges Facing the Security Services during the Current Decade (Arabic) • Crime in a Rapidly Changing World (Arabic)
2004	• Universal Declaration on Human Genome and Human Rights (Arabic) • Privatization and Used in the Security Sphere [sic] (Arabic) • Electronic Referral Systems between Police and the Social Sector (Arabic)
2005	• Early Warning Systems Effective Mechanism to Address the Potential Security Crisis (Arabic) • Develop a Mechanism to Take Investment Decisions and Its Impact on Enhancing the Security of Businessmen (Arabic) • Construction and Management Task Forces (Arabic)

(continued)

TABLE 3.1 *(continued)*

Year	Title
	• Expulsion of Aliens between State Sovereignty and Security Duty (Arabic)
2006	• Repercussions for the Security Problems of Slums (Arabic)
2007	• Globalization and Tourism (Arabic) • Early Warning Signs for Youth Violence: Fact, Fiction, or Fad (Arabic)

Source: Dubai police, General Headquarters, Research and Studies Centre (www.dubaipo lice.gov.ae/academy_prod/showpage.jsp?objectID=10 [no longer available])

goes on to "highlight [the] types of crimes probably committed among people having the described demographic feature" (1999: 2). The male to female ratio increased substantially because of the large numbers of male construction workers entering the country. According to the study, this "biased" or imbalanced male to female ratio makes the national population susceptible to the following crimes: "robbery, drug traffic and addiction, prostitution, raping, child abuse" (1999: 2).

This coupling of the (especially male) expatriate presence with a threat to the national citizenry is a theme that recurs in a number of the different studies published by the Dubai police, especially on issues relating to the security of the family and children. Often this security threat is not directly linked to the migrants themselves, but rather to the larger demographic changes that are likely to lead to certain criminal activities that the police force should preempt and control. However, the rationale behind why certain crimes are more likely to occur illustrates that the cultural threat of migrants is often conflated with criminal activity.

This conflation of migration with a security threat is exemplified in the way that these studies use the issue of juvenile delinquency to demonstrate how the local population would be impacted by the presence of foreigners. For example, the study entitled "Juvenile Delinquency Indicators" aims to determine the dimensions and identify the causes of juvenile delinquency in the UAE in an effort to develop "a control plan ... along with the evaluation of the exerted efforts in order to contain the problem" (Abdullah 1996: 1). It defines a juvenile delinquent as "one who commits an offence punishable by effective laws if he or she is over seven and under 18 years old, unless he or she is mentally retarded or lacks consciousness or discernment" (1996: 1). It states: "the child is born with a mixture of good and bad tendencies. Educational, sociological, economic, psychological and family conditions surrounding him or her help support one of the two sides to surmount the other" (1996: 1). It also names a number of family-centric factors that lead to juvenile delinquency, including a "broken home, ill-breeding, a weak parent-child relationship, deprivation, low IQ, low social and economic standards, heredity, abnormal personality, and delinquent peer groups." It then specifies, "local factors related to our culture that may influence juveniles depending on the immediately surrounding conditions and their predisposition as well" (1996: 2). These "local" factors include "how to spend leisure time, traveling abroad without sufficient monitoring, housemaids and early sexual experiences, television and videos, lack of school supervision, rapid social changes, multitude and conflict of cultures, class differences, competitive struggle for money, limited impact of social clubs, recreational activities and summer services" (1996: 2). Of these "local" factors, the factors identified as the exposure to a multitude of cultures and the "housemaids and early sexual experiences" are related explicitly to the presence of a migrant workforce. The study also identifies the rate of females to males as a factor leading to juvenile delinquency. It states that this ratio is equal in "balanced societies" while "in labor-importing countries" the rate of males to females may be "3 or 4 times as great." This "unbalanced rate may be conducive to the commission of more sexual crimes and child sexual abuse" which also leads to juvenile delinquency (1996: 2). The study argues that it is important to measure the concentration of juvenile delinquents by national origin in order to develop preventative plans and define ways to control the problem and keep it from spreading.

The Dubai police reports illustrate how a key step in the institutional development of the security apparatus was to study specific criminal activities and link them to the presence of noncitizens (even if the crimes themselves are committed by nationals, as in the case of juvenile delinquency). The Dubai police chief (from 1980 to 2013), Dhahi Khalfan, has openly called for restrictions upon noncitizens in the UAE, arguing that the population imbalance poses a great threat to the culture, national identity, and domestic security of the UAE. Asked the question of whether he thinks that Arab identity is in danger he responded:

Yes, the foreigner presents his idea, culture and identity on the Gulf society. I will not hide from you a secret as a security man that there are criminal customs and cases that were never found or heard about in our Gulf society, for example ... the third sex. These customs and beliefs were brought to our communities with the number of increasing expats. It may be a normal habit and acceptable in their community, but it has undoubtedly formed a thorny issue in our Gulf society.[15]

In all of these formulations of migration as a national security threat, the threat posed oscillates between cultural and criminal.

The security forces have developed specific mechanisms for managing and preempting that criminal/cultural threat; by the early 2000s, the new federal Minister of Interior had redesigned the institutions of the MOI for that purpose. The federal MOI adopted and implemented a "new policing" strategy spearheaded by the Abu Dhabi police force. Under the leadership of the Minister of Interior, Sheikh Saif bin Zayed Al Nahyan, a "Strategic Management and Performance Improvement Department" was established to implement the "Visionary and Strategic Institutional Change" plan in 2002. The key goal of the plan was to introduce a new policing concept which has shifted the scope and role of the Abu Dhabi police (in Abu Dhabi and Al Ain) from simply the criminal investigations and traffic divisions to a more maximalist, comprehensive idea of security, community, and knowledge, creating a force which could manage threats preemptively as well as reactively. This new concept of policing (implemented with the help of 63 international consultants embedded in all levels of the police force) aimed to familiarize the police forces with the different populations that inhabit the UAE so that the forces would know how to actively prevent crimes and build community relationships. There were 78 different initiatives implemented through this strategic plan, which required an internal assessment of the weaknesses of the force and comprehensive studies and assessments of the external challenges that are posed by the UAE's changing demographic composition, open borders, and economic growth.

When asked about this new policing concept, officials explained that what instigated this initiative was not that crimes were already on the rise. Instead, it was "a reaction to the changing social fabric and social conditions and foresight to try to assess the new risks and the internal capabilities to actually deal with those risks, to control a population where the rate of demographic changes was happening faster than anywhere else in the world" (interview with key informant in Abu Dhabi police, December 9, 2010). In other words, the institutional change was a less

---

[15] This quote is from an Arabic interview on a Qatar Television show titled *Laqum Al Qarar* (The Decision Is Yours). Excerpts of this interview are available in English: "Non-citizens are the future threat of the entire Gulf: HE Dahi Khalfan Tamim" (*The Peninsula* 2010).

a response to the increase in crimes because of migrants, and more a response to the *predicted* increases in crime because of migrants. A major component of the strategy for change involved extensive training initiatives for members of the police force, including diplomas (master's and PhD programs received abroad). It also included training the Abu Dhabi police forces with other police forces in locales as varied as the United Kingdom, Singapore, Finland, and Malaysia: "anywhere that police forces are specialized in an area of law enforcement that was seen as beneficial to the new challenges facing the UAE" (interview with key informant, December 9, 2010). Moreover, in addition to receiving training in law, strategic studies, political science, public administration, international relations, forensics, crime scene investigations, and other technical fields, the program embedded police officers in intensive language and cultural studies (fieldwork or exchange) so that they could come back to the UAE and be the community liaisons for the nationalities that were represented. Officers were embedded in places like China and Bangladesh living with host families, learning their languages, heritage, and tools for how to understand and communicate with these populations for the purposes of better management. They were also attempting to get a sense of what kind of relationship existed between those populations and their local security forces, to be able to tailor the Abu Dhabi police department's (ADPD) interactions with members of those specific communities that reside in the UAE. There were over 300 police officers studying in these language and cultural exchanges and another 400 members of the force in bachelor, master's, or PhD programs at the time of the interview in 2010.

This new concept of policing has led to the establishment of, in the words of my informant, a "community police" force that is "more effective by being more proactive" and by connecting with communities to gain trust and build lasting relationships. In 2009 and 2010, a human rights division was also introduced to the police department. From the standpoint of institutional development, the plan has been highly successful at implementing a great deal of change in a very concentrated amount of time and the ADPD has been a forerunner in the majority of excellence categories and rankings that the Abu Dhabi government uses to assess its institutions. What is striking about this new policing concept is that the Strategic Management and Performance Improvement Department of the ADPD recognizes that the UAE is and will continue to be an extremely diverse society and therefore does not aim to alleviate this heterogeneity but rather to manage it. In other words, what emerges with these policing practices is a kind of "controlled heterogeneity" – the emphasis is on disaggregating the mass of "migrants" into manageable units by national origin, and governing a heterogeneous population by making those units legible.

3.5 MANAGING HETEROGENEITY: LEGIBILITY AND SURVEILLANCE

A key aspect of this preemptive approach to managing a large and diverse population has been the increasing regulation, identification, and cataloging of expatriate populations by building a unified identity management system across the federation. To achieve this, a new and independent federal authority, the Emirates Identity Authority (EIDA), was established to develop and administer the population register and national ID card project.[16] It was mandated to create a comprehensive database that contains the individual's name, nationality, signature, fingerprints, eye-scan, birth date, gender, work visa status, labor card, health card, and occupation, as well as all health records, criminal records, and personal records from all of the UAE's ministries.

The official categorization of the expatriate workforce that was employed for the ID project provides a sense of the lens through which the federal state views, catalogs, and groups its noncitizens. The EIDA officially classified the population into five separate groups for the registration phases. The first group to have access to the national ID card comprises Emirati citizens, but only those citizens who can prove their nationality with a *khulāṣat al-qayd* (family book). This first group of citizens is followed by foreign residents, who are classified into four groups. Group 1 is made up of "white-collar" professionals and their families. The schedule specifies that these noncitizens should be holders of higher qualifications (diploma and above) and technical specializations in specified fields including consultancy, medical services, and law. Group 2 is made up of all residents employed in the private sector at administrative and vocational positions and their families. Group 3 is made up of domestic workers and other residents employed in the private sector undertaking "nonprofessional jobs" and their families. This group

---

[16] The EIDA is now the Federal Authority for Identity and Citizenship (ICA). This institution changed after Federal Decree-Law No. 3 of 2017 added new functions to the institution, including citizenship affairs, passports, and entry and residency of foreigners. www.ica.gov.ae/en/emirates-id/about-emirates-id.aspx

includes housemaids, drivers, fishermen, and taxi drivers. Group 4 is for "all unskilled labor, without exceptions," primarily encompassing construction workers. With few exceptions, Arab and Western noncitizens are unlikely to be found in groups 3 and 4.

Continuing with this documentation and identification of its population, the federal government is aiming to make the UAE the first country in the world to build a universal DNA database of all its residents, at a projected rate of 1 million per year. The DNA profiles are to be stored indefinitely even after noncitizens leave the country, and according to the newspaper *The National*, there have been plans to share some of the information with other governments or Interpol, depending on specific treaties or cooperation agreements. The program was initiated as a security directive, which means that it bypassed the legislative process entirely (Youssef and Shaheen 2009). This DNA gathering is used for multiple purposes. It is most commonly used for the evidentiary procedures of criminal investigations, and more recently it has been used to screen couples to attempt to prevent genetic diseases. But it also makes the population more legible and can provide authorities with what seems like a definitive answer about who belongs to which group. Indeed, in addition to being part of the procedure for naturalization applications, DNA testing is being used to trace the lineages of potential Emirati citizens residing outside the country.[17]

As part of a larger preemptive security strategy, this DNA-gathering initiative was designed to rank sections of the population based on security assessments of the threats those individuals likely pose. Dr. Ahmed Marzooqi, the program's director, explained to *The National*, "we will divide the population into certain groups and we will test them based on priority" (Youssef and Shaheen 2009). Marzooqi stated that this program will be used to not only solve but also prevent crimes, starting with minors. "Most criminals start when they are young," Marzooqi said. "If we can identify them at that age, then we can help in their rehabilitation

---

[17] In an effort to increase the number of Emiratis, the federal government used DNA testing to identify "true" Emiratis who reside outside of the UAE. A special committee, comprising members from the Ministry of Interior, was set up to locate the children of Emirati men (and foreign mothers) born abroad. The committee traveled to Oman, Qatar, and Saudi Arabia, to check the authenticity of marriage and birth certificates, and to conduct DNA tests that verify the "heritage" of the applicants. "The most recent trip was conducted as part of a program to strengthen the connection of foreign Emirati children with their native land" (*The National*, January 16, 2010). The committee identified 23 children who would become Emirati citizens in the Gulf, with plans to evaluate claims in Mumbai, Egypt, and Syria.

before the level of their crimes increase." Like earlier initiatives targeting family social security and juvenile delinquents, this project also aims to be a way of identifying, cataloging, and managing likely criminals. The ID system, population register, and DNA database are all initiatives that increase population legibility by creating integrated "profiles" of individuals that are organized into groups and ranked and marked for their priority based on calculations of national security. In addition to requiring agencies that manage the day-to-day workings of these initiatives (such as EIDA and the DNA division of Abu Dhabi police), this effort must be sustained through ever-growing capacities for surveillance and intelligence gathering.

The security industry is one of the largest sectors in the UAE, and the federal government dispenses large undisclosed sums on contracts for maintaining this apparatus as well as adopting the latest surveillance technologies. Every year, Abu Dhabi hosts the International Security National Resilience conference (ISNR), where Col Ishaq al Beshir, the director of operations for the Critical National Infrastructure Authority (CNIA), announced in 2010 that an AED 33 million (USD 9 m) security camera system would be installed across the capital in all critical infrastructure sites (Dajani 2010). This surveillance capacity is extending beyond camera networks and becoming increasingly diversified and integrated. For example, in the aftermath of the Arab Spring, the "Advanced Integrated System" was actively promoted in Abu Dhabi as a way of preventing non-state groups from organizing through social media by a company called ATS. It is a program that provides security forces with a comprehensive electronic profile of all individuals in a particular geographic scope. The system collates data from any number of electronic sources including but not limited to data taken from traffic cameras, smoke detectors, work and school absences, mobile phone texts, internet browsing habits, Facebook posts, tweets and Twitter-following patterns, GPS coordinates from mobile phone usage, and even driving patterns (from radio frequency identification tagging or RIFD inserted in license plates).

3.6 NATURALIZATION AS A NATIONAL SECURITY ISSUE

The previous sections summarize the main institutional developments that have accompanied the UAE's economic growth and the demographic impact of its guest worker program. In particular, the different agencies of the UAE's MOI have taken active roles in responding to the demographic changes and in developing preemptive policing strategies that include community policing, extensive surveillance networks, and increasingly individualized and standardized forms of identification. This background is important for understanding how the security forces came to be in charge of vetting candidates for naturalization and why naturalization is treated as a matter of national security.

The federal security forces play a central role in assessing and determining whether long-term residents should be granted access to citizenship rights. Naturalization in the UAE is extremely difficult. But despite being highly regulated and exclusionary, naturalization does occur in an ad hoc, case-by-case manner. According to the publicly available Federal Law No. 17 of 1972, naturalization is a possibility for Arab noncitizens after ten years of continuous lawful residence in the UAE, and after thirty years of residing legally in the UAE for non-Arab noncitizens (with the condition that they are Muslim and proficient in the Arabic language), and in both cases only if they have exhibited good conduct without convictions for offenses involving dishonor or dishonesty. However, interviews in 2010 with civil servants in the Dubai Naturalization and Residency Administration (DNRD) revealed that in practice Arab noncitizens from non-GCC countries are eligible for naturalization only after thirty years (as opposed to the stated ten) of continuous residence in the UAE, and GCC citizens are eligible after seven years of continuous residence in the UAE. Contrary to the codified law, civil servants were open about the fact that in practice there were no criteria for non-Arab or non-Muslim noncitizens to apply for citizenship and that those candidates cannot go through the emirate-level naturalization departments to initiate a case (although the naturalization of non-Arabs does occur sporadically through sovereign intervention). Applicants have to demonstrate that they have been completely integrated and assimilated into Emirati culture, and demonstrate their allegiance to the Emirates through their language, values, culture, and way of comporting themselves (respectful conduct). They have to study and be familiar with the history, and usually have children born in the country.

The security forces of the MOI are entrusted with assessing these determinations. Moreover, since applications are made and processed through the emirate-level government before they are forwarded to the federal government, this condition of continuous residence in the UAE without any substantial breaks is conditional upon residing in the same emirate for that entire period of time (seven years or thirty years). There are also three categories or gradations of this nationality (*jinsiya*) that are marked in one's booklet: Emirati by "rule of law" (*biḥukm al-qānūn*) (these are the citizens who can trace their lineages to 1925), citizen by marriage (this is only available for foreign women because Emirati women cannot pass citizenship to their non-Emirati husbands), and citizenship through naturalization. The passport is the document that marks and identifies an individual as an Emirati internationally, but internally, the nationality (*jinsiya*) booklet is essential for proving that one is indeed a citizen and eligible to gain access to the welfare services and funds provided to citizens. If an individual acquires citizenship through naturalization, then they had to demonstrate their allegiance to the UAE by forfeiting any other passport or ties to another nationality. And if, after having gone through this process, an individual receives Emirati citizenship and renounces it for another passport at any other point in time, then they will not be able to get this citizenship back or pass it on to their children (interview with key informant, April 12, 2010).

By all accounts, especially those of the civil servants working in the Dubai Naturalization and Residency Department, acquiring Emirati citizenship is an exceptionally difficult process. The entire process – from the actual legal criteria for eligibility, to where and how to file the applications, to how factors like allegiance or assimilation are measured – is extremely opaque. Moreover, while in other legal arenas there are lawyers specialized in assisting individuals through the process, this is not the case when it comes to naturalization. As one lawyer explained in a written communication:

kindly be advised that there are no lawyers in the UAE working in the area of citizenship acquisition as the Department of Immigration and Naturalization has the sole discretion regarding this issue. Thus, applicants are required to personally apply where the aforementioned government authority has the sole discretion of accepting or rejecting applications without explanations as the criteria are only known to them. (Email exchange, April 8, 2010)

In interviews, civil servants explained that naturalization does not require a court system or otherwise involve legal professionals because whether or not an individual is naturalized is not a legal-juridical determination. Rather, it is treated as an issue of internal "national security" that requires the execution of a sovereign political decision (*qarār siyāsī*).

A prominent Emirati lawyer and activist interviewed also reiterated this view and expanded upon why (in her opinion) naturalization was not (and should not be) determined by the court system. She explained that naturalization was not a legal decision that could be determined by a judge, because ultimately it does not hinge on whether an individual has met certain "objective" criteria (such as extended continuous residence). Rather, the single most important factor in determining whether an individual could be a citizen was their allegiance (*al-walā'*) to the UAE. And that kind of determination is a political one – it must be made by the head of state and internal security forces who are responsible for protecting the sovereignty, integrity, and safety of the national society. Each individual has to be individually assessed for their loyalty, patriotism, and benefit or threat to the society. She argued that the criteria for selection and evaluation had to be secretive because naturalization was essentially an issue of "national security" (*'amn al-dawla*) (telephone interview with key informant, April 10, 2010).

This framing of naturalization as an issue of national security has also been instantiated in the public statements of the Minister of Interior, Sheikh Saif bin Zayed Al Nahyan. In 2008 he was quoted making two public statements in the Arabic newspaper *Emarat Alyoum*: "*al-walā' sharṭ al-tajnīs*" (Allegiance is a condition of naturalization) and "*Al-dustur yasmah bi-saheb al-jinsiyya miman la ya'mal bi-istihqaqatiha*" (The constitution allows for the confiscation of citizenship from those who do not abide by its requisites). These statements were made in reference to the ministry's initiatives to establish a systematic naturalization procedure for the *bidūn*. The statements point to an imperative need to create a mechanism for the naturalization of the *bidūn* because many of them were "good people" who contributed to the UAE and truly desire being part of Emirati society. However, he argued that it was equally necessary to make sure that this naturalization mechanism was not "taken advantage of" by those who wanted to profit from the state's resources without feeling any real allegiance to the nation. Because of this danger, the constitution empowered the federal government with the right to confiscate citizenship from any individual who did not respect this privilege or act in accordance with its requisites (*Emarat Alyoum* 2008). These statements clearly link the protection of naturalization with the need to protect the UAE's national security, but internal security is broadly construed to include not only the preservation of righteous and respectful Islamic conduct and cultural and linguistic assimilation, but also the absence of criminal behavior and any evidence of political dissidence.

The securitization of the naturalization process in the UAE has meant that, in practice, foreign residents do not apply for citizenship. Those who are embroiled in the process are largely older minority groups who were present in the UAE territories prior to the formation of the union. Since the question of who was a citizen in 1971 was a contested one, acquiring full Emirati citizenship requires a dual process of emirate- and federal-level approvals. This has created a limbo zone of people who have been incorporated at the local level, but are still waiting for the federal approval of their citizenship cases. For many of those who are caught in limbo in between legal categories (the *bidūn*, children of Emirati women, and ethnic minorities) the attempt to naturalize has meant being subject to repeated rounds of interviews and security vetting from the federal MOI. The written law states that individuals are eligible for naturalization after seven years of residency but civil servants acknowledge in interviews that the minimum is actually thirty years of residency in the same emirate. Interviews with those undergoing the process, however, make clear that – when it comes to cases originating outside of Abu Dhabi – even those who have exceeded this thirty-year threshold continue to have to wait for federal approval. The security vetting they must undergo makes time itself the obstacle to entry; candidates wait, over years and decades, for iterative security checks to be completed and for a resolution of their citizenship cases – one that is constantly postponed.

3.7 CONCLUDING REMARKS

This chapter examines how migration and security come to be interlinked in the UAE, illustrating the factors that make it increasingly difficult to inhabit an ambiguous legal status over time. The chapter begins by examining how migration flows came to be associated with national security threats, even prior to the formation of the UAE. The British records demonstrate how political interests shaped the pattern of migration flows into the region; both the British authorities and Trucial State rulers were invested in preserving British hegemony and suppressing labor strikes, Arab nationalism, and insurrectionary threats. In response to the growing number of migrants entering the Trucial coastline, the British authorities and Trucial State rulers also began building an infrastructure for migration enforcement. This meant not only policing the shoreline, but also developing domestic identity checks to police the interior.

As the UAE has matured as the union, the mobilization of resources toward migration enforcement – especially the growth of surveillance and identity management capacities – has had a restrictive effect on the contours of Emirati citizenship. In particular, the securitization of naturalization as a protected realm of national security has foreclosed access to Emirati citizenship in two key ways.

First, foreign residents are overwhelmingly excluded from being eligible for naturalization, even if they have resided in the country for over thirty years. As Chapter 4 explores, this foreclosure of naturalization as a path for long-term residents has not meant that all migrants are only temporarily in the country. On the contrary, the guest worker program in the UAE has – like most other guest worker programs – led to permanent settlement. However, even those migrants who have resided in the UAE over generations cannot translate their permanent residency into permanent rights.

Secondly, while many of the security initiatives discussed in this chapter were targeted at new migrant flows after independence, the securitization of naturalization procedures has made it increasingly difficult for non-Arab minorities to gain federal recognition of their citizenship rights. As Chapter 5 explores in greater depth, for those caught in limbo in between legal statuses, waiting for citizenship has structured every aspect of their lives. This practice illustrates how time is deployed to not only construct, but also police national boundaries. If the institutionalization of a "countdown deadline" of 1925 is how time was used to define the UAE's national boundary, then the strategic deployment of delays is how time is being used to monitor and police the contours of Emirati citizenship.

4

Permanently Deportable: The Formal and Informal Institutions of the *Kafāla* System

Time, or duration of residency, is one of the predominant ways of accruing membership rights in a political community. However, it is legal status that determines how political entities *count* the unfolding of time – states can withhold rights by refusing to recognize the time spent of particular individuals or groups. This chapter examines the formal and informal institutions of the *kafāla* guest worker program in the UAE to explain how and why temporary legal statuses become protracted over time. An attention to duration of residency and the intergenerational settlement of noncitizens is important because a migrant who has resided in the UAE for forty years (or was born there) can no longer be considered a "guest" – but without access to citizenship they are not a citizen either. People fall into a limbo legal status when their short-term residency permits are constantly renewed, even over generations, but this residency does not translate into a secure path to permanent rights and citizenship. In such cases an individual is not temporary but permanently deportable.

While previous chapters have focused on national incorporation from the lens of a within-case comparison across different Trucial States or emirates, this chapter widens the scope of inquiry beyond the UAE to encompass the other Gulf states of the Gulf Cooperation Council (GCC). The chapter contextualizes the UAE by drawing important similarities across the GCC cases when it comes to citizenship and immigration policies. This is not to suggest that there are not important differences among these distinct states, which vary economically, socially, and politically. The structure of the GCC as a security umbrella is itself under strain with the emergence of a schism between Qatar on the one hand and Saudi Arabia, the UAE, and Bahrain on the other.[1] Even prior to this rift, the Gulf states differed in when and how each state was formed.[2] The relative strength and structure of different domestic political and religious institutions also differs across these cases.[3] Each GCC country's oil reserves are of a different size and were not discovered at the same time.[4] Moreover, the GCC that unites these six states has not institutionalized common standards in immigration policy in the way the European Union has (attempted to) for its member states.

However, despite these differences, all of the GCC states share a key common feature: they all use the *kafāla* and overwhelmingly depend on foreign labor forces. The region's aggregate population has increased more than tenfold in a little over half a century (from 4 million in 1950 to 40 million in 2005), making it the highest growth rate of anywhere in the world during that period (Kapiszewski 2006). Noncitizens now outnumber citizens in four out of the six GCC states – the UAE, Qatar, Kuwait, and (to a lesser extent) Bahrain (see Table 4.1). Noncitizen workers represent between 38 percent (Saudi Arabia) and 87 percent (United Arab Emirates and Qatar) of

[1] In June 2017 Saudi Arabia, the UAE, Bahrain, and Egypt imposed a land, sea, and air blockade on Qatar. The root of the fissure lies in the different sides that Qatar and Saudi Arabia have taken in different proxy conflicts across the region since 2011, with both states vying to fill the power vacuum caused by the Arab Spring.

[2] Saudi Arabia was united by the conquest of Al Saud in 1932; Kuwait was a British protectorate that gained independence in 1961; the remaining four states – Bahrain, Oman, Qatar, and the United Arab Emirates – all gained independence from Britain in 1971.

[3] Although all six states are monarchies, the domestic political landscapes diverge significantly. To name a few notable differences: Kuwait has had the most powerful independent merchant class and now the strongest parliament in the region. In Saudi Arabia the religious establishment holds more control than in the remaining states. And the states also differ in structure – the UAE is a federation while the rest are unitary.

[4] Collectively, the six GCC states have approximately 45 percent of the world's proven oil reserves. Oil was discovered in Bahrain in 1932, Kuwait and Saudi Arabia in 1938, Qatar in 1940, the UAE in 1958, and Oman in 1967. According to 2017 estimates, Saudi Arabia is the world's second largest (net) oil producer with one-fifth of the world's oil reserves. The UAE possesses nearly 10 percent of the world's total oil reserves, and is the eighth largest oil producer. Within the UAE, the emirate of Abu Dhabi controls more than 85 percent of the oil output capacity and more than 90 percent of its reserves. Kuwait has the world's sixth largest oil reserves and ranks as tenth largest oil producer globally. Qatar is thirteenth in the global ranking of oil production, but it holds the world's third largest natural gas reserves and is the single largest supplier of liquefied natural gas. Oman ranks twenty-first in global oil production. Finally, Bahrain, as the first to discover oil and the smallest territory, ranks fifty-seventh in global oil production, and it exports much of its oil in the form of refined petroleum products. Source: US Energy Information Administration (n.d.).

TABLE 4.1 *GCC citizens and noncitizens in absolute numbers and percentages (2016–2018)*[1]

	Citizens	%	Noncitizens	%	Total population
Bahrain	677,506	45.1%	823,610	54.9%	1,501,116
Kuwait	1,398,952	30.1%	3,241,463	69.8%	4,640,415
Oman	2,606,585	56%	2,049,548	44%	4,656,133
Qatar	348,479	12.7%	2,395,453	87.3%	2,743,932
Saudi Arabia	20,768,627	62.2%	12,645,033	37.8%	33,413,660
UAE	1,153,576	12.6%	7,967,600	87.4%	9,121,176
GCC Total	26,953,725	48.1%	29,122,707	51.9%	56,076,432

1 Aggregate (and estimates) provided by GLMM demographic database: https://gulfmigra tion.org/gcc-total-population-and-percentage-of-nationals-and-non-nationals-in-gcc-coun tries-national-statistics-2017-2018-with-numbers/
Sources: (1) Bahrain: Central Informatics Organisation, mid-2017
(2) Kuwait: Public Authority for Civil Information (PACI), November 2018
(3) Oman: National Center for Statistics and Information (NSCI), November 2018
(4) Qatar: Ministry of Development Planning and Statistics, October 2018
(5) Saudi Arabia: General Authority for Statistics, Demographic Survey end of 2016
(6) UAE: Federal Competitiveness and Statistical Authority (FCSA), end of 2016

the domestic labor forces in the region. As a result, all six states have segmented labor markets, with a low rate of citizen participation, and rising unemployment rates among citizens. Meanwhile, a large portion of the regional workforce is employed in construction, utilities, government institutions, and other service sectors – only 1 percent of the workforce is employed in the oil and gas sector, which produces 47 percent of the GCC's aggregate GDP (Al Khouri 2010: 4). These labor market similarities arise out of the GCC states' analogous implementation of their guest worker programs.

Officially, the noncitizens residing in the Gulf are not immigrants, but temporary contractual laborers with little or no recourse to permanent settlement or citizenship. They enter the country as guest workers under fixed-term employment contracts and are obliged to leave upon the termination of their work. Their stay is regulated through the *kafāla* or sponsorship system, which makes an individual Gulf national citizen or company sponsor (known as the *kafīl*) legally and economically responsible for the foreign worker for the duration of the contract period.

While the structure of the *kafāla* enables Gulf governments to maintain some formal/legal control over how long individual workers can reside in the country, the guest worker program as a whole is far from the temporary measure it was envisioned to be. Rather, following the trend of most other guest worker schemes, the *kafāla* has produced a structural dependence on foreign labor that is not subsiding despite public discontent and rising unemployment rates among Gulf citizens. Since the 1990s, Gulf governments have attempted to alleviate their dependence on migrant labor through campaigns aimed at training and nationalizing their labor forces. The general approach has been through job training programs and government quotas on the number of citizens that private businesses must employ.[5] However, these policies have been largely unsuccessful and the presence of noncitizens has continued to grow in both absolute and relative terms.

In no other region of the world do citizens comprise such a small proportion of the population. While this "demographic imbalance" makes the Gulf unique, large-scale migrant labor flows are certainly not exceptional to the GCC. Other receiving regions like North America, Europe, and Oceania have all expanded through migration that offers a path to permanent residency. What differentiates the Gulf is not its demographic expansion through migration, but rather the degree to which the region's governments have been able to exclude foreign workers from being integrated into the national citizenry. It is thus not the scale of immigration, but rather "the exceptional closure of local societies that makes the Gulf states unique" (Fargues 2011: 274). The exclusion or noninclusion of foreign workers is not the result of an essential characteristic of Gulf societies, but rather that of a deliberate policy of restricting citizenship. The social closure of citizenship had to be erected and continually enforced through specific policies and institutions that differentially impact the wide variety of noncitizens and the local populations.

This chapter examines the formal and informal institutions that support the inward flows of large numbers of foreign laborers while excluding noncitizens from full integration into Gulf societies. This analysis builds upon research in comparative politics that has exposed the insufficiency of studying only formal institutions, with scholars turning to informal institutions to explain why political outcomes may diverge from the predictions generated by formal rules and laws (Helmke and Levitsky 2004; Lauth 2000; Tsai 2006). Informal institutions are defined as "socially shared rules,

---

[5] For an overview of workforce nationalization campaigns in the GCC states see (Shah 2008); for an overview of labor market governance see Dito (2008).

usually unwritten, that are created, communicated, and enforced outside of officially sanctioned channels" (Helmke and Levitsky 2004: 727). These informal rules and practices become institutions through daily repetition rather than codification; they are not the same as weak institutions, nor are they reducible to culture (shared values are too broad), or informal organizations (criminal or mafia networks are actors, not rules that govern behavior). Informal institutions interact with formal institutions to shape political outcomes in a variety of ways. At times, informal institutions create or strengthen incentives to comply with formal rules, adding to the self-reinforcing path dependence of formal institutions. At other times, however, informal institutions enable actors to behave in ways that alter the substantive effects of formal rules, without directly violating them.

The institution of the *kafāla* is defined by a set of laws and regulations – the formal rules that actors have to abide by. Based on these formal regulations, the predicted outcome would be that foreign workers are in the Gulf for short periods of time. However, as this chapter explores, the Gulf states formally sanction temporary legal statuses that become permanent through the repetition and diffusion of coping strategies and operating procedures over time. Despite formal limitations on the residency of foreign workers, in practice national firms and citizen sponsors extend the duration of foreign residency by repeatedly renewing labor contracts. Moreover, the private sector often depends on migrant kinship networks to recruit new workers, which means local sponsors are critically involved in informally creating family settlement for migrant families. Because of the sponsorship structure of the *kafāla* system, citizen sponsors simultaneously play a critical role in both of these opposing dynamics, at once aiding in the enforcement of and undoing the restrictions on the residency and settlement of noncitizens. Thus, while the noncitizen labor forces are described as being formally "temporary," in reality a large segment of this population is actually durably settled in the region, often with their families, over generations.

4.1 GUEST WORKERS VERSUS PERMANENT MIGRANTS: HOW TEMPORARY IS "TEMPORARY CONTRACTUAL LABOR"?

A letter from the former permanent representative of the UAE to the United Nations, Nasser Al-Shamsi, to Human Rights Watch helps illustrate the stance of Gulf governments toward noncitizens residing in the region:

First of all, workers hosted by the UAE and other GCC countries cannot be considered migrant workers, as they work on a temporary basis and according to fixed-term employment contracts. Upon expiration of these contracts, they return to their home countries. Therefore, the immigration laws applicable in Western countries cannot be applied to these workers ... the internationally accepted concept of migration does not apply to them. (Human Rights Watch 2006: 70–71)

Al-Shamsi argues that there is a clear legal distinction between temporary contractual laborers and migrants – one that the noncitizens in the Gulf are themselves aware of prior to accepting employment in the region. He goes on to note that this formal distinction is recognized and protected by several international agreements between sending and receiving countries. He cites the findings of the Third Asian Ministerial Consultation Conference (2005) held by the International Organization for Migration (IOM) to argue that the temporary residency of expatriate workers has "become one of the agreed upon concepts of International Migration Organization concerning foreign labor working in the GCC" (Human Rights Watch 2006: 70).

What distinguishes a temporary contractual laborer from a permanent migrant worker? Contrary to what is suggested by the terms "temporary" and "permanent," the difference has less to do with the duration of stay and more to do with the formal and legal restrictions that structure the nature of a noncitizen's stay. In theory, guest worker programs are designed to increase the supply of a labor force without increasing the number of permanent residents in a population. They are supposed to produce only a temporary surge in the demographic makeup of a receiving country for a specific developmental purpose when the domestic labor force cannot meet the demand. Guest workers generally do not have free access to the labor market. Restrictions on visas prohibit them from applying for permanent residence or naturalization or bringing their families with them. In contrast, open or permanent migration schemes lead to the incorporation of immigrants and their families and impact the receiving country demographically, culturally, socially, and politically. These ideal-type models rarely maintain coherence in reality. Indeed, as a general trend, migration that begins as temporary quickly takes on a more permanent quality as governments struggle to control settlement once people have entered the country.

The term "guest worker" is a literal translation of the German "*Gastarbeiter*" and Germany's guest worker program of the 1960s and 1970s is often cited as one of the illustrative examples of how governments struggle to prevent the permanent settlement of temporary workers. The United Kingdom, Switzerland, and France also developed guest worker schemes in the second half of the twentieth century, ultimately leading to a European recruitment ban in 1973–1974 (Castles 1986; Martin and Miller 1980). The US government implemented guest worker programs prior to these European cases, beginning with the Mexico-US Bracero program to supply farmers to US farms from 1917 to 1921 and again from 1946 to 1967 (Martin 2001). In all of these cases, the employers' need for guest workers lasted longer and proved to be larger than originally expected. Guest worker programs tend to become permanent for two reasons: expansion of initial demand and dependence. The initial demand for workers grows and adapts with the promise of an almost unbridled labor supply. This dynamic is operating in the GCC across all economic sectors. The most illustrative examples are found in the construction industry, where foreign workers have permitted governments to implement ambitious building projects – such as the tallest building in the world – without having the indigenous manpower to meet these goals. The dependence upon foreign labor can also discourage innovation and the application of new and more efficient technologies in specific sectors. Relatedly, dependence occurs because employers in the receiving country come to rely on foreign workers, and those workers in turn form attachments to the receiving country, as do their families, who now depend on the remittances sent home. Summing up the German experience, Max Frisch said, "We asked for workers, and we got people" (cited in Martin 2001: 3).

This is no less true of the people who work in the Gulf. The governments of the GCC may not officially recognize noncitizens as migrants, but de facto settlement is occurring across the region. While temporary guest workers in the United States and Europe have to a large extent managed to leverage the long duration of their stay to gradually gain legal access to citizenship, this transition is not happening in the Gulf. The discrepancy in these two outcomes is not due to the more naturally "welcoming" nature of the liberal governments of the United States and Western Europe. These rights were often extended in spite of government efforts to circumscribe residency and deport workers. Temporary workers were able to legalize their status by pitting one state institution against another. The intervention of domestic courts played (and continues to play) an integral role in preventing deportations and shaping migration enforcement.[6] European courts directly challenged national decisions and policies on migration enforcement. European norms on family reunification and the general convergence of a common immigration and asylum policy also hampered government attempts to deport workers. The European Court of Human Rights also plays an important role in checking national migration enforcement, often aligning with domestic courts.[7] These court decisions, combined with the efforts of civil rights groups, produced new citizens out of former foreign guest workers in Europe and the United States. Such avenues for legal permanent settlement and integration are largely foreclosed for migrants in the Gulf – including those migrants who have worked and lived in the region prior to the formation of these nation states. The difference in these outcomes is due to key differences in the state institutions that shape the enforcement and implementation of migration policies.

4.2 FORMAL INSTITUTIONS OF THE KAFĀLA: BUILDING AND ENFORCING TEMPORARY RESIDENCY

Across the Gulf, the formal institution of the *kafāla* has two key defining structural features. First, the *kafāla* regulates foreign labor through citizen sponsorships; no individual can enter the country for work without

---

[6] For example, in 2012 the Supreme Court judges in the United Kingdom dealt a "hammer blow" to Home Office attempts to reduce the number of migrant workers entering the United Kingdom. In a case against Hussain Zulfiquar Alvi (a man of Pakistani origin who was refused a renewal of his work permit in 2010) the judges ruled that ministers could not ban non-European workers from the country unless the regulations used to reject their claim had first been shown to parliament. This seminal decision means that applicants whose visa claims were denied as far back as 2008 (when the points-based system was introduced) could appeal against their decisions. See Warrell (2012).

[7] For example in 2011, the First Chamber of the European Court of Justice issued a decision that Italy cannot criminally punish a third-country national for illegally staying in the national territory in violation of an order to leave within a given period. The court ruled that EU Directive 2008/115 precluded the ability of any member state to imprison a third-party national on the sole basis of having stayed in the country after being issued a deportation order. The Italian law in question was enacted as part of a "security package" ("pachetto sicurezza") of immigration laws that punishes migrants who violate the terms of their residency with one to four years in prison. The court's ruling in the case of Hassen El Dridi alias Soufi Karim (Case C-61/11 PPU, 28 April 2011) has repercussions for migration enforcement in Italy and across the union. Italy's interior minister Roberto Maroni criticized the decision for making expulsions "difficult or impossible" but the ECJ decision is consistent with Italian court rulings, including the Constitutional Court and the Supreme Court. See for an overview, Migrants at Sea (2011); court decision: http://curia .europa.eu/juris/liste.jsf?language=en&num=C-61/11; and EU Directive: http://eur-lex.europa.eu/LexUriServ/LexUriServ.do?uri=OJ:L:2008:348:0098:0107:EN:PDF.

a national sponsor and job secured prior to entry. The key feature of the sponsorship system is mobility restriction – once inside the country, foreign workers are unable to change jobs without their national sponsors' consent. Herein lies the key to the sponsors' (monopsonistic) power over individual migrants – the primary reason that this sponsorship system has been criticized by human rights organizations for facilitating the exploitation of foreign workers. This sponsorship arrangement also functions as a built-in enforcement mechanism for temporary residency by holding individual citizens directly responsible for the residency violations of individual noncitizens. Second, the *kafāla* is centrally administered and regulated through the Ministries of Interior of each of the Gulf states. This means that the same institution that decides to permit or revoke residency can also enforce those decisions without any outside intervention by the courts or other institutions. Effectively, the combination of these two formal aspects of the *kafāla* means that the mechanisms for enforcing temporary residency are widely dispersed while the authority over residency decisions is highly concentrated.

4.2.1 Citizen Sponsors and Dispersed Enforcement

In the early 1970s, at the precise moment when European states were moving away from guest worker schemes, the Gulf states formalized, expanded, and entrenched their guest worker system. Guest workers, who were already present in the oil industry since the 1930s, were now brought in to assist in virtually every aspect of state-building, providing labor for infrastructural development, education, healthcare, and transportation. By now the *kafāla* is an extensive and institutionalized inter-Asian guest worker scheme that moves millions of people and generates billions of dollars for sending and receiving countries annually.

At the base of this extensive structure are individual-level linkages between Gulf citizens (or national firms) and noncitizen workers. This is an integral structural feature of the guest worker system in the Gulf.[8]

---

[8] Citizen sponsorships have been used to enforce migration elsewhere. Notably, Italy experimented with a similar sponsorship system as part of a package of legal reforms in 1998 that were aimed to manage the country's shift from being a primarily migrant-sending to a migrant-receiving country. Law No 186/98 was the first attempt at implementing a coherent immigration policy for integrating migrants, establishing quotas, and more successfully restricting undocumented immigration. The Italian sponsorship system was less rigid than the *kafāla*, but the principle was the same: a citizen, an institution, an NGO "invites" a migrant to work, and is financially responsible for their salary,

Indeed, the words *kafāla* (sponsorship) and *kafīl* (sponsor) come from the Arabic root *k-f-l*, meaning to be a guardian, vouch for, or otherwise take responsibility for someone. Several sources suggest that the *kafāla* emerges out of the Bedouin customs of temporarily granting strangers shelter, food, protection, and even tribal affiliation for specific purposes (Heeg 2011: 6, citing Longva 1997). Individual-level linkages between the citizens and their "guests" thus build upon tribal narratives of hospitality, and fit in well with the official state nationalisms of the Arab Gulf states. The British archives (see the methodological appendix) also show that the *kafāla* at least partly originates from the British system of No Objection Certificates (NOCs).

Regardless of its origin, the *kafāla* system and use of citizenship sponsorships provides Gulf governments with a widely dispersed mechanism for enforcing the temporary residency of noncitizens. In this system, the residency of a foreign worker is merged with and tied to their labor contract. It is not an open migration scheme that allows foreign workers to have residency visas to legally enter the country and then compete in the labor market for jobs. Rather, each noncitizen worker enters the country already tied to a particular job that is sponsored by a national citizen or company (*kafīl*). Private citizens and companies are involved in the recruitment, residency, and repatriation of migrants. Whether through direct recruitment or through recruitment agencies, the sponsor-employer identifies the noncitizen worker they would like to hire and then applies for a visa on behalf of that specific worker. In so doing, the *kafīl* agrees to assume the legal and economic responsibility for the worker for the duration of their stay in the country and inform the Ministry of Interior (MOI) of any change in the labor contract (expiry, renewal, or cancellation), or in the worker's domicile or civil status. The *kafīl* is financially responsible for repatriating the worker as soon as their contract is fulfilled or terminated. This process of "vouching" for someone is not unlike the enforcement mechanism that is used by banks or bail-bonds when they require a third party to cosign on a loan or bond with the borrower and be held responsible in the case of defection. The cost of migrant deportation is thus externalized from the state to the private sector. In interviews with the MOI in the UAE and the Labor Market

Regulatory Authority in Bahrain, civil servants explained that the state keeps a small coffer of funds to deport people, but that those funds are eventually replenished when sponsors are tracked down and fined for their repatriation. This system thus externalizes the costs of deportation to individual employers (at little cost to the state) in contrast to the privatization of deportation through state-contracted companies (at a much higher cost to the state), as is increasingly the case in Europe and the United States.[9] This sponsorship arrangement effectively privatizes some of the costs of migration enforcement by directly holding individual citizens financially and legally accountable for each and every noncitizen. Citizen sponsors are thus a very important appendage of the state in the enforcement of temporary residency; "through the *kafāla*, states delegate to private citizens the surveillance of migration" (Shah and Fargues 2011: 268).

The *kafāla* has been criticized by the international community for constricting the mobility of labor and rendering foreign employees vulnerable to physical abuse, wage discrimination, and deportation (Turner and Human Rights Watch 2007; Longva 1999; Rahman 2010). The dependence upon sponsors can breed human rights violations because the system is highly discretionary; it depends upon the idiosyncratic nature of individuals who may subject workers to abuse and exploitation. While the cost of a visa (also known as a visa bond) is supposed to be paid by the sponsor, there is little protection against externalizing these costs to the migrants themselves. Moreover, even if the sponsor does not externalize these costs to migrants directly, recruitment agencies and sub-recruiters in the sending countries often charge migrants for seeking employment in the Gulf. The costs of paying for visas to enter the Gulf can be so high that some guest workers incur large debts to gain employment and are effectively forced to stay in unfavorable work environments until their debts are paid off. And since their right to work is tied to their residency, workers have little recourse to contest unpaid wages or the retention of their passports – despite the fact that all of the Gulf states have made it illegal for employers to withhold the passports of their foreign

[9] Migrant detention and deportation has grown into a lucrative industry over the past three decades in the United States and Europe with an increasing dependence upon a handful of large transnational security corporations (Bloom 2015). The use of private security companies for migrant detention is oligopolistically concentrated in three companies: Geo Group Limited, G4S, and Serco (Menz 2011).

employees. There are labor laws that protect foreign workers and enable them to sue their employers, but since the employer and sponsor are the same person, it means that while the trial is pending the plaintiff is unemployed and forbidden to work for anyone else. And "a sponsor may resort to pre-emptive measures, such as accusing the worker of some morally reprehensible behavior that could lead to his or her deportation" (Longva 1999: 22). Even if a foreign worker successfully wins a court case against an employer, the outcome of the conflict will mean the termination of their employment and hence their residency visa. The worker will thus have to return to their country of origin and repeat the costly recruitment process once again.

Since the sponsorship system holds individual citizens responsible for repatriating guest workers, Gulf governments are formally able to discourage visa overstaying and evade one of the most notoriously difficult aspects of migration enforcement.[10] However, this mechanism completely depends upon citizens to comply with the terms of sponsorship, and thus the very structural feature that is used to enforce the restrictions on residency can also be used to subvert those restrictions. The second half of this chapter explains how citizen/noncitizen linkages are also a key mechanism for extending the residency of noncitizens. The *kafāla* relationship, since it was institutionalized legally, has always been accompanied by systematic informal practices that allow the private sector to counter the restrictions the state has placed on the residency and family settlement of foreign workers.

4.2.2 The Ministry of Interior and Centralized Administration

Concretely, the centralization of the *kafāla* under the purview of the MOI works in the following way: citizens and citizen majority–owned companies in the Gulf apply for labor permits through the Ministries of Labor, but the approval for the residency permit must come from the Ministries of Interior, which issue individualized security clearances and permits. It is thus the Ministry of Interior – not the Ministry of Labor, or the Ministry of Justice – that wields the ultimate authority over how long an individual worker can stay in the country under a labor contract. Since the MOI also controls the domestic security forces, this means that the same institution that administers residency decisions also has the necessary resources at its

---

[10] Nearly half of the estimated 12 million undocumented aliens in the United States are visa overstays (Brown 2010: 88).

disposal for enforcing those decisions.[11] Once a residency permit has been denied or revoked, the MOI does not have to coordinate with a separate government entity to find, remove, and deport the guest worker (now deemed an "illegal" or an "infiltrator"). More importantly, in addition to being able to unilaterally make and enforce deportation decisions, it is this same institution, the MOI, that also wields the authority to decide upon and enforce naturalization decisions.[12] All of the avenues for legal residency are centralized and controlled by the state security apparatus. This highly centralized control over the citizen/noncitizen boundary has meant that the Gulf states have increased their labor forces without expanding their citizenries. "Decades of intense, but temporary, migration have resulted in citizens and non-nationals growing as two separate entities without a new, mixed, population emerging from their co-existence" (Fargues 2011: 280).[13] In other words, the UAE's and larger region's current challenge of a "demographic imbalance" is an unintended consequence of its successes in enforcing migration policy and preventing migrant incorporation.

4.3 INFORMAL INSTITUTIONS: NAVIGATING AND SUBVERTING TEMPORARY RESIDENCY

If the formal institutions of the *kafāla* sufficiently explained migration outcomes in the Gulf, we would expect the official stance of Gulf governments to hold – that is, all noncitizens are temporary workers who leave

---

[11] In the Emirati law from 1973, the Ministry of Interior is explicitly entrusted with doing so – "Article 25. Minister of Interior may detain the alien, against whom a deportation order has been issued, for a period not exceeding two weeks, if he considers this detention is essential for executing the deportation order." Similarly Article 22: "Local security authorities in member Emirates and federal security authorities, each within its frame of concern, shall stop and search any vessel, if these authorities suspect that this vessel may carry persons who have committed crimes punishable under the provisions of this law, or attempting to commit such crimes. The authorities may arrest these persons and request the vessel to enter the nearest port in the country."

[12] For a case-by-case explanation of the naturalization laws in each of the GCC states, see Parolin (2009) or Fargues and Brouwer (2011) for a summary. In general, naturalizations were more inclusive from the 1950s to the 1970s. After the 1970s, in response to massive numbers of guest workers, the legislation on nationality across the GCC became more restrictive.

[13] Intermarriage rates are lower for Gulf women than Gulf men. This is due to the higher informal restrictions on Gulf women marrying foreign men from their families and the broader society, and this trend is further entrenched by the fact that women lose the ability to transfer citizenship to their children when they marry foreigners. In the UAE in particular, religious sheikhs must have permission to marry Emirati women to foreign men.

after a fixed period of time and do not turn into permanent migrants. Instead, "the Gulf countries are experiencing that many guest-workers gradually transform into immigrants, but governments do not yet formally acknowledge this fact" (Fargues and Brouwer 2011: 240). Over the course of the past forty years, there has been a continuous rise in the number of noncitizens residing in the region, and increasingly, they are joined by their spouses, giving birth to a second (and even third) generation of immigrants, and finding informal ways of staying past retirement. While data on the indicators of permanent migration is sporadic and scarce, the official figures and studies that do exist suggest that noncitizens are informally, yet systematically, turning into permanent migrants. Section 4.3.1 briefly highlights findings from publications that aim to measure the degree to which temporary labor migrants are turning into permanent immigrants.The available national census data from all six states indicate that de facto permanent settlement is occurring across the GCC. There are two indicators for measuring the extent to which temporary contractual workers are gradually turning into permanent migrants:

(1) Long duration of residency, measured as
     a over ten years of residence
     b past the retirement age of 65
(2) Family settlement, measured through
     a migration of nonnational spouses
     b birth or migration of noncitizen children under the age of 15.

4.3.1 Duration of Residency and Settlement

Official data on the duration of residency for noncitizens is not widely available. Many ethnographic studies show that foreign communities in the Gulf are developing sustained ties to the host country and stay well beyond the usual estimate of ten years of residency. Andrew Gardner's work on the Indian diaspora and Sharon Nagy's work on the Filipino diaspora both suggest that foreign communities in Bahrain are well entrenched and have been for decades (Gardner 2008; Nagy 2010). Likewise, Hélène Thiollet's research (2010) on the everyday forms of belonging in Saudi Arabia demonstrates that national belonging is not limited to those who are formally included in the body politic – an argument that Neha Vora (2013) also makes about Indians in Dubai

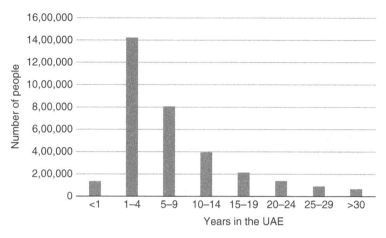

FIGURE 4.1 Duration of residency in the UAE (2005) Source: National Bureau of Statistics, UAE Ministry of Economy, 2005. Available in GLMM database: https://gulfmigration.org/uae-non-emirati-population-by-sex-age-group-and-duration-of-stay-in-the-uae-five-year-periods-2005

The UAE is the only Gulf state that has published data on the duration of residency in its 2005 census (though the National Bureau of Statistics has not included any more recent data on this in subsequent publications). Figure 4.1 presents the noncitizen population by length of duration in the UAE. Based on this data, approximately a third (28%) of the total non-citizen population has lived in the UAE for over ten years, indicating that noncitizens are not as "transitory" as official accounts suggest. Second, the modal duration of residence is one to four years, with 44 percent of the population residing in the UAE for a period within that range. However, since the migrant population almost doubled from 1995 to 2005, it is unsurprising that many migrants were recent arrivals in the 2005 census.[14] By now the stock of longer-term residents is likely even higher given that inward migration flows have declined as a proportion of the total population. Moreover, approximately 15 percent of the individuals who resided in the UAE for one to four years are under the age of 15 (age data not shown in figure), so they are children of migrants rather than temporary contractual workers. Indeed, about a fifth of the total

---

[14] See Figure 3.1 in Chapter 3. The noncitizen population in the UAE increased from 1,823,711 in 1995 to 3,280,932 in 2005 according to figures released by the National Bureau of Statistics (Ministry of Economy). https://gulfmigration.org/uae-population-by-nationality-emirati-non-emirati-at-census-dates-1975-2005-and-2010-estimate.

population of noncitizens in the UAE is under nineteen years old, and over half of that group (53%) have resided in the country for fifteen to nineteen years. This suggests that they were likely born in the country or migrated at a very young age. A final observation concerns the aging noncitizen population. In absolute numbers by 2005 estimates, 30,524 people (8%) are over sixty years old. About a third of this group (29%) have resided in the UAE for over thirty years and an additional 35 percent have spent anywhere between ten and twenty-nine years of their lives in the UAE. This suggests that there is an aging population of migrants who have spent most of their working lives in the UAE and are approaching the age where they will either have to find a new place to relocate or find a way to informally stay past retirement. Forty percent of them are already over the official retirement age of 65.[15]

To assess the degree to which settlement past retirement is occurring across the GCC, Table 4.2 presents the most recent census data on the 65-and-over age group by citizenship status (citizen or noncitizen) in each state (with the exception of Qatar since these estimates are not publicly available). The age composition of the total population is generally skewed toward the working ages (15–65). This youth bulge is characteristic of most states in the Middle East more broadly. Among citizens in the Gulf, the over-65 population is already small (between 4% in Bahrain and 2% in Kuwait and the UAE), and this proportion shrinks even more in the case of noncitizens. Noncitizens over the age of 65 years old make up barely 1 percent of the total noncitizen population in each country. However, among the 65-and-older age group, there is a sizable noncitizen presence in at least two cases. Noncitizens make up approximately a third of the over-65 population in the UAE (35%) and Kuwait (32%). In the remaining three cases for which estimates are available, noncitizens make up approximately 10 percent of the over-65 population. These findings suggest that foreign communities are most settled in the UAE and Kuwait, although Fargues and Brouwer (2011) also find that Saudi Arabia has high levels of settlement past the working ages.[16]

---

[15] There are a variety of restrictions placed on the renewal of labor contracts and residency visas for noncitizens after they have reached the retirement age of 65 (and in some cases upon reaching the age of 60). The specific restrictions vary across countries, economic sectors, and professions.

[16] There are large undocumented Burmese and African multigeneration populations in the Western Province cities of Saudi Arabia (especially Mecca and Jeddah) who are not counted in the official census data.

TABLE 4.2 *Population over 65 years of age by citizenship status*

Country	Nationals over 65	Noncitizens over 65	Total population over 65	Percentage of noncitizens in over 65 population	National population over 65 as proportion of total national population	Noncitizens over 65 as proportion of total noncitizen population
Bahrain (2010)	23,577	2,657	26,234	10%	4%	<1% (0.3%)
Kuwait (2005)	24,916	11,903	36,819	32%	2%	<1% (0.8%)
Oman (2010)	68,681	5,132	73,813	7%	3%	<1% (0.6%)
Saudi Arabia (2007)	609,573	66,342	675,915	10%	3%	1%
United Arab Emirates (2005)	21,728	11,801	33,529	35%	2%	<1% (0.3%)

4.3.2 Family Settlement: Spouses and Children

The second way to measure the extent to which noncitizens in the Gulf are becoming permanent migrants is family settlement through the immigration of noncitizen spouses and the birth or migration of noncitizen children. There is no data that directly links individual guest workers with their dependent spouses. The possibility of family settlement is generally more available to high-skilled workers in the private sector and is not permitted for all categories of temporary workers, especially domestic workers and construction workers. Aggregating the official data (2008) on noncitizen women and children outside the labor force (which is only available for Bahrain, Oman, and the UAE), Baldwin-Edwards (2011) calculates the proportion of the nonworking, noncitizen population under 15 as a proxy for family presence (see Table 4.3).

In Bahrain and the UAE, the data suggest that roughly half of the nonworking noncitizens are under the age of 15. The remaining are either spouses (this data is based on the assumption that these spouses are female) or older children who are outside of the labor market. As Baldwin-Edwards points out, in the case of Oman the data does not make sense as there are more children than the total population of noncitizens outside of the labor force even though the calculations use the same official source for both figures.

Another proxy for family settlement is the proportion of noncitizens under the age of 15, illustrated in Table 4.4 above. The presence of noncitizen children suggests that there is a growing second generation of immigrants, and the available data likely underestimates the size of this second generation as they do not reveal the presence of

TABLE 4.3 *Noncitizen population not working (all ages) and foreign children*
<15 in the GCC, 2008

	Saudi Arabia	Kuwait	Bahrain	Oman	Qatar	UAE
Foreign population not in labor force	2,410.0	624.0	111.0	91.0	284.0	1,285.0
Of which aged 0–14	—	—	53.1	106.6	—	486.7

Source: Baldwin-Edwards 2011: 30

TABLE 4.4 *Children under 15 years of age by nationality (2015–2016)*[1]

Country	Citizens under 15 as proportion of citizen population	Noncitizens under 15 as proportion of noncitizen population	Noncitizens under 15 as proportion of total population
Bahrain (mid-2016)	32%	9%	25%
Kuwait (2016)	36%	13%	46%
Oman (mid-2016)	36%	5%	9%
Qatar (2010)	40%	9%	58%
Saudi Arabia (2016)	30%	15%	23%
UAE (2005)	38%	15%	61%
GCC total	32%	13%	27%

1 Citizen and noncitizen populations by aggregated age groups in GCC countries. Aggregate (and estimates) provided by GLMM demographic database: https://gulfmigration.org/gcc-national-non-national-populations-aggregated-age-groups-gcc-countries-national-statistics-2005-2016

those born in the region who are now well over the age of 15 and counted as part of the population of "guest workers" in the labor force. The majority of the noncitizen population is found in the working age group of 15–65, but Table 4.4 reveals several points about noncitizen children in particular.

First, noncitizen children make up anywhere between approximately 10 to 60 percent of the total population in the Gulf states, and between 5 to 15 percent of the population of noncitizens. Noncitizen children account for a sizeable proportion of the total youth population in the Gulf, comprising approximately 3 million of the 11 million children under the age of fifteen in the region (almost a third of the region's youth). In Oman and Saudi Arabia, the only two states in which citizens outnumber noncitizens, noncitizen children are still a minority of the youth population (9% and 26%). However, in Kuwait migrants make up almost half of the population under fifteen years old, and in the UAE and Qatar they are already the majority of the country's youth.

This census data, as well as the studies of Baldwin-Edwards (2011) and Fargues and Brouwer (2011), all indicate that there is a growing population of young noncitizens for whom "return" migration is meaningless because they have spent most – if not all – of their lives in the Gulf. This assessment can only be fully confirmed when the governments of the GCC collect data on family reunification and make it publicly available. However, since the official data lumps all noncitizens into one group, what it does not and cannot show is that this transition from temporary worker to permanent migrant is not occurring uniformly for all noncitizens.

The extent to which noncitizens are able to reside in the Gulf for long periods of time with their families is highly differentiated across the labor force. Two informal institutions critically shape noncitizen access to permanent residency and family settlement – one complements the *kafāla*'s formal institutions, the other subverts them.

4.3.3 Hierarchies of Noncitizen Residency

The first of these institutions is the informal hierarchy of the labor force, determined by the national origin, ethnicity, class, education, and/or skill level of noncitizens. This hierarchy sets the unwritten rules for how both state bureaucracies and private firms and individuals respond to noncitizens and citizens alike. In order to make sense of and differentiate between members of an extremely heterogeneous labor force, state and non-state actors systematically utilize shared understandings about the "reservation wage" or "value" of labor, determined by national origin and skill level. In some cases, the sending countries also help codify and set the wage differentials for a specific occupation.[17] This informal hierarchy of the value of labor explains why the *kafāla* has systematically produced patterns of institutional discrimination or exclusion against citizens themselves (including the preference for and higher wages paid to "white-collar" European and American noncitizens over citizens in the private sector).

As a complementary informal institution, this hierarchy "'fill[s] in the gaps' left by formal institutions – addressing problems or contingencies that are not explicitly dealt with in the formal rules – without violating the overarching formal rules" (Helmke and Levitsky 2003:12). In other words, though these racial hierarchies are not codified in the formal laws

---

[17] For a discussion of the Philippine government's approach to preparing its citizens for work in the Gulf, see Watanbe (2010).

of the Gulf, they provide bureaucracies with an unwritten script for how to deal with diverse populations. Different procedures and restrictions apply to different groups of noncitizens. Critically, a noncitizen's national origin, ethnicity, socioeconomic status, and education fundamentally structure their interactions with the state. These factors impact everything from what kind of health screening they must undergo, how often they must renew their residency permits, how susceptible they are to deportation and arrest, how easily they can gain access to state resources or police protection, whether they can be accompanied by family members, even what spheres of consumption they have access to.

For example, when it comes to accessing spheres of consumption, malls in the UAE, Qatar, and Kuwait often display signs that explicitly bar construction workers from entering, or have designated "family days" that prevent unaccompanied single men ("bachelors") from entering the commercial space. These "family days" occur on Fridays, which are often the only day many migrant workers have off. In practice, family day policies are largely applied to South Asian men, and Arab and white men are not stopped from entering malls even if they are not accompanied by their families.

The informal hierarchy of the labor force appears across sectors, but the racialization and stratification of nationalities in the sphere of domestic work is particularly stark; evidence of this hierarchy not only appears in the everyday discourses that surround which maids or nannies are "cleanest" or otherwise desirable, but also codified in minimum wage levels. In the UAE, the minimum wage in 2012 for a domestic worker from the Philippines was AED 1,500 per month (408 USD); for an Indian domestic worker this minimum wage dropped to AED 1,100 per month (299 USD); and for a Nepali domestic worker it decreased even more to AED 900 (245 USD).[18] The UAE hosts approximately 146,000 female migrant domestic workers, largely from the Philippines, Indonesia, India, Bangladesh, Sri Lanka, Nepal, and Ethiopia. Human rights organizations have documented widespread abuses against women in this sector in particular (Human Rights Watch 2006). Because of this sizeable presence of domestic workers, women from these large sending countries have a decidedly different

---

[18] These figures were published in *999*, a magazine produced for expatriates by the Ministry of Interior in Abu Dhabi (Kumar 2012).

experience than white or Arab women in the UAE and can be associated with domestic work even if they do not partake in that work. Even without official data confirming the racialization of the workforce, these patterns are palpable to residents and often seep into their discourses as a naturalized order:

one has to live in Dubai for only a few days to notice how the workforce is racially labeled and how professional stereotypes define ethnic groups. It is not uncommon to assume a Brit in the UAE is a high-ranking executive with a leisurely life, while a Lebanese is an aggressive businessman. Only in this country is "construction worker" interchangeable with "Indian" or "housemaid" with "Filipina." It is vile and reductionist, and most disturbing when on the tongues of schoolchildren. (Kaabour 2009)

While the government of the UAE, both on the federal and local levels, does not explicitly identify sectors of the economy with national origin, noncitizens are often grouped by their skill level and sector of the economy – a grouping that does contain patterns of national origin. Indeed, this way of segmenting and categorizing the workforce (e.g., "white-collar" versus "non-professional" workers) was precisely how the federal government divided all of its residents in order to issue the UAE's national ID in 2008.

The foreign resident populations in the Gulf are far from monolithic; they are "fragmented first by nationality and then further divided by ethnicity, education, employment, and economics. In some instances, economics – earning power – and education connect people from disparate ethnic and national origins, while in others, ethnicity and employment are so inextricably connected that education is immaterial" (Bristol Rhys 2010: 25). This hierarchy melds with preexisting ideologies about genealogy, nationhood, and citizenship that state-building initiatives have successfully instantiated in the public sphere and civic culture of the Gulf. The stratification of the labor force is not only expressed through the actions and words of Gulf citizens – hierarchies also travel with migrants themselves. Bristol Rhys notes how some foreign communities (citing Indians, Egyptians, and Pakistanis in the UAE) have reproduced in the Gulf the socioeconomic hierarchies that structure and stratify society in their home countries. She argues that "the labor policies and practices of the UAE appear to have reinforced class divisions within migrant communities rather than, as one might anticipate, the development of transcendent transnational identities, a new ethos of commonality predicated on the shared experience of migration" (2010: 25). These ethnic and socioeconomic hierarchies of noncitizens complement the formal rules of the *kafāla* by reducing people to their work and legitimating migrant exclusion as being a part of the "natural order" of things.

4.3.4 Citizen Sponsors and Extensions of Residency

Noncitizen access to permanent residency is also structured by the degree to which a particular migrant has access to a supportive sponsor who wants to extend their residency. The literature on the *kafāla* tends to emphasize the antagonistic dimensions of interpersonal relations between citizens and noncitizens because the sponsorship system makes particular groups of noncitizens highly vulnerable to abuse – especially in the spheres of domestic and construction work.[19] It is critical to document the systematic abuses these workers face and this growing literature has done much to illuminate the structural violence of the *kafāla* as it impacts lower-income workers. However, focusing solely on the abuses occurring in those sectors or treating them as representative of the entire system glosses over the complexity of the multidimensional power relations between citizens and noncitizens that the *kafāla* produces.

The dominant narrative paints a stark picture of segregation between citizens and noncitizens that is transgressed daily. Citizens interact and build relationships with noncitizens in every aspect of their lives: in the domestic sphere, in the workplace, in the service industry, in restaurants, in malls, in mosques, on the streets – everywhere. Particular economic sectors (like farming or construction) that employ temporary guest workers tend become permanent immigration channels because employers in the receiving country come to rely on foreign workers, and those workers build attachments to the host country. In the Gulf this interdependence takes on much larger dimensions – entire economies have been built on citizen/noncitizen attachments. Thus while the formal institutions of the *kafāla* are designed to uproot migrants, citizens and noncitizens also simultaneously continuously form linkages that work against these restrictions. Citizens' goals can align with those of noncitizens to facilitate permanent migration – even as competition and hierarchical relations between these groups are reproduced.

---

[19] For research on domestic workers see Chin (1998); Ehrenreich and Hochschild (2004); Esim and Smith (2004). For research on construction workers see Degorge (2006); Heeg (2011); Human Rights Watch (2006); Keane and McGeehan (2008).

One example of how citizens can informally subvert the rules of the *kafāla* is by renewing residency permits iteratively to allow migrants to continue living in the country, at times even after they have unofficially retired. For example, one elderly Emirati woman from Abu Dhabi, Badriya, explained that she was in an ongoing battle with the authorities to receive approval for a visa to sponsor a new domestic worker (interview with Badriya, July 25, 2010). When pressed as to why she could not sponsor any more domestic workers she revealed that she was already sponsoring five people – far above the allotted quota for one woman now that her children were outside of the house. In reality, however, three out of the five people she sponsored were either close to or already over the age of 65, and having lived with Badriya for decades, none of them wanted to return to the abstract "home" they had left behind in what is now India. Moreover, two of the elderly migrants had children in the country working in Badriya's sisters' houses so she did not want to separate the family. Instead of canceling their visas or paying for their flights to India after the age of 65 as she is supposed to, Badriya is instead creating an informal form of postretirement settlement by dragging her feet and refusing to comply with the rules. The Ministries of Labor do not have the authority to regulate domestic work in the Gulf because it falls under the protected private sphere of the home, making it difficult for Gulf governments to enforce regulations. Herein lies the ability for sponsors to abuse domestic workers – but also their ability to protect them, albeit in ad hoc and informal ways. In this case, unquantifiable human linkages and emotional attachments explain why the national sponsor prolongs noncitizen residency beyond the formal restrictions placed by the state. While most of the narratives about domestic workers focus on the very real abuses these migrants face in the Gulf, less attention has gone to the fact that people form emotional attachments, especially when they live together for so many years and partake in the intimacy of raising children and sharing a home.

Emotional attachment is not the only reason that a *kafīl* might choose to extend the residency of their sponsored guest worker. Employers prefer to limit the turnover of guest workers for several reasons; they aim to minimize the costs of training new employees, and sustainable economic ties are often built upon important social ties of trust and partnership. Ties between citizens and noncitizens can also enable family settlement to occur as citizens depend upon the noncitizens that work for them to vet and choose new employees from the same sending country. For example,

Vora's analysis of the elite Indian diaspora in Dubai demonstrates that Indian business owners are not only well entrenched, they are a crucial facet of governing lower-income Indian migrants who they recruit and manage, acting in many ways as unofficial *kafīls* on behalf of silent national sponsors (Vora 2010). Moreover, citizens do not only align with other foreign elites; the networks they build can enable specific groups of less privileged noncitizens who would otherwise not have access to family settlement to bring their families with them to work in the same or related households.

For example, domestic workers do not have the right to family settlement; formally their visas do not allow them to be accompanied by their children or spouses. However, informally, a very common way that Gulf citizens recruit domestic workers is through the recommendation or family connections of domestic workers who are already in the country. While the official data does not capture this form of family settlement or permanent residency, the use of kinship ties, both on the sides of guest workers and *kafīls*, is a dominant way of vetting and recruiting migrants, creating networks of migrant families layered on top of national families. These networks provide an additional form of security for both employers and employees – as one *kafīl* vouches for another and one migrant vouches for another they create an added informal layer of social trust and protection against crimes like migrant abuse or theft from the *kafīl*.

Profit-seeking and trust networks can transform the *kafīl* from an enforcer of restricted residency into a conduit for extending noncitizen residency. Firms and citizens work alongside noncitizens to negotiate and evade the formal rules of the *kafāla* without openly breaking them. These accommodating informal institutions have enabled noncitizens to systematically settle in the Gulf by tempering and modifying the formal restrictions on their settlement from the bottom up.

4.4 REFORMS TO THE SPONSORSHIP SYSTEM

While the enforcement of expansive migration and exclusionary citizenship policies may initially buffer the power of Gulf governments, depending upon noncitizens without extending permanent residency or citizenship rights necessarily also makes these economies vulnerable. It can have an especially crippling effect on the economy in times of crisis because linking residency to work contracts means that individuals have to leave the country almost as soon as they lose their jobs. The linking of residency and employment makes Gulf banks especially vulnerable to loan defections. That is why, for example, the quintessential image of the economic crisis in Dubai is abandoned cars – not unemployment lines. This stark image of capital flight is as true today during Dubai's current economic crisis as it was in 2008. Moreover, the overwhelming dependence upon foreign labor impedes the development of an indigenous labor force, and all of the Gulf governments have struggled with integrating national workers into the labor force.

In response to some of the challenges associated with the dependency on guest workers, several Gulf governments have instituted reforms to ease the restrictions of the *kafāla* system. In 2006, Bahrain officially abolished the *kafāla* and established a government agency, the Labor Market Regulation Authority (LMRA), to manage the guest worker program. However, this reform has not substantively eradicated the sponsorship model, since all noncitizens still require national sponsors. The reform has nonetheless lessened some of the barriers against switching national employers, and migrant workers no longer have to leave the country in order to change jobs.[20]

More recently, several Gulf states have announced the introduction of longer-term visas and some moves toward the establishment of permanent residency rights. In 2016, Bahrain announced that for certain companies 100 percent foreign ownership will be allowed. Meanwhile, in 2017 the government of Saudi Arabia announced a plan for a green card–like permanent residency program and Qatar approved a law granting permanent residency to some skilled workers. To prevent capital flight and compete with Qatar in particular, the federal government of the UAE also recently announced that foreign residents will be able to own their own businesses, and in some cases will be entitled to ten-year residency permits.[21] These efforts are targeted at retaining the more economically privileged and high-skilled "white-collar" professionals rather than the entire guest worker population. Though most of these reforms are new and their impact has yet to be assessed there is little evidence to suggest that any of the Gulf states are likely to entirely eliminate the *kafāla* in the foreseeable future.

---

[20] See Act No. 19 With Regard to the Regulation of the Labour Market (Kingdom of Bahrain 2006).

[21] For more on these initiatives see Ismail and Pacheco (2018); Lewis (2018).

4.5 CONCLUDING REMARKS

The interaction of formal and informal institutions illustrates how, despite strongly enforced formal restrictions on residency, some groups of noncitizens are gradually settling in the Gulf. Noncitizens are able to permanently reside with their families in the region, but this is occurring in a highly differentiated way across the labor force. There are two structural features of the *kafāla* that make it an effective formal institution; the first is its centralized administration through the Ministries of Interior and the second is its diffused enforcement through citizen sponsors. Even though these structural features make it so that the rules of the *kafāla* are routinely enforced and complied with, the very mechanisms that lead to migration enforcement can be used to subvert these restrictions. The effectiveness of temporary residency policies is shaped and tempered by two informal institutions. First, the hierarchy of labor value (or the racial wage) is a complementary informal institution driven by both state and non-state actors to differentiate in the treatment of an extremely diverse labor force. These unwritten rules critically shape which groups of non-citizens have access to more permanent forms of residency and family settlement and which ones experience the full force of stringent citizenship and settlement policies. A second informal institution competes with and subverts restrictive settlement policies; citizens use their roles as sponsors to extend the temporary residency of noncitizens when it suits their interests. The interaction of formal and informal institutions means that a large proportion of the labor force in the UAE and other Gulf states are temporary on paper only. This chapter demonstrates the importance of legal status for determining how time – or duration of residency – is counted by political entities. Instead of becoming permanent residents or citizens, the *kafāla* turns people into permanently deportable "guests."

5

"Ta ʿāl Bachir" (Come Tomorrow): The Politics of Waiting for Identity Papers

The previous chapter addressed the exclusion of the foreign resident populations from citizenship in the UAE; their time spent (or duration of residency) does not count toward citizenship because the guest worker population is explicitly excluded from being eligible for citizenship. This discussion illustrates that it is not simply the time spent in a polity that leads an individual to accrue rights; it is legal status that mitigates how that time is counted and valued by a political entity. While the previous chapter addressed how people can fall into a limbo status when they are permanently on "temporary" legal statuses, this chapter examines another way that the asynchronicities of time are used to exclude individuals from the national citizenry.

Specifically, this chapter examines the use of delays as a means of policing the citizen/noncitizen boundary. People can fall into a limbo status when they have citizenship cases that are constantly postponed, rather than ever being approved or denied outright. Unlike guest workers, the populations discussed in this chapter are, on paper, eligible for citizenship, and embroiled in the naturalization process – but their entry into the citizenry and access to full rights is continually postponed. As discussed in Chapter 3, if a UAE resident cannot trace their paternal lineage to the Arab tribes of 1925 (the "countdown deadline" for nationality), then they must undergo a naturalization process, even if they were born in the country and can trace their family's settlement over generations. During the naturalization process candidates must undergo a rigorous security vetting and receive approvals for citizenship from both the emirate and federal levels. While the federal law states that this process can only be initiated after seven years of residency in the UAE, civil servants acknowledge that the minimum is actually thirty years of residency in the same emirate. Moreover, interviews with those undergoing the process reveal that many have exceeded this thirty-year threshold and continue to wait for citizenship.

The postponement of cases in the naturalization process illustrates how bureaucrats deploy temporal obstacles that place people in a limbo status; the waiting at once entangles these individuals into the web of the state, while also effectively excluding them from the national body politic. This chapter addresses this tactic of delays to examine what it means to wait for citizenship for a protracted time period from the perspective of those undergoing the process. This is achieved through interviews with naturalization candidates and an analysis of an archive representing a vast paper trail that documents one community's efforts to secure access to Emirati citizenship – the papers of waiting for papers. This archive provides a protracted view of one refugee community's experience of waiting, and the problems associated with waiting for citizenship over time, especially over generations.

5.1 THE PATTERN OF WAITING FOR CITIZENSHIP: ABU DHABI VERSUS DUBAI AND THE NORTHERN EMIRATES

As discussed in Chapter 2, different emirates have historically had competing visions of who should be counted as a citizen. From the outset, Abu Dhabi's vision of the citizenry has been more ethnically homogenous and focused on Arab genealogy than that of Dubai or the Northern Emirates. As a result, the UAE did not have a unified citizenship and immigration policy at its formation; there were two policies, one for Abu Dhabi and another for the rest of the emirates. The naturalization policy was also stratified, with individuals becoming citizens first through their emirate of residency before gaining federal nationality.

The result of this dual system is that some resident populations were granted citizenship by the rulers of Dubai, Sharjah, Ras al Khaimah, Fujairah, Ajman, and Umm Al Quwain, but were never approved to receive the nationality document from the federal government located in Abu Dhabi. Some members of this group are ethnic minorities (now commonly referred to as the stateless *bidūn*); they are the descendants of Persian, Baluchi, and East African merchants and slaves who were residing in the Trucial State territories prior to the formation of the modern Emirati state. Others are the children of Emirati women who are married to the *bidūn* or other non-Emirati men. Yet another subset of this population comprises the waves of migrants (especially from Yemen, Zanzibar, Uganda, and other parts of East Africa) who entered the UAE during the early phases of state formation, when the *kafāla* system was not as consolidated or uniformly applied. These heterogeneous populations are united only in what they all lack – the nationality document or a "family book" (*khulāṣat al-qayd*) that traces each family's lineage to the UAE's founding tribes. Without family books, members of this population (of approximately 80,000 to 120,000 people) are not able to gain access to any of the benefits associated with citizenship in the UAE. They are neither citizens nor guest workers, residing in a liminal zone in between the state's official population categories.

The pattern of pending naturalization cases reveals key political dynamics between the elite rulers in the federation, with all of the stalled cases originating from emirates other than Abu Dhabi. I argue that the postponement of these cases is itself a strategy of exclusion. By keeping the citizenship cases of the remaining emirates pending, as opposed to excluding or including those individuals, the federal government does not outwardly reject people who have been accepted by the rulers of Dubai, Ras al Khaimah, Sharjah, Ajman, Fujairah, and Umm Al Quwain, but it does not incorporate them as full citizens either. Saying "no" would mean acknowledging that Abu Dhabi does not recognize their authority and sovereignty to define the membership of their jurisdictions. Instead of being rejected, these cases are instead left pending, and in many cases are still in "security processing" four decades after the formation of the union.

If the postponement of these cases were not a deliberate policy of exclusion but simply a sign of bureaucratic inefficiency, then waiting times would be randomly distributed across the population. Instead, from the interviews and archives a discernible pattern emerges – the naturalization cases from Abu Dhabi are resolved (either accepted or rejected), while the cases from other emirates are left pending. No naturalization candidates with pending cases from Abu Dhabi could be identified.[1]

Moreover, this pattern is also confirmed by the differential treatment experienced by minorities in Dubai and Abu Dhabi. The same refugee group that was resettled in Abu Dhabi and Dubai from Uganda at the same time (1973) now has distinct citizenship outcomes. The citizenship

---

[1] This is not to say that there are no stateless persons or people with an irregular legal status in Abu Dhabi. The author identified several Palestinian families residing in Abu Dhabi who are effectively stateless. However, in contrast to those interviewed from the other emirates, the Palestinians interviewed in Abu Dhabi did not apply for Emirati citizenship, explaining that they were never given any indication that they would be eligible. They also did not receive (and were not encouraged to apply for) Union of Comoros passports.

cases of the Abu Dhabi group have been resolved – these families were not granted citizenship by the Emirati government and were instead referred to the United Nations High Commissioner for Refugees (UNHCR) for resettlement to the United States and other countries in 2008–2009. Meanwhile, the members of the Dubai group are still waiting for a resolution of their citizenship cases – these families were issued Union of Comoros passports in 2008–2009. Like the *bidūn*, members of this refugee community in Dubai were informed that their Comoros passports were an interim step toward Emirati citizenship and that, based on their good behavior, they would eventually receive Emirati identity documents. In other words, while the Abu Dhabi group has received a resolution to their citizenship cases, the Dubai group continues in their four-decade-long wait for Emirati citizenship.

5.1.1 Interviews with Naturalization Applicants

This section utilizes interviews with naturalization applicants to illustrate the federal government's preference for Abu Dhabi's naturalization cases. Collectively the interviews identify three points about the variation in incorporation outcomes. First, the venue of the case and the ethnic background of the candidate matter because of differences in local patterns of incorporation – as the union has matured Abu Dhabi's more homogenous Arab vision of the citizenry has become the hegemonic one. Relatedly, timing also matters because citizenship laws were less restrictive during earlier periods of state formation than in later periods. And finally, changes in elite leadership also matter because the earlier generation of ruling elites in each emirate placed greater weight on the "national dilemma," or issue of minority incorporation, than subsequent rulers.

The interviews revealed that the candidates who have naturalization cases that have been stalled for long periods of time, and who received Union of Comoros passports, all instigated their cases in emirates other than Abu Dhabi. This assessment is based on interviews with sixty-eight (former or current) naturalization candidates in the UAE conducted from 2009 to 2011.[2] Of these sixty-eight naturalization candidates, six applicants were from Abu Dhabi, twenty-nine of the applicants were from Dubai, eighteen were from Sharjah, ten were from Ras al Khaimah, and five were from Ajman

---

[2] From 2012 to 2016 my team also conducted an additional twenty-two phone interviews with new interviewees who received Comoros passports between 2008 and 2009.

(no candidates were identified from Fujairah). Fourteen were born elsewhere but had arrived in the UAE prior to the formation of the state in 1971, and the remaining fifty-four were born in the UAE. Twenty-three of the sixty-eight naturalization applicants had Emirati mothers.

Of the sixty-eight candidates interviewed, only six people had secured a passport and family book, and all of them had cases that originated in Abu Dhabi. Meanwhile, the remaining sixty-two cases from outside the Emirate of Abu Dhabi all continue to have pending naturalization cases. The federal identity regularization drive of 2008 did not resolve these citizenship cases; instead they all received Union of Comoros passports and were told by Ministry of Interior officials that this was a necessary step in the process of acquiring Emirati citizenship.

While only the Ministry of Interior (MOI) knows the exact criteria for choosing to stall a citizenship case or approve it, from the perspective of those undergoing the process, the emirate of residence appeared to be the decisive factor in whether or not a citizenship claim was successful. In interviews with naturalization applicants, respondents consistently attributed their failure to gain Emirati citizenship to the fact that they were not Abu Dhabi residents, but instead filed their citizenship claims through Dubai, Sharjah, Umm Al Quwain, Ras al Khaimah, or Ajman. This pattern was similar across different ethnic minorities. This point was made stronger by the fact that at times members of the same family and minority group experienced different citizenship outcomes based on where they applied.

For example, all six of the candidates who had successful naturalization cases had migrated to Abu Dhabi in the late 1960s and received citizenship by the early 1970s. Though all six individuals were born in Yemen the location of birth on their Emirati passports is specified as *Al-ʿAyn*.[3] These interviewees are all related to a naturalization candidate, Mariam, who is based in Dubai and still has not received citizenship, despite her family's arrival from Yemen at the same time. Now in her mid-twenties, Mariam works as a receptionist in Dubai. For Mariam, access to citizenship hinges on whether one's family pledged allegiance to Sheikh Zayed of Abu Dhabi or Sheikh Rashid of Dubai: "The Yemenis in Abu Dhabi, those are the ones who became citizens, not us" (Interview with

---

[3] *Al-ʿAyn* is located on the UAE's border with Oman. The region was also historically controlled by the Al Nahyan, and today it is the second largest city of the Emirate of Abu Dhabi, after the city of Abu Dhabi.

Mariam, March 10, 2011). During the early phases of state formation, the Emirate of Abu Dhabi was more inclusive toward certain tribal Arab migrants who appeared to have at least some loose affiliation with the tribes on the Trucial State shoreline. This allowed for the naturalization of some Yemeni tribes (as well as some Omani and Najdi tribes) as citizens of Abu Dhabi in the early period of state formation. Sheikh Zayed recruited some of these tribes into the military and security forces, especially during the late 1960s and early 1970s.

Dresch and Piscatori (2005) also find that while Sheikh Rashid of Dubai had a more heterogeneous understanding of the national citizenry and privileged groups who were already resident in Dubai, Sheikh Zayed had a more genealogical (*nasab*) understanding of the citizenry which allowed for some targeted naturalizations of Yemenis in particular. In an effort to increase the population of Abu Dhabi, citizenship was granted to tribes connected with the Bani Yas: "The Manāhīl, whose range extended to Hadramawt, are an obvious case. As the UAE took form, however, the immediate post-colonial order in South Yemen was collapsing ... and people from such Yemeni tribes as Yāfiʿ and ʿAwlaqī, who had no shared history with Abu Dhabi, were recruited also" (Dresch and Piscatori 2005: 142). During earlier phases of state formation, Arab tribes from outside the Trucial coastline were recruited to join Abu Dhabi's new institutions and this became a conduit for gaining Emirati citizenship.

Abu Dhabi's expansions of the citizenry were specifically targeted at other Arabs, which meant that new migrants who could fulfill this genealogical Arab imaginary could gain citizenship, but it also meant that other migrant groups and resident populations who were not considered Arab were not granted this same privilege. The different citizenship outcomes for these early Yemeni migrants (inclusion in Abu Dhabi, exclusion of their peers in Dubai) only appear to hold for Arab tribes. For other non-Arab minority groups who migrated to the Trucial coastline at the same time, their inclusion was stalled regardless of the venue of the citizenship case. For example, several waves of Zanzibaris who migrated to Abu Dhabi and Dubai in the mid-1960s continue to wait for Emirati citizenship.[4] This suggests that the most likely conditions for gaining citizenship were both (1) residency in and allegiance to Abu Dhabi and (2) Arab tribal genealogy. Non-Arabs in Abu Dhabi did not receive the

---

[4] The author did not interview members of the Zanzibari community in Abu Dhabi, but their cases appear in the archive presented in this chapter. Their cases were also constantly referenced in interviews with other ethnic minorities.

same access to citizenship; nor did the Arab migrants (like Mariam's immediate family) who levied their citizenship claims through Dubai.

In Mariam's view, the possibility of inclusion has continued to recede as the UAE has developed into a union. For her, the turning point in her citizenship case was not Abu Dhabi's accumulation of oil wealth or the formation of the federation and independence – it was the death of Dubai's former ruler, Sheikh Rashid Bin Saeed Al Maktoum. "After Sheikh Rashid died, things became different for those of us from Dubai. We had a chance when Sheikh Rashid was alive, he really cared, now there really isn't a chance at all." Mariam viewed the death of Sheikh Rashid in 1990 as the turning point in her naturalization case because she felt that he had been invested in including all of his subjects into the new union. She viewed his successors as being driven more by the new developments in Dubai's rapid economic growth and the Dubai "brand," and less interested in the older power struggles (the national dilemma) that went into the formation of the union.

Bader also reiterated this distinction between Abu Dhabi and the remaining emirates. He currently works as a driver for a private company in Sharjah. He was born in Ras al Khaimah and is ethnically Baluchi. He explained, "My father was a policeman, and my parents have been here since before independence. But we are Baluchis from Ras al Khaimah, they don't see us as *Emirati* Emirati in Abu Dhabi" (interview with Bader, April 11, 2011). In Bader's assessment, his family could not become citizens of the UAE because they were outside the national imaginary of what citizens should be (descendants of Arab tribes) in the eyes of the decision-makers in Abu Dhabi. Bader also spent time explaining that in his view, the Baluchis *were* "Arab," with roots stemming from the Arabian Peninsula, but they are not acknowledged as such. He juxtaposed his family's current position to what he characterized as a more inclusive period of his parents' belonging during the 1950s and 1960s. The relationship between individual families and the political authority was more personalized, direct, and circumscribed to the jurisdiction of the ruler in one Trucial State. In his view, as the ruling families were coming to an agreement about national identity, the non-Arab minorities who were concentrated in Dubai and the Northern Emirates were forsaken as subjects of the new federal state. Since his family members were issued passports but never family books, Bader saw his family's inclusion in the citizenry as being one of the concessions Ras al Khaimah has made in order to join the union. Bader views his Baluchi ethnicity as a barrier to his inclusion in the Emirati "nation," but not a barrier to his inclusion in the Emirate of Ras al Khaimah.

Sultan argued that it was one's ethnicity and the timing of one's allegiance to a particular ruling tribe/emirate that mattered more than ethnic affiliation on its own. Sultan is in his late twenties and sells perfumes online. He was born in Dubai to an ethnically Persian father and an Arab mother (whose own father came from a recognized tribe). His father was a trader who would frequently shuffle back and forth from Dubai to Bandar Abbas (a port city on the southern coast of Iran). He recalled the stories his father told him about waves of population movements from Dubai and the Northern Emirates to Abu Dhabi in the early 1960s. He said his father staked his belonging and allegiance to the Al Maktoum of Dubai as something that could not be changed, and suspiciously regarded people who switched their belonging, insisting that they were motivated by financial gain: "We aren't like that. The calculating ones went to Abu Dhabi. But we are from Dubai. Maybe if my family had gone to Abu Dhabi like the others much earlier we would be in a different situation. But you can't just change your allegiance like you can your change clothes. We are from Dubai" (interview with Sultan, May 9, 2010).

Sultan's characterization of the act of moving between emirates as being an indication of "changing allegiances" is also found in the British records; especially after 1966, the Trucial State rulers were continually in dispute over the changing allegiances of tribes and families who moved to Abu Dhabi as the oil wealth trickled in. This interview illustrates that not only is the venue of a citizenship case important, but also the timing of migration, as those who pledged allegiance to the Al Nahyan of Abu Dhabi during earlier periods of state formation were more likely to be included as citizens of the new state.

5.1.2 The Case of Asian-Ugandan Refugees: Dubai versus Abu Dhabi

The assessment that the venue of a citizenship case and the ethnic background of the applicant largely explain the variation in citizenship outcomes also holds for an Asian-Ugandan refugee group that was resettled in Abu Dhabi and Dubai at the same time. Focusing on this small community of less than 100 people allows for a sharper comparison between the policies of Dubai and Abu Dhabi, as the members of the same ethnic group who arrived at the same time have had different citizenship outcomes based on which emirate they originally settled in. The elders of this community have effectively become stateless twice in their lives: once rapidly, when Idi Amin expelled them from Uganda in 1972, and again slowly, as they settled for four decades in Dubai and Abu Dhabi, waiting for citizenship documents.

These families were part of a population that the UNHCR referred to as "Asians of undetermined nationality" in the wake of their expulsion from Uganda (UN High Commissioner for Refugees 1974: para. 152), which was ordered and administered by the former Ugandan dictator Idi Amin in 1972.[5] "Asian-Ugandan" is a common signifier used for those expelled by Idi Amin, but unlike the South Asians in East Africa who arrived with the British Empire, the members of this particular group are ethnic Baluchis, and their families moved from South Asia to East Africa with the Omani Empire at some unidentified point in time prior to the nineteenth century. They settled for generations in Zanzibar, Uganda, and elsewhere in East Africa until Omani and British imperial rule gave way to national formation in both East Africa and the Gulf. When Idi Amin expelled them from Uganda for not being "African" enough to fit into the new state's national imaginary, they were resettled by the Aga Khan Foundation, Red Cross, and UNHCR in Dubai and Abu Dhabi.

By the time they arrived in 1973, the UAE was only two years old as a union, and it did not yet have a robust identity management infrastructure or centralized citizenship and immigration system. The decision to be settled in Dubai or Abu Dhabi – which was not perceived as a significant difference when the community first arrived – has made all of the difference for their current legal statuses. The community was split between Dubai (62 people) and Abu Dhabi (28 people) (document on file, December 27, 2003). Both groups had temporary protection under the rulers' offices of Dubai and Abu Dhabi and both initially received financial support for housing and education. However, the Dubai ruler's office was proactive in integrating this population and issued UAE passports to members of the community in 1997, making sure that they had residency rights and work authorization similar to Emirati citizens in Dubai. Though this group continued to wait for the federally issued family book, the UNHCR considered the Emirati passports to be equivalent to Emirati citizenship and closed these sixty-two case files with the judgment that a durable solution had been found.

---

[5] "Uganda: A Decree to Cancel Entry Permits and Certificates of Residence Held by Certain Persons in Uganda and for other Purposes Connected Therewith" (August 9, 1972. www .jstor.org/stable/20691015?seq=1#page_scan_tab_contents.

Meanwhile, no similar provisions were made for the group in Abu Dhabi. In an internal UNHCR memo sent from Abu Dhabi, an official explains what they perceived to be the reason for this difference in treatment. Referring to the Dubai government's decision to issue passports to the Asian-Ugandans in Dubai, they explained:

This step was not welcomed by Abu Dhabi Authorities and the Ugandan refugees residing in Abu Dhabi did not benefit from the same decision. We believe that the Authorities did not want to create a precedent, which could be invoked by the other categories in need of travel documents such as the Bedoons, or other refugees living in the country (Palestinians, Somalis, etc.). (Document on file, December 27, 2003)

The memo goes on to explain that without Emirati passports the Ugandan-Asians in Abu Dhabi were "suffering from many difficulties" including the fact that both public and private employers would not recognize their ad hoc documents and their children were being denied the right to continue their studies at UAE universities.

While both subgroups waited for full citizenship for decades, the federal government's identity regularization drive definitively ended the "waiting time" for the Abu Dhabi group while extending it for the Dubai group. Specifically, in 2003 the Ministry of Foreign Affairs in Abu Dhabi started the process of referring the cases of six families (28 people) to the UNHCR for resettlement, and these individuals have since moved to the United States and other refugee-resettling countries. Meanwhile, the remaining families (62 people) who were settled in Dubai have since lost any privileges of Emirati citizenship that they used to be able to exercise at the local level in Dubai. Instead of receiving the family books that they were expecting to get from the federal government, they received Union of Comoros passports. In other words, the identity standardization drive provided a clear answer for the Asian-Ugandans in Abu Dhabi about their Emirati citizenship cases – "no" – while the Asian-Ugandans in Dubai were grouped with the larger population of stateless minorities who were told to "wait."

Ironically, the Abu Dhabi group is now in the more privileged position. For the Asian-Ugandan community in Dubai a clear "no" in the form of an official government referral of these cases to the UNHCR may actually be helpful. It would allow them to start the refugee resettlement process yet again. As it stands, the UNHCR Abu Dhabi office that resettled the Abu Dhabi group has not resettled the members of the Asian-Ugandan group in Dubai. In 2015, our legal team approached the UNHCR headquarters in Geneva and in Abu Dhabi to understand why the records reflect this difference in treatment of the same refugee group and to gain clarity on the UNHCR's stance on the Union of Comoros passports. While not providing any official stance, staff from the UNHCR in Abu Dhabi acknowledged that they knew the UAE has been paying the Union of the Comoros for these foreign passports, but they believed that by 2020 the passports "would no longer be around," and all those who are eligible for UAE citizenship will receive it (written communication, October 26, 2016).[6]

What appears to have happened in the case of the Asian-Ugandans in Dubai is less of a targeted persecution of a minority group by a state, and much more the outcome of the sweeping arm of regularization that groups a variety of cases into one category. In terms of their identity documents, the Dubai group is now indistinguishable from other stateless minorities, including those who never received passports.

While the venue of the citizenship case is the most important factor, the comparison between the citizenship outcomes of the Asian-Ugandans and Yemenis in Abu Dhabi illustrates that ethnicity is a key factor because it sets the boundaries of who can be considered a citizen within Abu Dhabi. While the Yemenis in Abu Dhabi received citizenship, the Yemenis in Dubai are still waiting. While the Asian-Ugandans in Abu Dhabi who arrived at the same time as the Yemenis have been firmly excluded from Emirati citizenship, the Asian-Ugandans in Dubai are also still waiting for a resolution for their citizenship cases. This lends further indication that the citizenship cases initiated through Abu Dhabi are more likely to be resolved (either included or excluded), while those initiated through other emirates are more likely to be left pending.

5.2 POSTPONING CITIZENSHIP: DELIBERATE STRATEGY OR NO STRATEGY AT ALL?

Is the federal government's postponement of citizenship cases a deliberate strategy of exclusion? Or is it simply a manifestation of the fact that ruling elites in Abu Dhabi did not have a coherent strategy of how to respond to internal minorities until the identity regularization drive and outsourcing

---

[6] One of our informants wrote Kuzmova (head of legal team) an email summarizing their conversation with the UNHCR: "They said that according to Shk Saif from the ministry of interior, comoros passports are part of the clean up. They said that UAE paid the Comoros government for the passports and UAE will not pay them for these forever. As per their communication with Shk Saif, they learned that by 2020, there won't be any more bedoun or comoros passports issued in UAE (only UAE and expats). They also mentioned that files of comoros passport holders will be reviewed and those eligible for UAE citizenship will get it" (anonymous informant, October 26, 2016, anonymized gender).

of passports in 2008? These two scenarios are not mutually exclusive – postponement is a tactic that is most useful when there is no overarching strategy. From the civil servants who meet with candidates face to face all the way up to the ruling elites who have the authority to resolve these cases, delaying and buying time is the de facto position and modus operandi of bureaucrats who have to deal with cases that they do not know how to (or want to) resolve.

The case of the Asian-Ugandans in Abu Dhabi, who finally received a clear "no" about their citizenship cases, suggests that the federal government's delaying of citizenship cases was due to the lack of a strategy until its multifaceted identity regularization campaign of the mid-2000s. There may have been the desire to exclude these Asian-Ugandans from being eligible for citizenship, but there was no coherent plan for how to achieve that exclusion until the identity regularization drive. The federal MOI's foot-dragging and delays that likely began as an unintended consequence of not wanting to include non-Arab minorities has now coalesced into a strategy that uses waiting as the mechanism of exclusion.

For the Asian Ugandans in Dubai and other groups with limbo legal statuses, the waiting has not stopped with the federal government's formation of an identity regularization strategy. In other words, even when a clearly deliberate strategy for dealing with this limbo population was created – the outsourcing of passports from the Union of the Comoros – it has functioned as a way of further postponing these citizenship cases. The Comoros Islands passport recipients are effectively stateless, as they have no ability to reside in the Comoros Islands or seek diplomatic protection from the Comoros government. Instead, the passport recipients have been informed that their foreign passports are only an interim step in the naturalization process, and they thus continue to wait for Emirati citizenship.

By making this argument – that the identity regularization strategy further postpones the incorporation of this limbo population – I am not suggesting that ruling elites in Abu Dhabi intend to include these minorities eventually. On the contrary, the evidence suggests that excluding these minorities from the Emirati citizenry was (and continues to be) the goal, and that they have attempted to achieve that goal through outsourcing. And from the perspective of inter-emirate rivalry, Abu Dhabi's decision to give individuals who had emirate-level citizenship documents foreign passports certainly further denies the rights of Dubai and the Northern Emirates. The act of outsourcing passports renders these domestic populations "foreign," consolidating Abu Dhabi's hegemony over the union and its power to dictate the boundaries of the nation.

The point is, however, that this attempt to exclude a population from the national body politic has not led to the expulsion of that same group from the territory. This limbo population is not being systematically deported, or forcibly displaced. Most important is the fact that passport recipients are informed that these passports are only temporary, leading people to believe and hope that they will eventually receive Emirati citizenship if only they are compliant and patient. As I expand upon further in the next section, it is precisely that uncertainty about whether they have been excluded and their abiding hope for inclusion that make waiting such a powerful political strategy. By continually postponing the outright denial of citizenship, people are neither fully excluded nor included, but instead continue to be suspended in a limbo demographic zone – with foreign passports that now codify their permanently "temporary" status.

5.3 WAITING: THE MECHANICS OF CONDITIONAL INCLUSION

How are delays used to police and reshape citizen/noncitizen boundaries? This section draws on the existing literature on waiting and in-depth interviews with naturalization applicants to explain the power dynamics of waiting from the perspective of those who have been caught in limbo, waiting for identity documents for decades.

In the social science literature, the use of delays has been understudied as a political strategy in its own right. Instead bureaucratic delays have most frequently been treated as institutional "inefficiencies," leading studies to largely focus on identifying ways of decreasing waiting time (through monitoring, transparency, competition, bribes), rather than examining waiting as the end in itself (Ahlin and Bose 2007; Bose 2004; Yanez-Pagans and Machicado-Salas 2014). The scant attention waiting has received as a deliberate political strategy is surprising because time has played a central role in studies of the state since the 1980s, thanks in large part to the sustained engagement with diachronic processes from a variety of traditions.[7] This extant literature has largely focused on identifying the causes and patterns of institutional change and stability, that is, how time

---

[7] This includes historical institutionalism in political science, rational choice institutionalism in economics, and sociological institutionalism in sociology. By now a rich and extensive social science literature on formal and informal institutions demonstrates how time shapes state institutions and political outcomes (Blyth and Varghese 1999; Hall and Taylor 1996; Helmke and Levitsky 2004; Mahoney 2000; March and Olsen 1984; Pierson 2000; Steinmo, Thelen, and Longstreth 1992; Tsai 2006).

unfolds in state institutions – rather than the way states *use* and deploy time for political purposes.

A notable exception is the work of Javier Auyero (2012), who extensively examines delays as a poverty-regulation strategy in *Patients of the State*: a sociological account of the extended waiting that poor people seeking social services must endure in Argentina. Auyero argues that waiting represents the "temporal processes in and through which political subordination is reproduced" (2). The individuals he interviews in Argentina describe their situations in remarkably similar ways as interviewees waiting for citizenship in the UAE: "they know that they have to avoid making trouble, and they know, as many people told me, that they have to 'keep coming and wait, wait, wait'" (Auyero 2012: 9).

Mansour, a member of the Asian-Ugandan refugee community who is now in his eighties, has spent the better part of this life waiting for citizenship. He expressed the same emphasis on needing to not only wait but also come back iteratively. Relaying a conversation with a security official in the federal Ministry of interior, Mansour impersonates the bureaucrat by cupping hands as if holding a passport and mimics putting it in a desk drawer:

MANSOUR "*Inzīn, inzīn, inzīn, inzīn* [OK, OK, OK, OK] ... OK, *Insha'allah* [OK, God Willing] ... Come back in a week and I will see." [pause, Mansour speaks as himself] One day I asked these people, "Why don't you say 'yes' or 'no'?" Because if you go for an interview, or a job application, somebody he will see the papers and then write on it, and give it to the secretary or whoever – what do you call it – HR?

INTERVIEWER Yes.

MANSOUR He will say: "no, this is not my selection" on the spot. But here I said, why don't you say "no" right away? And he said, in Arabic it is some kind of shame to say "no" to a man directly to his face – *'Ayb!* [shame].

But my friend, you are killing this man with kindness.

Again, he will die in despair, because you are giving him hopes that are not there! And you are smiling [mimics stamping papers]: "OK, *insha'allah, insha'allah, bīṣīr khayr, līṣīr khayr* [good shall come, good shall come], *anta ta'āl bachir* [you come tomorrow] ... *ta'āl bachir, always ta'āl bachir*" [come tomorrow, always come tomorrow] ... that's normal.

So you will go until you get tired. And you will give up.

They know how to make you give up without forcing you, or without
telling you – "no." But they will make you tired, and you will feel "no."
So you will give up yourself – and he's not to be blamed, because *you*
didn't go back. (Interview with Mansour, October 22, 2012)

In this vignette, Mansour makes several important points about how
waiting functions as a form of political subordination. The first point
is that the candidate is never told "no" – they are told *"insha'allah"*
(God willing) and that they should come back again. This creates the
hope that if only they keep coming back enough times there will be
a resolution, even if the repetition of the same action has not changed
the outcome before. The hope entraps the individual into coming back
again and again and makes it challenging to identify what one's
options actually are in the situation. As Mansour notes, the hope itself
leads to despair – by *not* saying no, "you are killing this man with
kindness." Auyero's conversations with people who spent long periods
in waiting rooms points to a similar pattern: "Rosa ended our hour-
long conversation crying, saying, 'I'm a grown-up person, and they
tell me [come] tomorrow, [come] tomorrow, [come] tomorrow'"
(2012: 114).

Waiting means relinquishing control over one's time to the whims of
someone else, and in so doing, one recognizes their power, and submits
to it. Waiting, especially for protracted periods, creates a life of structured uncertainty that siphons one's choices into surrendering to someone else's rhythm or giving up and selecting out of the process. The
emphasis placed on coming back means that the responsibility lies with
the individual candidate rather than the bureaucrat dealing with the case
(as Mansour puts it, "he is not to be blamed, because *you* didn't go
back").

In this form of social control the means of exclusion is not formal
foreclosure, but self-selection. Denial works through numbing exhaus-
tion, by tiring people's patience and obfuscating how long the process
will take, rendering it impossible to calculate how much time is too
much time spent, after which it becomes irrational to renege.
Postponement is effective because waiting is both materially and psychologically costly, and when the costs of waiting outweigh the perceived benefits, people will self-select out of the process. This is
a point that Piven and Cloward (1971) and Auyero (2012) show in
their studies of welfare distribution in the United States and Argentina
respectively; postponements, additional screenings, and changes in the

patterns of processing times wear people out so that they do not gain benefits that they are formally entitled to.

Another recurring theme in the interviews was the way waiting structures the conduct of both those who wait and those who are waited upon. Smiling and dissimulation more generally are key mechanisms of circumlocution, representing the polite veneer that masks the indignant and dull realities of waiting time. In the conversation quoted above, Mansour notes that the civil servants smile and tell him to keep trying even when they know his case will never be resolved. Smiling was a recurring trope in my extended conversations with many other interviewees; in each case the person found something about the smile and dangling promise of a resolution to be especially degrading, like placating a child whom you never intend to indulge. For example, Khadija explains:

Everyone is very polite. They often say they understand how difficult it is to do anything without paperwork and they will do anything they can to help us. They smile and tell you "really there is no problem, don't be so worried." You also have to be polite, you have to sit and smile and wait, and sit and smile and wait, and sit and smile and wait. (Interview with Khadija, March 1, 2011)

It is not just the civil servants who smile; smiling or good conduct more generally is also how people are expected to perform their waiting time. Likewise Auyero finds that "repeated trips to state offices and interactions with state officials and courts teach poor people that if they are to get a hold of resources crucial to their survival, they will have to *comply by waiting, usually silently*" (Auyero 2012: 62). Failure or success is framed as a reflection of whether or not the applicant is truly dedicated to what they claim to be waiting for. One is taught to self-regulate behavior, either to perform the conduct of the "obedient" patient or finally renege and exit the waiting queue.

Domination not only occurs when you make someone wait, but can control how they wait. Power is exerted over those who wait patiently, civilly, and gladly. It is not enough to wait; they have to wait with a smile, and continue to smile even when the only tidbits of sparse information are negative. The longer the duration of their patience, the more irrational their waiting, the deeper the level of their perceived allegiance and obedience. The concept of allegiance is a key condition of Emirati citizenship and a recurring theme in the interviews. The question of what constitutes good and appropriate "conduct" is central to debates about citizenship and who is deserving of it. Ibrahim explains how waiting for citizenship structures one's behavior:

You have to hold your tongue – not just when you are being interviewed but all of the time. You have to be on your best behavior all of the time. My friends can relax but I never do, I always have to think about what I am doing – what I am wearing, how I'm driving, what I am saying, whether I will offend someone. When we were younger we were in school I was the same as everyone else, now they are living their lives and I am waiting to start mine. (Interview with Ibrahim, December 11, 2010)

This emphasis on good conduct means that the self-regulatory power of waiting works outside of the waiting room and seeps into people's everyday lives. This concern with good conduct is not simply a fear that is projected by individual applicants – naturalized citizens (and even those with more secure citizenship status) can be (and have been) denaturalized for behaving in any way that is perceived to disrespect the state and ruling elites. In addition to influencing how identity documents are withdrawn, this focus on "good conduct" also appears when documents are issued.

Figure 5.1 shows a document that had to be signed by the Asian-Ugandan refugees in Dubai prior to receiving their first UAE passports in 1997. The document specifies the conditions for holding the passport through a testimony of "good conduct." In particular, the passport recipients are told to be discreet about their acquisition of Emirati passports and not bring too much attention to the fact that they possess them ("there will not be any show-off incidents"). Abdullah (now deceased) was an Emirati who worked in the Dubai ruler's office and had access to these records. He explained why this document was drawn up by the ruler's office in Dubai: "To your questions, this document was drawn up by the late Mr. Duff from fear the recipients of UAE passports would jump the gun and start behaving as if they have secured full UAE nationality by displaying themselves as UAE nationals. So to protect them this document was drawn up just for Ugandans" (Abdullah, written communication, September 9, 2015).

Abdullah and Mr. Duff (a British advisor to Sheikh Rashid bin Saeed Al Maktoum, the ruler of Dubai at the time) drafted the "Statement of Good Conduct" before issuing passports to the refugee community that were secured by the ruler's office in Dubai. Abdullah viewed the document (and the imposition of silence and obedience upon others that it implied) as a way of protecting the members of this vulnerable community. The underlying message was a reminder that their citizenship was precarious and revocable and their access to its associated rights could be withdrawn.

Another recurring trope in interviews and the secondary literature is the insistence that the constant postponements and delays are caused by

STATEMENT OF GOOD CONDUCT

I,.., having been

issued with UAE passport #...........................dated................declare the
following:

That the usage of the above passport is strictly for travel & identity purposes
only. Under no circumstances will I at any time commit any deeds which infringe
upon abuse or misuse of this document which has been provided for its privilege
as intended. I will keep it at home under the safe custody and will not expose it
for any loans, liens or any such usages and that there will not be any show-off
incidents or expositions which render as abuse of this document.

I further, declare if I am found to have committed any abuse or misuse of this
passport that the good offices of HH The Ruler will have the right to revoke this
privilege of providing this document and that I fully understand I will not be
entitled to any other passport privileges anymore. It is expressly understood that
this privilege and others will be terminated instantly.

Name: ....

Signature: ....

Date: ....

Witnessed by:

Name: ....

Signature: ....

Date: ....

FIGURE 5.1 Testimony of good conduct

forces beyond the control of the civil servant. Delays are often implemented through redirections; the individual is directed to a different counter or
agency, or told the case is in the hands of a higher authority in a different
jurisdiction. One of the challenges to acquiring citizenship in the UAE is the
lack of clarity about the process itself; it has circuitous routes that require
iterative rounds of checks and approvals in a multilevel state. The multiple
layers of jurisdictions and unclear formal and informal criteria for inclusion help explain delays. As Mansour put it "nobody knows in whose
court the ball is supposed to be played" (interview with Mansour:

October 22, 2018). He explained that with regard to the treatment of his particular community – the Asian Ugandans in Abu Dhabi – the Ministry of Foreign Affairs alleged that they never got a reply from the MOI regarding the case of the refugees; for its part, the MOI alleged that as soon as the ruler's *diwan* (Sheikh Zayed's private office in Abu Dhabi) decreed the issuance of passports, the MOI would immediately issue them; when the refugees went to the *diwan* they were told that the cases were held up in the Ministry of Interior or Foreign Affairs, and so on. Each part of the bureaucracy would evade responsibility and redirect the individuals to another office. Meanwhile, the candidates would have to take time off work to visit the merry-go-round of offices over and over again.

Political subordination unfolds through this temporal process: the indeterminate waiting is reproduced daily, creating a permanent sense of insecurity. Any new laws or announcements of naturalizations are held as morsels of hope – attempts to read into the signs of whether a resolution will finally come about. Each time a new directive or law is announced, or people hear of successful cases, the news circulates and creates more uncertainty, convincing some people that the only resolution will come from silently and obediently waiting. Auyero observes a similar dynamic in his study in Argentina: "it would be very difficult to make sense of poor people's constant waiting if not for the fact that, for a few of them, waiting 'pays off.' ... events demonstrate to neighbors that 'something is happening' and that their waiting is not totally futile" (2012: 147). One example of a development that has given people an indication that waiting "pays off" occurred in 2011, when the UAE became the fifth Arab state (and only Gulf state) to reform its law to allow women to confer nationality to their children. Reports in local newspapers and on Twitter created a ripple of hope among the community of stateless children of Emirati women. Years later, however, none of the interviewees for this book who have Emirati mothers (n = 23) had been conferred citizenship; they all still carried Union of Comoros passports and were waiting for developments on their Emirati citizenship cases.

Whether or not waiting is indeed productive, one thing is certain – waiting has material and psychological costs that are compounded over time. Materially, waiting requires taking time off work, and incurs transportation costs, childcare costs, and food costs (while one waits in a waiting room). Outside of the waiting room, waiting for citizenship also incurs costs for photocopies, keeping and storing paperwork, translating and notarizing documents, postage costs, and registration fees. When documents are not renewed, people are cut off from education, healthcare, legal employment, and other state benefits. At a certain point, the costs outweigh the benefits of the good or service that is waited upon, causing the individual to opt out of the process. This is why market research has been so invested in understanding waiting – because the private sector loses money when they lose "waiters."

In examining the psychology of decisions to abandon waiting for services, Janakiraman, Meyer, and Hoch (2011) find that waiting generates two opposing psychic forces: escalating displeasure with waiting (waiting disutility) versus an escalating commitment to a wait that has been initiated (completion commitment). The authors argue that abandonments are most likely near the midpoint of waits, which is suboptimal for many waiting time distributions. The decision to abandon waiting thus requires the decision-maker to be able to calculate (at least an approximation of) how long the process will take. With particularly long waiting periods, especially ones that extend over generations, this calculation becomes exceedingly difficult. The punitive power of waiting "is met in its most extreme forms when a person is not only kept waiting but is also kept ignorant as to how long he must wait'" (Schwartz 1975: 38, reprinted in Auyero 2012: 78). Psychologically, uncertain waits feel longer than known, finite waits, and unfair waits feel longer than what individuals perceive to be "fair" ones (Maister 1985).

Waiting is thus most effective as a form of political subordination when individuals are unable to make sense of how long they have to wait or why. The only way to end that domination is to opt out and abandon the service altogether. But this ability to renege from the waiting line requires the demand for the service to be elastic and for there to be alternative options for those who wait. Those in limbo do not perceive their demand for Emirati citizenship to be "elastic" or see it as one of several viable options. Instead they view themselves as Emirati, and continue to wait patiently for their legal status to reflect that sense of national identity.

5.4 THE PAPERS OF WAITING FOR PAPERS

Waiting for citizenship creates an expansive document trail of the efforts to gain access to the right identity papers – the papers of waiting for papers. While those without a secure legal status are often referred to as "undocumented," this case illustrates that precarious access to citizenship actually generates documentation. Having an ad hoc or irregular legal status forces people to collect masses of identity verification materials. While someone with a secure citizenship status – whether as a citizen or foreign worker – can travel and interact with public and private institutions by producing only one valid identity document, those with insecure citizenship need a plethora of paperwork to access basic state services. They must constantly find ways of explaining and "proving" their identities to civil servants. The remainder of this chapter analyzes the paper trail of one Dubai-based refugee community's efforts to secure access to Emirati citizenship from 1973 to 2016.

Over the course of three years of sorting and coding from 2013 to 2016, approximately two thousand documents have been summarized, translated (when necessary), chronicled into a comprehensive timeline, and indexed for content. This archive has been organized to provide a quantitative basis for understanding the analytics of waiting. These records provide a unique synoptic overview of a protracted process of waiting over generations using previously unused records from a subdivision of the Dubai ruler's office (*diwan*). This archive originated as the records of Mr. William R. Duff (aka Bill), a prominent British advisor to Sheikh Rashid bin Saeed Al Maktoum, the ruler of Dubai from 1958 to 1990. Over the course of his career, Duff held many different positions in the Dubai ruler's office. He served as inspector general in the Dubai Ports and Customs, he was a finance expert, central accounts director, and the head of a little-known offshoot called the Ugandan Refugee Liaison Office.[8] The records of the Ugandan Refugee Liaison Office consist of the paperwork that Duff accumulated in his efforts to integrate the Asian-Ugandan community since they first arrived in Dubai and Abu Dhabi in 1973. The vast majority of these records focus on the Dubai group that Duff took responsibility for, with references to the Abu Dhabi group in the letters and testimonies. Information about the Abu Dhabi group was thus supplemented by extended interviews with Mansour, who was a part of the Abu Dhabi group and lived in the UAE from 1973 to 2009, before he was resettled to the United States.[9]

---

[8] When Duff first became financial adviser to Sheikh Rashid in 1960, Dubai was still part of the British protectorate of the Trucial States. He worked and lived in the UAE for 52 years until his passing in 2014, helping transform the emirate into the commercial hub it has come to be. Duff's early tasks included establishing a customs department and overseeing electrification and street-lighting. He helped manage the spending on transport infrastructure and public amenities and played a key role in planning the Jebel Ali free trade zone, which would eventually become one of the world's busiest commercial ports.

[9] While the main difference between the Dubai and Abu Dhabi groups is that the Abu Dhabi group has been resettled outside of the UAE, there were also differences in the treatment of these groups in terms of work authorization and housing and education. Significantly, the

The archive reveals the informal but active role that the local actors of the ruler's office took in matters of refugee resettlement or integration. Even when there was no established refugee resettlement policy in place, a web of public actors had to manage the real problems of human displacement. Different civil servants were responding to different challenges: Abu Dhabi officials were concerned with document fraud, open borders, and all of the associated security risks of having a transitory population. Meanwhile, the Dubai ruler's office had to deal with stowaways who arrived in the Dubai ports, and the civil servants in the ruler's central office developed ad hoc accommodations to deal with people fleeing conflicts.

Duff's informal role in refugee integration and resettlement involved more than simply collecting paperwork; it involved dealing with the entire bureaucracy of the burgeoning UAE federal state and UN offices (especially the United Nations Development Program [UNDP] and UNHCR). He was primarily in charge of first the Zanzibaris and then the Ugandans, but the documents illustrate that he later informally took on the role of refugee liaison for other groups, especially before the UNHCR office in Abu Dhabi was established. The archive contains information on the Ugandan refugees who arrived in 1973 (and to a lesser extent the Zanzibaris) who arrived prior to the formation of the UAE. UNHCR and archival documents show that the Zanzibaris who were treated as refugees arrived from 1965 to 1968, before the union was formed in 1971. The individual rulers of the emirates accepted Zanzibari and Ugandan refugees, but this arrangement stopped as the UAE's policies on refugees became more consolidated. As a result, the records show that by 1974 Zanzibaris who arrived in Dubai were no longer accepted as refugees and did not receive the same protection as the Ugandan Asian group. Likewise, later flows of stowaways in ships fleeing conflicts in Somalia and Iraq were treated as "unauthorized" cases and not referred to the ruler's office for sponsorship and Emirati citizenship. Even with these later arrivals, however, the Dubai ruler's office took an active role in coordinating with UNDP and then UNHCR to resettle people to other countries.

Figure 5.2 demonstrates the number of documents that have been collected over the past four decades, providing a quantitative measure of

Dubai government allowed this group to own businesses and properties like Emirati nationals, while the Abu Dhabi group was limited to government and private salaried jobs.

the records generated over time. One of the key challenges to coding this archive was the repetition of the records over the years: what is the accurate timestamp for a document that is created in 1974, but sent for the fourth time in 1995? The research team addressed this by providing two different total numbers for the visualizations, 854 unique records or 1925 individual papers. The total of 854 was arrived at by excluding all duplications of documents, counting multipage documents as one and assigning a date only to the first page, dating personal identification papers by the year of their issuance (rather than when they were sent), and inferring, as much as possible, illegible dates from the context of the documents. Figure 5.2 (n = 854 records) provides the distribution of unique records that were generated about the Asian-Ugandans and other refugee cases from 1967 to 2011.

This figure illustrates that the need to exchange documents ebbed and flowed with changes in the issuance of identity documents or changes in the state bureaucracy. For example, the decline in communications from 1997 to 2007 is an outcome of the Dubai group's ability to secure Emirati passports. Another decline in documents reflects the fact that the Ugandan Refugee Liaison Office was officially closed in 2005.

While this figure provides an accurate sense of the chronological distribution of the records, it also underestimates the volume of paperwork that was stored and sorted (n = 1925). The materiality of these records – the sheer quantity of papers that had to be collected by those who were waiting for papers – is not ancillary to the barriers to acquiring citizenship. The confusion over which papers had to be presented at which time, how many copies were necessary each time, and how many times they had to be sent and to whom is precisely what makes waiting for citizenship so difficult to manage. Many of the records consisted of multipage documents where different individual sheets of paper served different functions (e.g., an ID document may be affixed to documents requesting education support), and certain documents (such as copies of IDs or lists identifying all family members) were affixed to a large number of transmissions. To capture the real volume of the paperwork and the variety of functions that these papers were used for, the rest of the visualizations are based on the larger n (1925) where each and every individual sheet of paper has been coded.[10]

---

[10] Some of the visualizations have a slightly smaller n of 1910, just short of the full archive of 1925 documents. The reason for this gap is the number of only partially legible or illegible documents in the records.

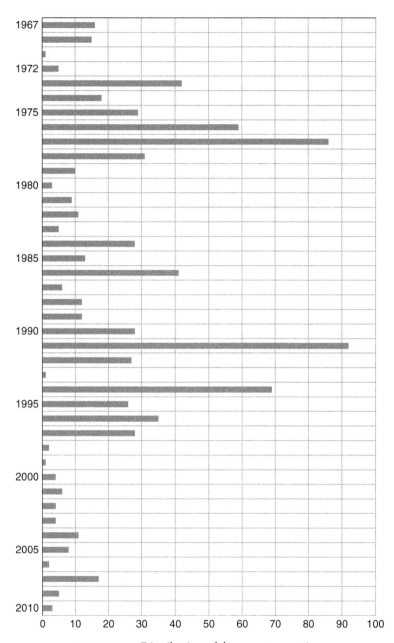

FIGURE 5.2 Distribution of documents over time

Many of the documents generated soon after resettlement to Dubai (especially those evidencing Sheikh Rashid's approval of the refugees to have Emirati citizenship) have been reproduced and attached to subsequent letters, requests, and applications. Particularly repetitive are the permits issued on the "Ruler's Court – Government of Dubai" letterhead and addressed to various government agencies in Dubai over the years. The Dubai government agencies that repeatedly required letters from the Ruler's Court for the issuance of various licenses and permits included:

- Dubai municipality
- Passports and Immigration Office (the name often varies to "Immigration and Passports Office" and later changes to "Naturalization and Residency Department")
- Ministry of Labor and Social Affairs
- Dubai traffic police (for the issuance of driver's licenses)
- Financial Development Department (beginning in the 1990s).

Approximately 20 percent of the archive is made up of duplicate records. The degree of duplication in the records helps illustrate the repetitiveness and hopelessness of having to iteratively present and send the same documents and hope for a different outcome. This repetition points to the constant need for copies, the need for storage space, and the navigation of paperwork that goes into a life spent waiting for citizenship.

5.4.1 Ugandan Refugee Liaison Office: Storing and Navigating Paperwork

How and why did a local authority in a state that does not officially recognize refugees or grant asylum create a refugee liaison office? This offshoot of the Dubai ruler's office grew out of the informal problem-solving efforts of the Dubai authorities that attempted to secure identity documents and social services for the families they were responsible for. By 1979 a new agency was created to manage the logistics of storing the masses of paperwork that the Asian-Ugandan cases had already generated after only six years. The new division designated employees who would navigate the increasingly complex bureaucratic procedures for acquiring identity documents, housing, employment, healthcare, and education on behalf of the refugees. The requests of the local authorities and refugees themselves were constantly shuffled from one jurisdiction to another, with the need to coordinate with other local authorities like the Dubai police, or federal authorities from the MOI, or international actors like (at first) the UNDP in Abu Dhabi, and once it was established in the UAE, the UNHCR. Many of these documents also had to be in both English and Arabic, so the exchanges also required a constant coordination with translation services.

Figure 5.3 provides a network map of the letters contained in the archive. The lines illustrate the connections between institutions and the arrows are used to show that letters were being exchanged in both directions. All the documents that have a recipient and sender were coded as letters. The majority of these are hard copies of posted letters, but the archive also includes faxes, telex transfers, and at least one printed-out email (the transition from hard copies to digital communication via email led to a decline in the number of letters in the archive from the mid-1990s onwards). This network map demonstrates how many different local, federal, nongovernmental and intergovernmental institutions had to intervene in order to allow these families to settle in Dubai. There is no central node in the network of letters; while the Refugee Liaison Office often initiated requests, other branches of the Dubai government (including the ruler's office, the Dubai police, the Dubai municipality, central accounts, and the finance department) were all active in the process of directly vouching for this community or lobbying for different aspects of their integration in the UAE. These letters reflect appeals to renew expired identity documents, and requests for educational assistance, employment, medical support, and housing. One pattern that emerges is that it was often unclear which authority was responsible for accommodating these refugees, including who should pay for different aspects of the refugees' lives. Various educational, housing, and health costs were paid for by the UNDP, UNHCR, Dubai ruler's office, or the Ministry of Foreign Affairs in Abu Dhabi (for the Abu Dhabi group). Even the local officials writing the letters did not necessarily know the correct path for how to accommodate this population, generating more and more documents that circulated between different agencies and institutions. For example, the Dubai ruler's office exchanged dozens of letters about who would pay for the schooling of the Asian Ugandan refugees who were under the age of 18. The Refugee Liaison subsection of the ruler's office had to coordinate with the UNHCR in Beirut, Cairo, or Amman and with each individual private school for each individual child, every semester, for many years until the UN stopped paying for these fees. The UNHCR argued that after gaining Emirati passports in 1997, children from this population became eligible for public schooling – a right their local brokers again had to negotiate

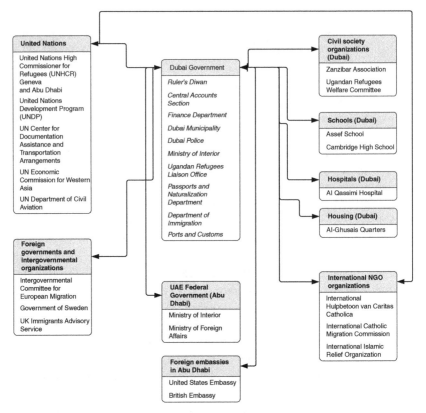

FIGURE 5.3 Network map of letters between institutions

with paperwork. In short, the network map reveals a multiplicity of actors and illustrates how complicated it can be to navigate basic access to public services when people do not have a clear legal status. The attempts to accommodate even a very small community can generate thousands of documents over the years. The sheer quantity of paperwork and the efforts required for accommodating this population led to the creation of a new subdivision within the Dubai ruler's office. The fact that a new division had to be built shows that even with a formal promise from the ruler of Dubai that this refugee community would be treated like Emirati citizens, the logistics of actually securing services for people who do not fit into a state's extant population categories was exceptionally difficult and required a high degree of coordination.

Several letters in the archive, exchanged in October 1979, shed light on the impetus behind the establishment of a refugee liaison office. This exchange clarifies that Duff's role (and therefore the role of the ruler of Dubai for whom Duff acted as a proxy) was as a local sponsor rather than a sovereign authority who could definitively resolve the citizenship cases. The first record that references this office is a letter from Duff, under the letterhead of the Central Accounts Section of the Government of Dubai, and it is addressed as a "Notice to All the Ugandan Refugees" (October 15, 1979). In the letter Duff explains that "an office has been established outside the premises of this section in order to deal more effectively with all matters concerning the refugees. It will operate under the title 'UGANDA LIASION OFFICE'."[11] The letter specifies that the office will be administered by two personnel and lists their names. It provides the physical address of the new office building, hours of operation, and a new phone number. The notice also states that new identification documents "are now being prepared and will be ready in due course; however, there will be new data forms to be completed prior to the issuance of these documents." This would not be the first or last time the refugees would receive notice that their identity documents were to be expected shortly, pending yet another new step in the acquisition process.

In response to this notice, Duff receives an angry letter three days later that is signed by several members of the community. They start by acknowledging the establishment of the office: "every one of us here believes that this kind of arrangement makes it easier for you to deal with our matters."[12] They go on, however, to contest the choice of liaison personnel, revealing rivalries between members of their own community. It is worth reproducing Duff's rejoinder here (figure 5.4) because he makes several key points that clarify the purpose behind the establishment of the refugee office and reveals his community-driven strategy for facilitating refugee settlement. Duff's tone is stern, and he begins defining the office by what is it is not: "It is <u>not</u> an office of 'mediation'; it is an official branch of the Ugandan Section in my office, which has taken over the job of keeping my records and, because of lack of room in my office, has set up a new office."[13] Duff shows that, first,

---

[11] The name of the office subsequently morphed into Ugandan Refugee Liaison Office.

[12] Ugandan refugee heads of family to William R. Duff, "Re: Notice to All the Ugandan Refugees," October 18, 1979.

[13] "Re: Re: Notice to All the Ugandan Refugees," October 27, 1979. On file with author.

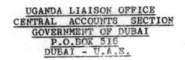

UGANDA LIAISON OFFICE
CENTRAL   ACCOUNTS   SECTION
GOVERNMENT OF DUBAI
P.O.BOX 516
DUBAI - U.A.E.

Dear Sirs,

I fear you have misunderstood the purpose of my establishment of the Ugandan Liaison Office. It is **not** an office of
"mediation"; it is an official branch of the Ugandan
Section in my office, which has taken over the job of keeping
my records and, because of lack of room in my office, has set
up in a new office.

I am also well aware that there are feuds and rivalries
amongst you - I have not been very impressed by your sense of
loyalty to each other, nor do I consider that the signatories
to the letter are so blameless as to entitle them to sit in
judgement on others.

Decisions will still be taken by my office but I intend this
new Section to keep my records You are free to choose your
own committee and appoint any number of mediators - any
cooperation between yourselves to better your lot is very
welcome and it will of course make the life of my office
easier too.

However any attempt to refuse the provision of reasonable
information to my appointed officer will inevitably delay the
work of this Department on your behalf. You are of course
always free to approach anybody else for assistance, since
this Department has not nor does it wish to have any powers
of coercion, nor in fact has it ever been officially appointed
the exclusive authority in Dubai for Ugandan Refugees.

I can only repeat that, as your community becomes more dispersed
within the rest of the community here, a more systematic
collection of information is necessary, if your interests are
not to be neglected, and cooperation from you will benefit both
sides.

Yours faithfully,

W. R. DUFF
FINANCIAL EXPERT TO
THE GOVT. OF   DUBAI

WRD/sv
Date: ...27/10/1979

FIGURE 5.4 Letter regarding the establishment of the Ugandan Refugee Liaison
Office

the imperative for creating the new office was not actually an official decree but an ad hoc response for more storage space and a need for a more systematic treatment of a case with swelling paperwork. The masses of paperwork that had to be stored, and the necessary task of coordinating between so many different state actors and different families, meant this case was starting to become a logistical nightmare for Duff.

Duff continues by chiding the letter writers, acknowledging their rivalries and feuds and noting that he has "not been very impressed" by their "sense of loyalty to each other." He points out that they are free to appoint any number of mediators and he would welcome their efforts to collectivize, but warns that their refusal to provide information to his appointed officer would delay their cases. Duff clarifies that the responsibility that his office has taken is informal and that the refugees are not actually obliged to seek his help. His reference to not having any "coercion" over the refugees narrates his position as a local broker for citizenship rather than the authority that confers it. The local authority's role is also clarified in an earlier letter, when Duff writes to a hospital in Sharjah about one of the refugees in 1976. The letter specifies that the individual identified in the letter is "under the sponsorship of H.H. the Ruler of Dubai."[14] It goes on to say that while the individual's case has yet to be fully settled and "it is still under discussion between the Ministry of Foreign Affairs and the Ministry of Interior," there is nonetheless "no question of their being liable for deportation nor does the normal prohibition against employment" apply in this case.

5.4.2 Ugandan Refugee Welfare Committee: Collectivizing Waiting Time

Duff's exchanges about the rivalries between members of the Asian-Ugandan group reveal his strategy of interlinking the fates of the families into one distinct community for better chances of gaining citizenship. This strategic effort to frame the individualized process of citizenship acquisition into a collective good for a "deserving" community is evident across the archive. Duff ends the letter with a prescient warning about the importance of defining their community *as* a community: "I can only repeat that, as your community becomes

---

[14] "To Al-Qassimi Hospital Matron," October 30, 1976. On file with author.

more and more dispersed within the rest of the community here, a more systematic collection of information is necessary, if your interests are not to be neglected, and cooperation from you will benefit both sides." He fears that the refugees would have less and less chance of gaining citizenship if they were "dispersed" into the larger UAE community of stateless domestic minorities. As it turns out, this ends up becoming a well-founded fear for the members of the Dubai group, since they now have the same Union of Comoros passports as the *bidūn* in the UAE, and have lost any special privileges or protections they had prior to the federal government's identity regularization drive.

The archive reveals how Duff attempted to collectivize the "waiting time" of the Asian-Ugandan community over the years. This was done by attempting to make the efforts of one count for the efforts of others. One active strategy was to interlink the legal cases through the constant reproduction of "family lists" and other documents that tie the community together. This meant that when a request went out, a list of all the members of the community was appended to the letter. Over the years, the refugees themselves further collectivized to reduce the uncertainty brought on by their ambiguous legal statuses. In 1985 they established the Ugandan Refugee Welfare Committee (Figure 5.5). This committee did not have a political role – instead, like the Refugee Liaison Office, its main goal was to simply navigate the bureaucracy and help resolve the citizenship cases of the Asian-Ugandans.

The exchange between Duff and the refugees is important because it reveals that despite his efforts to collectivize their "waiting time," the members of this small community did not necessarily agree on all issues or the best strategy for attaining citizenship. One of the more powerful ways that waiting produces subordination is by creating fractures. This is due to the fact that the power of waiting unfolds by obfuscating one's options and shrouding determinations of "how much" waiting is too long for the option of reneging to be viable. The conflicting information and uncertainty that is endemic to this process has split the community and made collective action very difficult. The letters reveal that while all of the members of the Dubai group would have rather had Emirati citizenship and continue living in Dubai, some believed that this would happen if they continued to compliantly follow procedures and kept patiently waiting and demonstrating their allegiance to the UAE. Others believed that they would never gain full citizenship in the UAE and resettlement was the only way to ensure future generations had a secure citizenship status.

لجنـــة الـــرعايـــة الاجتمـاعيــه للــلاجئـــين الاوغديـــين

UGANDAN REFUGEES WELFARE COMMITTEE

C/o Ugandan Refugees Liason Office
P. O. Box 516
DUBAI (U. A. E.)
Telephone: 435758
Telex: 47605 SURE EM

مكتب شؤون اللاجئين الأوغنديين
ص . ب ١١٦
دبــي (الإمارات العربية المتحدة)
هاتف : ٤٣٥٧٥٨
تلكس : ٤٧٦٠٥

Ref. .... المرجع

Date 21.09.1985 التاريخ

    ARTICLES OF ASSOCIATION OF UGANDAN REFUGEES WELFARE COMMITTEE

    I.

    The name of this association is UGANDAN REFUGEES WELFARE COMMITTEE.

    II.

    The purposes for which this association is formed are :-

    (a)   To represent the Ugandan Refugee Community on the
          issue of travel documents.

    (b)   To meet with officials of the U.A.E. Government.

    (c)   To represent the Ugandan Refugee Community on all
          matters that require dealing with the
          Ugandan Refugee Liaison Office.

    (d)   To operate as a non-profit association which does not
          contemplate pecuniary gain or profit to committee members.

    III.

    The office for the transaction of the business of the
    association is to be located in DUBAI.

    IV.

    The Ugandan Refugees Welfare Committee and its
    Representatives will work closely with the Ugandan Refugees Liaison Office,
    also located in Dubai.

                                        ... contd.2/

FIGURE 5.5 Ugandan Refugee Welfare Committee Articles of Association

5.4.3 Identity Verification as a Precondition for Livelihood

Coding the entire archive by subject of each document reveals one very clear pattern: when someone does not have the "correct" ID, they

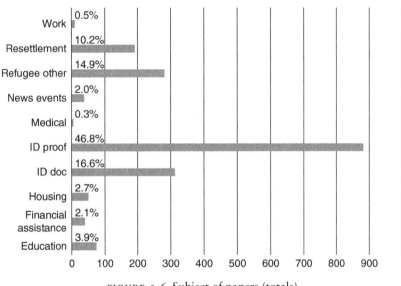

FIGURE 5.6 Subject of papers (totals)

constantly must prove that they are who they say they are. By far the most important path to any service arena was not direct negotiation about that specific state service or benefit, but the process of identity verification. Before even beginning negotiations about whether someone could gain access to a benefit and who would pay for it, the precondition was to establish the identity of the individuals in question. As the years accrued, more, not less, identity verification documents were needed to meet this basic precondition and supplement the community's identity documents. Figure 5.6 demonstrates the results of the coding of the archive by function of each paper, showing that the vast majority of the paperwork is related to Identity verification materials.

The bulk of the records in this archive – 63 percent – are copies of identity documents and testimonies of proof related to the identity verification process. The subject "ID DOC" was used to code any identity documents themselves – these make up 17 percent of the archive. Meanwhile, an additional 47 percent were supplementary documents that accompanied copies of IDs – these were coded as "ID PROOF." This category refers to all the additional documents that were required for verifying the identity of this population. These included long summaries about the original exodus from Uganda and how they entered the country, background checks, and testimonials vouching for the character of these individuals (from employers or prominent Emirati citizens), receipts from previous application rounds, and any proof that individuals had to show that they were who they said they were. This demonstrates how much effort was expended on the identity verification process, as opposed to resettlement attempts (10%) or specific arenas like housing (3%) or education (4%). The archive also contains numerous receipts that have been saved over the years, presumably to provide additional "proof." The majority of these slips state that a plea has been received and fees have been paid. Duff meticulously kept records to document and prove that the community has "served" its waiting time. The archive is a way of verifying that this community does indeed exist despite its lack of formal recognition.

5.5 CONCLUDING REMARKS

This chapter examines how waiting is used to police the boundaries of the Emirati citizenry. From the perspective of inter-emirate rivalries, this chapter shows how local authorities had greater control over who could belong to and reside in their jurisdictions during earlier periods of state formation. The federal government's attempt to resolve the issue of statelessness through an identity regularization drive grouped all subnational minority groups into one new larger group of Comoros Islands "guest workers." In so doing, ruling elites in Abu Dhabi have successfully diluted the power that local authorities – like the Dubai government – used to have over their own residents. Now, letters from local rulers or locally issued passports can no longer be used to leverage access to state services. As federal institutions have become more entrenched, the only acceptable forms of identity verification are federally issued identity documents that align with the state's binary population categories (citizen or guest worker).

Meanwhile, from the perspective of those who have been waiting for citizenship, they have gradually lost more and more rights. They can no longer access basic services, enroll their children in schools, or marry Emirati citizens or foreign residents without challenges. The psychological impact of waiting for that which never arrives means knowing something only through its absence – like the character of Godot in Beckett's (1955) classic literary work on waiting. If citizenship represents the relationship between individuals and the modern state, then for the individuals who have ambiguous legal statuses, citizenship is known only through its denial. This "denial" of citizenship is not experienced as an abandonment of state power, but rather an ever-increasing ensnarement and dependency upon the state.

6

Identity Regularization and Passport Outsourcing: Turning Minorities into Foreigners

The previous chapter illustrates how delays are used to police national boundaries. It examines the pattern of those who have been forced to wait for citizenship in the UAE to argue that Arab ethnicity and the venue of a case – specifically whether or not a citizenship claim was initiated in the Emirate of Abu Dhabi – largely determines whether that case was likely to have been approved for citizenship by the federal government. Citizenship cases that have been stalled for long periods of time have predominantly involved individuals of mixed or non-Arab descent with citizenship claims made in emirates other than Abu Dhabi. The substantial delays experienced by those undergoing naturalization procedures means that postponement – rather than outright denial – is the mechanism of exclusion.

Postponement is an evasive tactic and the de facto behavior of bureaucrats when there is no coherent strategy to address a specific policy problem. This chapter explains how a deliberate strategy or "solution" was eventually developed to address the problem of minority incorporation in the UAE. In the mid-2000s the Ministry of Interior (MOI) began an identity regularization plan that culminated with the outsourcing of pending citizenship cases to the Union of the Comoros in 2008. Why did the UAE outsource passports from the Union of the Comoros, and why did this occur when it did?

To explain the timing of the state's identity regularization drive, this chapter points to the importance of a change in the elite leadership of the federal MOI during a period when identity regularization campaigns became a much larger global trend. This combination of an internal change in the leadership of the security forces and external security pressures drove the UAE's MOI to attempt to eliminate any irregular statuses in the country. This case shows how identity regularization drives create critical junctures for elites to reassess the boundaries of national inclusion, allowing

expansions and contractions of the citizenry to occur through the depoliticized language of e-governance and identity management.

The UAE's identity regularization strategy of outsourcing passports
may have solved some aspects of the statelessness problem for the security
forces – specifically the need to harmonize all residents of the UAE so that
everyone neatly fits into the only official population categories of citizens
or foreign guest workers. However, from the perspective of those undergoing the process, the lived experience of this offshore solution is similar
to being continually ignored by the federal government. They continue to
wait for Emirati citizenship, but as "foreign" residents whose claims to
Emirati citizenship is made even more tenuous.

It should be emphasized that the Comoros passport recipients are not
citizens of the Union of the Comoros in any substantive way, because they
cannot access consular protection and they are not allowed to reside in the
Comoros Islands. The significance of a passport as a functioning identity
document is that it connects an individual to a sovereign authority who is
responsible for that individual; in this case, the UAE and Union of the
Comoros created passports that are disconnected from any political
entity. This use of outsourcing allows the UAE's federal government to
more formally abdicate responsibility for its domestic minorities, invent-
ing a class of permanently "temporary" residents in the process.

By outsourcing passports the UAE's federal authorities transformed the
informal limbo status experienced by those waiting for citizenship into
a codified legal status of permanent temporariness. These individuals are
permitted to continue residing in the country, but are now permanently
deportable and thus in a more precarious situation than if they only had
a local ID. This form of conditional inclusion has advantages for the state
over full inclusion or overt exclusion. Incorporation would make this
largely indigenous population eligible for the monetary and social benefits
of Emirati citizenship. This use of outsourcing is certainly a form of exclusion; it indicates that the federal government does not recognize the right of
individual emirates to define the boundaries of their citizenries. But this
form of exclusion falls short of stripping people of all documentation and
rendering them de jure stateless. Stripping individuals of all documentation
(or creating a different local ID) would challenge the state's ability to
eradicate all irregular statuses in the country. In other words, this use of
outsourcing creates a kind of conditional inclusion that allows the state to
evade the national dilemma (competing definitions of citizenship across the
federation) while solving the security dilemma (creating an exhaustive
accounting of all populations using the state's extant categories).

The next section presents an overview of the expected outcomes of identity regularization drives, examining some recent attempts by other governments to regularize legal statuses within their territories. The purpose of this comparative discussion is to contextualize how this case compares to other state responses to the question of minority incorporation when governments attempt to upgrade or expand their identity management systems. The chapter then addresses alternative explanations for the UAE's outsourcing of national identity documents, and proceeds to discuss the factors that explain the timing of this exchange in greater detail. The chapter then examines how both the problem the UAE faced (irregular legal statuses) and the solution it developed (outsourcing passports) compare to other cases. Finally, the chapter concludes by examining the impact of passport outsourcing on the individuals who received these passports, providing a side-by-side comparison of the rights associated with Emirati and Comoros passports.

6.1 IDENTITY REGULARIZATION: EXPECTED OUTCOMES

At its core, the problem that the UAE government was responding to when it outsourced citizenship cases is a gap between how the population is imagined and its actual composition. This disjuncture between nations as distinct and bounded "imagined communities" (Anderson 2006) and the heterogeneous reality of modern societies problematizes the very presence of certain groups. This is why millions of people cannot acquire citizenship despite generations of residency in their countries of birth (Berkeley 2009; Flaim 2017; Lawrance 2017; Sadiq 2017). This gap emerges because there is a time lag between the design of the nation-state system and the application of national citizenship. As Torpey explains, "in order to be implemented in practice, the notion of national communities must be codified in documents rather than merely 'imagined'" (2000: 6). In other words, as national citizenship is codified in documents and an infrastructure for identity management is actually built, exclusions occur. It is not only stateless populations who are caught in the margins; a "variety of marginalized groups (immigrants, minorities, homeless, the poor) experience a gap between formalized institutional citizenship and their actual lived reality" (Sadiq 2017: 166). Individuals can persist with an irregular legal status when there is not the infrastructure and technology to actually enforce legal status – especially when it comes to accessing public services or earning a livelihood at the local level. But as governments respond to a variety of concerns (ranging from border enforcement and national security to effective welfare allocation) the initiatives to strengthen identity management infrastructures have also brought cases of ambiguous and in-between legal statuses to the fore.

Identity regularization campaigns are designed to provide authorities with a comprehensive vision of their populations and create uniformity in the identification procedures that unlock access to state services and benefits. In addition to being used for migration enforcement and domestic security purposes, identity regularization campaigns are also a necessary prerequisite for the adoption of digital governance structures that can streamline access to public services and prevent welfare fraud. Identity regularization thus requires a concerted and coordinated multi-ministry effort to identify all the inhabitants of a territory and register their identities.

The UAE is the first and (at the time of publication) only state that has outsourced the identity documents of its own residents to another state. However, this use of outsourcing occurred as part of a larger identity regularization drive – and such drives are increasingly common in other parts of the world. There are three common types of identity registration drives, which are often found as progressive stages of one extended regularization campaign: (1) first, authorities begin issuing new national IDs to all inhabitants; (2) then, they identify and register populations with irregular legal statuses; (3) finally, they create sorting mechanisms for providing amnesty and documentation to some people who have irregular statuses, while targeting others for deportation. Registration campaigns that begin with a blanket registration of the entire population are usually deployed for the purpose of issuing a new or upgraded local ID – this was not only the case with the adoption of new biometric national ID cards in the UAE in 2006, but also in Argentina in 2012 and in India in 2014.[1] Identity registration campaigns can also specifically target one subset of the population with ambiguous or irregular legal statuses, as with the stateless registrations undertaken by the UAE in 2008, Taiwan in 2013 (Pan and Jui-chin 2013), and Sri Lanka in 2003 and 2009 (Wolozin 2014). The same process that enables some groups to have greater access to identity documents and (as a result) government services also often involves the active criminalization of other groups as being "illegals," as

---

[1] In Argentina an executive order was passed in 2011 to create a new biometric ID card, the Federal System of Biometric Identification for Security (SIBIOS). What followed was a multi-ministerial push to collect and store the biometric data (fingerprints and face scans) of all Argentines and foreign visitors. See Avaro (2014).

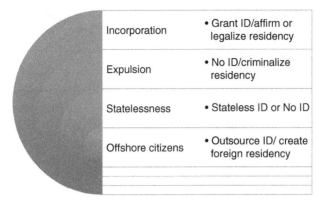

Incorporation	• Grant ID/affirm or legalize residency
Expulsion	• No ID/criminalize residency
Statelessness	• Stateless ID or No ID
Offshore citizens	• Outsource ID/ create foreign residency

FIGURE 6.1 Identity regularization outcomes

observed in Israel in 2002, Saudi Arabia in 2013, and the United States in 2017.[2]

In other words, identity regularization is a multifaceted process that for some can mean the issuance of an identity document, but for others can mean deportation, arrest, and/or the loss of residence and livelihood. During regularization campaigns states typically respond to their residents in one of three ways: document and incorporate as citizens, deport as "illegals," or ignore (i.e., refuse to issue identity documents creating statelessness). This case of "offshore citizens" shows how the UAE and Union of the Comoros have created a fourth option in national incorporation – using outsourced identity documents to transform domestic minorities into "foreign residents" (Figure 6.1).

To contextualize this case of outsourcing identity documents, the remainder of this section provides a brief overview of the outcomes of identity regularization drives elsewhere that occurred during a similar time frame. This discussion is used to show that questions of national incorporation are not fully resolved during the critical juncture of a national founding; the national dilemma of who should be included in a citizenry is revived during identity regularization campaigns. Identity regularization processes create critical junctures for elites to reassess the boundaries of national inclusion. Governments can use identity regularization to reassess which of their residents should have access to valid identity documents – and who should no longer be allowed to reside in the

---

[2] For the executive order in the United States see Trump (2017); on Israel see Willen (2010); see the "Deportation" subsection later in this section for more information on Israel and Saudi Arabia.

territory. The reissuance of identity documents allows political entities to expand or contract the boundaries of a citizenry through the seemingly depoliticized process of technological upgrades in identity management.

Incorporation: The first expected outcome of identity registration drives is that states will document and more fully integrate their populations into the national body politic. The World Bank estimates that over 2 billion people in the developing world lack a national ID – a problem that disproportionately impacts women and children from poor rural areas in Africa and Asia (Dahan 2015: 1). Without a form of national identification, residents are unable to participate in elections or access healthcare, education, financial services, welfare benefits, or economic development initiatives. International development agencies have encouraged developing countries to adopt biometric ID cards to "leapfrog" technologies and build integrated identity management infrastructures. By 2010 there were 160 cases where biometric identification was adopted in developing countries for economic, political, or social purposes (Gelb and Clark 2013). India provides perhaps the best example of a massive identity registration campaign. Since introducing the *Aadhaar* biometric ID card in 2014, the government of India has used biometric identity registrations for food and fuel subsidies and banking purposes, and as of January 2017 1.1 billion cards have been issued (Parussini 2017). Proponents of biometric identity registration cards argue that such drives enable the state to have a more direct interaction with its citizens, providing benefits to rural or nomadic populations who have never had birth certificates or any form of national identification. Identity registration drives can thus be a way of transforming disenfranchised and isolated populations into national citizens who have a connection to a national authority for the first time.

Deportation: A second outcome of identity regularization is the expulsion or deportation of resident populations. For example, Saudi Arabia not only has the largest number of labor migrants in the Gulf (approximately 10 million), but also the largest number of irregular migrants due to the overstaying of religious pilgrims to Mecca (Gulf Labor Markets and Migration 2015). Since 2013, the Saudi government has begun a series of identity regularization campaigns that culminated with an estimated 5 million deportations in 2017 (*Al-Arabiya* 2017; Middle East Monitor 2017). The mobilization of resources required in such campaigns shows that the status of becoming "illegal" requires an active process of targeting on behalf of state authorities (often with the complicity and assistance of the private sector and NGOs). The same identity regularization drives that provide amnesty and documentation for some residents render others "illegal." In the United States, for example, President Obama's 2012 executive action on Deferred Action for Childhood Arrivals (DACA) provided an amnesty for some long-term irregular migrants to regularize their status and continue residing in the United States legally. This extension of amnesty to select irregular migrants was coupled with the mass mobilization of resources toward the deportation of other irregular migrants who did not meet the DACA requirements.[3] Indeed, official figures on deportations suggest that a record number of immigrants were deported under the Obama administration – just over 3 million, larger than the 2 million removals under President George W. Bush.[4] Identity regularization drives thus often have the dual effect of extending rights to some residents while actively criminalizing others.

Statelessness: In addition to incorporation and expulsion, a third outcome of identity regularization is statelessness. As states strengthen their identity management infrastructures, the very mechanisms put in place to eradicate irregular legal statuses can have the opposite effect. In her research on stateless highlanders in Thailand, Flaim finds that "protracted statelessness among highlanders persists, paradoxically, as a result of the bureaucratic practices and procedures that have been enacted to address it" (2017: 148). This is because the individuals in question are outside of the imagined community of the officials who determine citizenship status.

Identity regularization drives lead to statelessness in two ways. One way this occurs is when state officials "ignore" (i.e., actively avoid documenting)

---

[3] To have qualified for DACA, applicants must have arrived in the United States before their sixteenth birthday, they must have continuously lived in the United States since June 15, 2007, to the present day, they must be under thirty-one years of age as of June 15, 2007, they must have never had a lawful status in the United States on or before June 15, 2012, they must be in the process of obtaining or have already obtained a high school diploma or General Education Development (GED) or be honorably discharged from the US Armed Forces or US Coast Guard, they must have not committed a felony, significant misdemeanor, or three or more minor misdemeanors, and not pose a threat to national security or public safety, and lastly they must have been physically present in the United States on June 15, 2012, and at the time of their DACA request (US Citizenship and Immigration Services 2016).

[4] Obama's administration focused on removals more than returns. Removals involve the compulsory movement of a noncitizen out of the United States based on a formal court order. Removals have harsher penalties because they prevent individuals from re-entering for a specified period of time. Meanwhile, returns refer to individuals (typically Mexicans or Canadians) who were trying to enter illegally and were apprehended at their own border. Instead of being formally placed into proceedings, these individuals are turned around and prevented from entering the United States (US Department of Homeland Security 2016).

select populations during registration processes, rendering them effectively stateless and/or deportable during regularization campaigns. For example, in December 2013, the government of the Dominican Republic set out an eighteen-month "National Regularization Plan for Foreigners with Irregular Migration Status" aimed at weeding out "illegal" immigrants who had migrated to the Dominican Republic. The regularization campaign followed the Dominican Constitutional Court's September 2013 ruling (judgment 168–13) that determined that children born in the Dominican Republic to foreign parents who did not have legal statuses have never been entitled to Dominican nationality. The judgment changed the *jus soli* (citizenship by birth) basis of Dominican citizenship and was applied to people born since 1929, constituting a retroactive deprivation of nationality that disproportionately impacted Dominicans of Haitian descent. This is due to the fact that low-level bureaucrats in civil registries would routinely refuse to register children born to mothers of Haitian origin (Amnesty International 2015). Following the expiration of the regularization period in June 2015, the Dominican authorities began deportations of anyone who could not provide evidence of birth, leading to mass deportations of Dominicans of Haitian descent, with estimates ranging between 100,000 and 200,000 by 2016.[5] These populations could not prove either Dominican or Haitian citizenship and therefore became stateless. Though they did not have citizenship documents prior to the identity regularization campaign they could reside in the Dominican Republic; the resource-intensive identity regularization campaign is what targeted them, criminalized their presence, and rendered them effectively stateless.

Another way that identity regularization can lead to statelessness is when individuals are registered *as* stateless persons, codifying this status. Identity regularization initiatives can therefore have the impact of reifying the stateless status of some groups, foreclosing their access to benefits and protections that they could previously access. For example, beginning in 2005, all residents in Thailand were issued national ID cards. Stateless populations were included in the registration process, but officials can differentiate between stateless IDs and those belonging to other groups of residents (citizens, naturalized citizens, and legal foreign residents) based

---

[5] Amnesty International reports that as of May 26, 2016, 40,000 people were deported from the Dominican Republic to Haiti while at least another 66,000 returned "spontaneously" after receiving threats or being pressured to leave the country (Amnesty International 2016: 4). Meanwhile other news outlets have estimated the number of deportees to be closer to 200,000 (Castillo 2016).

on the first numbers of the sequence on the ID card (Harris 2013: 113). Harris found that when the Thai government made national IDs a requirement of accessing universal healthcare, stateless persons were effectively disenfranchised from government healthcare programs that they could previously access with other forms of identification like driving licenses or household registrations.

Outsourcing identity documents: In 2008–2009, the UAE and Union of the Comoros created a fourth outcome for identity regularization drives – instead of incorporating, deporting or ignoring residents with irregular legal statuses, the UAE imported passports from the Union of the Comoros to count its own minorities as "foreign residents." Indigenous and long-term residents with pending naturalization cases (many of whom had Emirati passports and other forms of identification) found themselves in the position of becoming citizens of a foreign state that they had no connection to. This process unfolded over three stages. First, the MOI announced a stateless registration drive, requiring anyone who was stateless or in the process of applying for UAE citizenship to register for a stateless ID card. Second, the MOI reaffirmed the government's prerogative to revoke citizenship on the basis of national security assessments, laying the groundwork for the confiscation of (or refusal to renew) Emirati passports from those who had them previously. Finally, the MOI issued Comoros passports to those with stateless IDs, informing them that these foreign passports represented an interim step in the path to Emirati citizenship – a stopgap measure that would provide them with documentation while their security checks were being processed for naturalization.

The UAE's stateless registration drive was part of a larger multifaceted identity regularization campaign that the federal government began in the mid-2000s. In 2004, a federal decree established the Emirates Identity Authority (EIDA), and by 2006 the authority began an identity registration campaign to introduce a new biometric national ID system that would link all government services to the new ID card.[6] National IDs were issued to only two categories of people: citizens and temporary foreign residents. To be issued a national ID, foreign residents had to

---

[6] Federal Decree No. 2 of 2004 established the Emirates Identity Authority, and Federal Decree No. 9 of 2006 dictated the creation of a population registration system and issuance of national IDs; see Federal Authority for Identity and Citizenship (2018). See Chapter 4 for more details on how the population was organized and segmented to implement the new national ID.

present a valid residency visa (identifying themselves and their national sponsor) and citizens had to present a "family book" (*khulāṣat al-qayd*) identifying their tribal lineage. That meant that all the individuals who have resided in the UAE without this family book – including the *bidūn*, children of Emirati women, and ethnic minorities – could not receive national IDs.

The new ID card infrastructure made it increasingly difficult for individuals without the national ID (but with other forms of identification like birth certificates and passports) to gain access to government services. Once the new national ID card was introduced it was deemed the only valid ID for UAE citizens in all interactions with the state – this included all interactions with the courts, attaining marriage licenses, accessing public education, and being able to apply for the robust economic privileges associated with citizenship. In response to the gap this new ID created, the federal MOI initiated a stateless registration drive in 2008 that sought to regularize the identity statuses of all residents. As the secretary general of the UAE Interior Minister's office at the time, Major General Nasser Al Nuaimi, announced, the ultimate goal was to eradicate any irregular legal statuses: "once the process is completed, there will only be three sets of people in the country – citizens, expatriates and visitors. The remaining will be considered illegal" (Absal 2008).

The primary aim of the identity registration campaign was thus not only to create a master population registry and issue national IDs, but also to exhaustively enumerate the resident population into a binary of only two legal categories of residents: citizens and temporary foreign residents. For those with irregular legal statuses, the identity registration drive "regularized" their status in the UAE, but instead of becoming citizens they became "guest workers." Upon receiving Union of Comoros passports they were informed that they could legally reside in the UAE, but in the same way as all other foreign residents. They would thus need to locate an Emirati family member or friend who could nominally function as a *kafīl* (national sponsor) to sponsor their (renewable) temporary residency visa.

Since this arrangement was never publicly acknowledged, it is difficult to count exactly how many people received Union of Comoros passports in the UAE. There are no official figures of the denominator (the total number of people who have applied for naturalization and are waiting for Emirati citizenship) nor the numerator (the total number of those individuals who have been issued Comoros passports by the UAE government). Estimates provided by a variety of sources suggest that these passports were issued to approximately 80,000–120,000 people living in the UAE –

a number that roughly corresponds to the size of the *bidūn* population in human rights and media reports.[7] Before explaining how this case of "offshore citizens" was implemented in further detail, the next section presents alternative explanations for why the UAE government outsourced foreign passports for its own residents.

6.2 ALTERNATIVE EXPLANATIONS

Why did the UAE government outsource its naturalization cases to the Union of the Comoros? This section evaluates two alternative explanations and presents my argument for why this passport outsourcing arrangement occurred.

6.2.1 Outsourcing for Incorporation

One possible explanation is that the UAE adopted these Union of Comoros passports as part of a larger plan to fully incorporate its "irregular" and stateless populations. In other words, these passports may have been issued to facilitate the registration of people undergoing naturalization in the UAE – providing the MOI with a way to document people as they wait for Emirati citizenship. Ethnographic and archival evidence supports the finding that these passports are designed for residency in the UAE, and some passport recipients do very much believe these foreign passports are a step toward achieving full Emirati citizenship. Out of sixty-two interviewees who received these Comoros passports in the UAE, all sixty-two report being assured by officials that these passports were an interim step in the naturalization process. Most held the belief that if they followed the proper procedure to attain these Comoros

---

[7] Interview with former Comoros Gulf Holding (CGH) employee, April 5, 2011 (Comoros passports issued to 20,000 families or approximately 80,000–100,000 people); Interview with Comoros passport recipient, March 3, 2012 (80,000–120,000 people). Investigative journalist Abrahamian (2015) estimates that 100,000 people received these passports. Refugees International estimates that there are between 10,000 and 100,000 *bidūn* in the UAE (Lynch 2010). Camilla Hall and Michael Peel (2012) cite an estimate of 30,000 to 100,000 thousand *bidūn* in the UAE. Laura van Waas (2010) does not give estimates but cites sources estimating the number of *bidūn* as 100,000. Finally, the US Department of State's Country Report on Human Rights Practices in the UAE for 2007 provides an estimate of "at least 20,000 stateless residents who either were without citizenship or had no proof of citizenship for any country" (US Department of State Bureau of Democracy, Human Rights, and Labor 2008). Each subsequent Department of State report on the UAE's human rights practices from 2008 to 2016 lists an unverified estimate of between 20,000 and 100,000 stateless individuals in the UAE.

passports then they would become full Emiratis in a few years, expecting to finally attain a new Emirati passport as well as the elusive "family book."

Moreover, at the same time as these passports were issued, several newspaper articles stated that naturalization applicants would "need a passport to get a passport," suggesting these Comoros Islands passports were a temporary measure. While the UAE government's role in issuing Union of Comoros passports was never officially acknowledged, officials from the MOI made public announcements in *Emarat Al Youm*, *Khaleej Times*, and the *Gulf News* stating that it was obligatory for people who apply for Emirati citizenship to show documentation of a previous nationality. The Minister of Interior Sheikh Saif bin Zayed Al Nahyan publicly commended Comoros passport recipient Hasan Abdul Rahman and recommended him for naturalization. Sheikh Saif was quoted saying, "We appreciate the initiative of Abdul Rahman, who has shown himself to be a law abiding person. The fact that he sought to correct his status to stay and work legally in the country proves that he is well intentioned" (*Khaleej Times* 2008). Abdul Rahman obtained a Comoros passport to enable him to work and stay legally in the UAE, while at the same time pursuing his UAE citizenship. This allowed him to have "a clean record" and the MOI publicly announced that it had thus recommended his approval for Emirati citizenship. In another example of being "rewarded" with Emirati citizenship after acquiring these foreign passports, the MOI's news service publicized that in 2008, Major General Nasser Al Nuaimi issued instructions to approve the naturalization cases of twenty-five MOI employees who had applied for Union of Comoros passports. Al Nuaimi commended their eagerness to apply for passports and regularize their legal status, saying that such behavior demonstrated a willingness to abide by the law (*Gulf News* 2008). Such announcements encouraged other applicants to go through the Union of Comoros consulate as a means of regularizing their status, spreading the belief that doing so meant "abiding by the law" and that this would lead them on the right path to eventually gain Emirati citizenship.

If these Comoros passports are designed simply as a conduit to Emirati citizenship, then it is not clear why the UAE's federal government would need to issue foreign passports as opposed to an internal document and local ID. If the UAE federal government's goal was to simply document its own resident population, then why involve a different sovereign state? Those who received Comoros passports and are still waiting for Emirati citizenship are largely domestic minorities of mixed descent (Persian, East

شروط المتقدمين للحصول على بطاقة التسجيل الخاصة:-

يجب على المتقدم الذي تنطبق عليه شروط التقديم ادناه تعبئة طلب التسجيل للبطاقة الخاصة وتعبئة جميع البيانات المطلوبة
بكل دقة وأمانة، ويتحمل المتقدم جميع التبعات النظامية لأي خطأ فيها

أولاً: - الاشخاص الحاصلين على جوازات سفر الدولة بدون الحصول على خلاصة قيد.

ثانياً:- الاشخاص الذين صدرت لهم مراسيم بمنحهم جنسية الدولة ولا يحملون جنسية دولة اخرى.

ثالثاً:- الاشخاص الذين تم استلام طلبات تجنيسهم وتم منحهم ايصال الاستفهام ولا يحملون جنسيات دول اخرى.

رابعاً:- كافة الاشخاص الذين سواءً سبق أن تقدموا للتسجيل أو لم يسبق تقدمهم للتسجيل من قبل من لا يحملون أوراق
ثبوتية.

خامساً:- جميع فئات من لا يحملون أوراقاً ثبوتية أو ما تعارف عليه بالـ "بدون".

ملاحظة مهمة:- يجب تعبئة طلب لكل فرد من افراد العائلة و حضور جميع افراد العائلة للموعد المحدد للتسجيل.

FIGURE 6.2 Application criteria for stateless registration (document on file)

African, South Asian) who are often referred to as stateless (*bidūn*). This population is not "undocumented" but rather partially or ambiguously incorporated. My interviewees held local documents like birth certificates, health records, school records, driving licenses, and in some cases even federally issued passports but are still waiting for the most crucial identity document – the *khulāṣat al-qayd* or "family book."

For the internal purposes of the state, a domestic ID like the stateless cards already makes this population legible to the authorities. Indeed, prior to issuing Union of Comoros passports, the government already held a stateless registration campaign and issued stateless IDs to the *bidūn* population. These IDs were frequently referred to as "gold" cards because of their color, and the application form from 2008 reveals at least five different categories of irregular legal statuses that the government had to contend with (Figure 6.2).[8] This includes (1) people who have UAE passports but not family books, (2) people who have a citizenship decree (*marsūm*) approving their UAE nationality but have not received family books and do not have nationality in another state, (3) people who have applied for naturalization and can present a receipt showing their case

[8] This stateless application form was provided by an unnamed informant who was born in Dubai. He received a gold card and now holds a Union of Comoros passport. This informant falls under category (1) of these groups, as he was issued several UAE passports over the years but was never issued a family book. (Passages were underlined by applicant.)

number and do not have nationality in another state, (4) all individuals who have either previously registered or have not previously registered but are not in possession of any identity documents, and (5) all segments of the population who do not hold any identity documents, otherwise known as the *bidūn*.

If the goal of the Comoros passports was to register people in preparation for full national incorporation, then this population was already registered through the statelessness drive and it is not clear what value was added by adopting a foreign passport. Instead of incorporation, the use of a foreign ID points to the fact that there was the intention to further exclude this population, rendering internal minorities deportable. This act of outsourcing allows the federal government to more formally abdicate its responsibilities toward the very diverse members of this group so that they are all grouped together as one artificial category of permanently temporary residents.

6.2.2 Outsourcing for Expulsion

A second possible explanation is that the UAE purchased passports to create a "deportation haven" in the Comoros Islands. In other words, this passport scheme was simply a new way for states to adopt the "expel" option and widen the deportability of the population. In this explanation the outsourced passports now allows the UAE to deport its own citizens and indigenous stateless minorities (*bidūn*). This is the interpretation adopted by some media sources that reported on these passports. A recent piece in *Foreign Affairs* claims that the UAE government "is paying the cash strapped Comoros to take stateless people like [Semira] off its hands" (Mahdavi 2016). The author predicts that this exchange will prove to be unsustainable because it means nearly 1 million stateless persons in the UAE and Kuwait will move to the Union of the Comoros (whose population is a mere 750,000). Meanwhile, in his story "Inside the $100 Million Scheme to Send the Middle East's Most Unwanted People to Africa," another reporter focuses less on the *bidūn* population and more on domestic political opponents (Salisbury 2015). He argues that this offshoring scheme was developed to allow the governments of the UAE and Kuwait to have a way of deporting denaturalized citizens: "Gulf States, intolerant even of critical tweets, are now punishing their own citizens by rendering them stateless" (Salisbury 2015). He characterizes the outsourced passports as being part of the political tactic of denaturalization that has been adopted by some Gulf states since 2011. In both of these explanations, outsourcing passports to the Union of the Comoros is a way of facilitating the deportation and physical relocation of segments of the UAE's resident population.

It would not be unprecedented for a state to pay another state to take its "undesirable" populations. For example, both the United States and Australia have offshored migration enforcement; both employ migrant interdiction and detention centers outside of their territories. The US base in Guantánamo Bay, Cuba, is an offshore migrant detention center that holds asylum seekers intercepted at sea by US Coast Guard vessels.[9] Meanwhile, the Australian government has offshore detention agreements with Nauru and Papua New Guinea to intercept and detain Australia-bound migrants.[10]

This explanation – that the UAE essentially purchased foreign passports to expel residents – would also align with the predicted outcomes offered by several social science theories about national incorporation. Primordialists would predict that the passport recipients, especially the *bidūn* (stateless), were excluded because of their perceived cultural or ethnic differences from the "core" national group. More security-driven theories would support Salisbury's claim that the UAE is expelling those who are perceived to be security threats.

Evidence from both the UAE and Comoros Islands, however, demonstrates that this exchange was not designed to relocate UAE residents to the Comoros Islands. On the contrary, the Union of Comoros passport recipients are *not allowed* to reside in the Comoros Islands as a stipulation of the program. Three different sources confirm that these Comoros

---

[9] This offshore site was an extension of the Reagan administration's program of intercepting Haitian boat migrants, moving South Florida's border protection to international waters and beyond the reach of the US courts. This tactic was explicitly used to evade judicial overview and effectively shielded immigration officials from lawsuits challenging comprehensive denials of Haitian asylum claims (Kahn 2018).

[10] The Australian government legislated offshore detention starting in 1992 to "deter" refugees and asylum seekers. Agreements with Nauru and Papua New Guinea were signed in 2001. Successive governments have prevented migrants arriving by boat from accessing asylum procedures, resulting in indefinite and mandatory detention of migrants in offshore private detention centers. Transnational human rights groups recently filed a communiqué in the International Criminal Court against the involved states for crimes against humanity under Article 15 of the Rome Statute. The claim documented overcrowded and unsanitary conditions of detention; abuse at the hands of guards and local gangs; sexual violence (including against children); inadequate access to food, water, and medical treatment; and extensive mental suffering of detainees (Achiume *et al.* 2017). Human rights groups make similar claims against EU practices of "offshoring detention" both at the borders and outside of the EU.

passports are designed for residency in the UAE and not for relocation to the Comoros Islands.

The first source of evidence about the nonresident status of these Comoros passports comes from the law of the Union of the Comoros. In July 2008 the national assembly met to debate and vote on a bill on the introduction of "economic citizenship" – "*Loi relative à la citoyenneté économique en Union des Comores*" (Law Concerning Economic Citizenship for the Union of the Comoros; Assemblée de l'Union 2008). Article 6 specifies that economic citizenship does not grant any rights to habitual residency in the Comoros at any given time.[11] The text discusses granting citizenship papers to "partners" of the Comoros, as long as these individuals do not have criminal records, belong to terrorist organizations, or threaten the social and cultural cohesion of the country. Those who benefit from economic citizenship would be able to obtain passports but cannot permanently reside in the Comoros, do not have the right to vote, and cannot serve in the armed forces or run for office. Atossa Abrahamian's investigative reporting on these passports in the Comoros and her interviews with Comorian officials also confirms that this Gulf citizenship agreement – which was passed by the parliament in November 2008 – did not include a provision for resettlement (Abrahamian 2015).

Additional evidence about the nonresident status of these passports comes from the United States Department of Homeland Security's (DHS) policy on Comorian passports issued to UAE residents. In response to an interviewee's visitor visa application to the United States, the DHS instructed the applicant to submit a passport waiver request in order to receive a US visa. The reason, stated in a form handed out during the visa interview, is straightforward: "DHS notes the Comoros economic citizenship travel document does not confer upon its holder the right to reside in the Comoros or return to that country after a stay in the United States. It therefore does not meet the definition of a passport as outlined in Immigration and Nationality Act Sectors 101 (a) (30) and 212 (a) (7) (B) (i)."[12]

---

[11] Article 6 in the original reads "*la citoyenneté économique est accordée sans condition de résidence habituelle aux Comores ni de stage. Elle ne peut être accordée qu'à l'étranger justifiant de sa résidence habituelle hors du territoire Comorien.*"

[12] Consulate General of the United States of America, Dubai, UAE, "Notice to Visa Applicant," February 3, 2016 (on file with author).

Other publications by US government bodies indicate that the issuance of Comoros passports to residents of the UAE has been a known concern for years. Notably, a Department of State report on human rights practices in the UAE found that stateless persons had been forced to take Comoros passports. Should these Emirati Comorians be deported, "the Republic of Comoros would not accept these persons, who would have to find refuge in another country" (US Department of State 2013).

Finally, a third source of evidence about the nonresident status of these passports comes from the case of a high-profile individual who received his Comoros passport in the UAE and was subsequently deported – but not to the Comoros Islands. Ahmad Abdul Khaleq is a *bidūn* blogger who was born and raised in the UAE. He became a vocal proponent of stateless rights online and in 2009 he began posting on a site called "UAE Hewar" (UAE dialogue) that was founded by Ahmed Mansour, a pro-democracy activist. In April 2011, Abdul Khaleq was arrested along with Mansour and three other people who had been posting on the site – the media referred to the group as the "UAE Five." They were charged with disruption of the public order and publicly insulting the country's rulers (a crime under the Emirati penal code), and were sentenced to two years in prison. They were subsequently pardoned by the president of the UAE, Sheikh Khalifa bin Zayed Al Nahyan, after serving eight months. Then in May 2012, Abdul Khaleq was instructed by officials from the MOI to come in with his family and apply for a Comoros passport. Like my interviewees, Abdul Khaleq reports being informed that if they applied for Comoros passports they would subsequently receive Emirati citizenship (Abrahamian 2015). He and his family members received Comoros passports and were instructed to locate a sponsor and apply for a residency visa. A few weeks later Abdul Khaleq was asked to come into the passport office again, but this time the authorities told him to wait outside alone. He was put in a car and driven to jail in the Wathba district of Abu Dhabi. While in jail, he was given the option of being deported to Afghanistan, Pakistan, or Iran. He rejected all of the options and subsequently was allowed the option of going to Thailand, landing in Bangkok on July 16, 2012. He was eventually granted asylum in Canada, and is currently based in London, Ontario. At no point was he given the option to travel to the Comoros Islands.[13]

[13] For more on Abdul Khaleq's case see chapter 3, "The Reluctant Cosmopolite," in Abrahamian 2015. See also Morris (2012) and US Department of State (2013).

Abdul Khaleq was targeted for deportation because of his political activism, but there is no indication that the UAE government is deporting Comoros passport holders en masse. In the aftermath of issuing these Union of Comoros passports, deportations of Comoros passport holders like Abdul Khaleq have been few and far between. The vast majority of the people who received these passports continue to live in the UAE, but like guest workers, their residency rights are contingent and revocable. These passports make the population deportable, but the specter of deportation is even more important than the actual act of expulsion. Deportability appears to be a key motivation behind this outsourcing arrangement. The constant threat of deportation regulates the behavior of passport recipients, creating a permanent sense of insecurity. Recipients can be expelled if they are perceived as being politically active, committing criminal acts or threatening state security. They are thus legal residents on sufferance – conditionally tolerated but not integrated with permanent or inalienable rights.

6.3 OUTSOURCING FOR CONDITIONAL INCLUSION: THE FLEXIBILITY OF AMBIGUITY

If the Comoros Islands do not serve as an offshore haven to expel populations to, then why did the UAE outsource its naturalization cases to the Union of the Comoros? I argue that these passports were not created for the purposes of incorporation (secure residency) or expulsion (nonresidency), but rather to codify the conditional inclusion of a population with contingent and revocable residency rights. This arrangement renders the population deportable, but instead of being forcibly relocated, they inhabit a permanently insecure and ambiguous legal position. The passport outsourcing codifies and formalizes permanent "temporary" residency into a legal citizenship status. This is a nominal citizenship status that exists on paper only and does not impart substantive rights. In other words, the UAE and Union of the Comoros have effectively rendered this population de facto stateless. However, the issuance of foreign passports provides the façade of citizenship while generating the UAE praise for addressing and "resolving" its statelessness problem.[14] This arrangement has also allowed the government of the Union of the Comoros to

---

[14] In 2008, the United Nations High Commissioner for Refugees (UNHCR) spokesperson William Spindler announced that the agency "welcomes UAE decision on stateless people" (Spindler 2008).

earn a substantial income. Academic analysis of the legality of this kind of interstate agreement has been scant, but at least one legal scholar has stated that this arrangement need *not* violate international law given the wide margin of discretion that states enjoy when it comes to determining nationality (Spiro 2014).

By creating "offshore citizens" Abu Dhabi was able to continue evading and postponing contestations about the boundaries of the Emirati citizenry, while addressing the need to document and monitor all residents. In other words, this arrangement allows the state to evade the national dilemma (competing definitions of citizenship across subnational units) while addressing the security dilemma (eliminating irregular legal statuses). As a political tactic, conditional inclusion is more powerful than either acceptance or rejection. First, because ambiguity is strategic, it allows the state to evade political impasses and pivot to selectively accommodate or exclude individuals as it sees fit. Second, because without a rejection or approval of their citizenship cases, the people who received these passports continue to obediently wait and hope for Emirati citizenship. And finally, third, because conditional inclusion leads to delays as opposed to denials, and delays deprive people of claimant rights (such as the right to state resources, own property, and vote) while allowing other aspects of residency (such as labor) to continue.

The legal ambiguity of these cases is not a part of a process toward a larger goal or end; it is a goal and end in itself. Political gains are reaped from ambiguous nationality and citizenship laws. As Shevel finds in her study of Russian citizenship in light of post-Soviet nation-building dilemmas, the Russian state found it most convenient to legalize "the ambiguous definition in the nation's boundaries 1999 law on compatriots and the 2010 amendments to it. The fuzzy definition of compatriots in the law allows Russia to pursue a variety of objectives and to target a variety of groups without solving the contradictions of existing nation-building discourses" (Shevel 2011: 179). Ambiguous citizenship laws allow ruling elites to pursue multiple and contradictory goals at the same time, often to respond to competing domestic constraints or dilemmas. In the case of the UAE, the evidence suggests that the legal ambiguity of these cases began in an ad hoc way because of the federal authority's response to the national dilemma by delaying naturalization cases. This delaying tactic turned into a deliberate strategy when the federal government codified the ambiguity of its "in-between" populations with the outsourcing of citizenship to the Union of the Comoros.

This case of "offshore citizens" could not have been purely motivated by monetary gains (or rather savings) because the agreement itself was quite costly. In order to outsource passports, the UAE's federal government paid not only the Union of the Comoros, but also a private company – Comoros Gulf Holding (CGH) – to facilitate the deal. According to interviews with a former CGH employee, this passport exchange was brokered with the UAE's MOI and was the single most lucrative deal of CGH's business portfolio. The UAE paid a reported 200 million USD to CGH to facilitate the initial printing of Comoros passports in 2008 (Abrahamian 2015; Interview with former Comoros Gulf Holding employee, April 5, 2011). In subsequent years the two governments worked directly together and removed CGH from its role as the liaison. The International Monetary Fund (IMF) reports show that there is an influx of cash into the Union of Comoros government coffers since 2009, with a spike occurring in 2012 (after CGH is no longer involved). The IMF reports that the Comoros government's revenue increased due to an "economic citizenship program" or ECP; "the ECP involved the selling of passports to foreign nationals in some Middle Eastern countries, mainly the United Arab Emirates. Revenues from the program declined steeply in 2013 following the imposition of tighter controls in response to earlier irregularities" (International Monetary Fund 2016).

Moreover, during the same time frame that the UAE's federal MOI purchased foreign passports for its own residents, it also invested time and resources to attempt to increase the size of the Emirati citizenry. The UAE's citizen/noncitizen ratio is heavily skewed toward foreigners, with noncitizens comprising 88.5 percent of the UAE's total population and 92 percent of its labor force (UAE National Bureau of Statistics 2010; UAE National Bureau of Statistics 2005). Public officials and the media refer to this ratio as the UAE's "demographic imbalance," and, as discussed in Chapter 3, security officials have constructed this "imbalance" as posing a national security threat. In an effort to increase the number of Emiratis during this same time period, the federal government used DNA testing to identify "true" Emiratis who reside outside of the UAE. A special committee, comprising members from the MOI, was set up to locate the children of Emirati men (and foreign mothers) born abroad. The committee traveled to Oman, Qatar, and Saudi Arabia, to check the authenticity of marriage and birth certificates, and to conduct DNA tests that verify the "heritage" of the applicants. "The most recent trip was conducted as part of a program to strengthen the connection of foreign Emirati children with their native land" (*The National* 2010). By 2010, the committee had identified twenty-three children who would become Emirati citizens in the Gulf, with plans to evaluate claims in Mumbai, Egypt, and Syria.

In other words, in a short time span, the federal government invested considerable resources into shaping the composition of the national body, adopting policies that on the one hand cull its size by effectively denaturalizing at least 100,000 people who were born in the country and are assimilated, while on the other hand creating specialized task forces to attempt to increase the size of the citizenry and locate "lost" citizens who meet the patrilineal criteria. What is measured with DNA is essentially a frozen snapshot of the Arab tribes of the UAE in 1925. This is, of course, only a partial view of the residents who actually resided in these territories at the time, but this empirical fact does not change the fact that the use of DNA to identify citizens means tracing a political pact with scientific precision as if it were a primordial truth. This suggests that the federal government was not so much invested in monetary gains as it was in reshaping the national body in a way that aligns with what ruling elites in Abu Dhabi view as the "rightful" and "true" Emiratis – those who *should* be allowed to benefit from the redistributive benefits of citizenship. Taken in this wider context, the people who received Comoros passports are excluded (not from residency but from claimant rights), because they are construed as being internal "others" who do not have the proper lineage and ethnic composition.

Scholars of national incorporation draw distinctions between groups that are targeted with assimilationist policies (conferring national citizenship but erasing group differences) and groups that are accommodated (conferring citizenship while establishing minority group rights) (Mylonas 2013). This variation does not exist in the UAE. There is no official acknowledgment of ethnic or cultural heterogeneity among citizens. Instead, as previous chapters illustrate, Emirati citizenship is being increasingly narrowly construed to refer to a homogenous tribal Arab population. This homogeneity is a social construction of nationalism, one that requires an active erasure of alternative ethnicities and histories.

The homogenizing force of modern Emirati nationalism is found in artifacts that are typical of nationalist projects elsewhere – national dress, historical narratives, museums, official language, and the arts. Physical spaces that point to alternative histories are Arabized and renamed to eliminate references to non-Arab ethnicities. For example, in 2013 the Bastakiya historical neighborhood in Dubai (where merchants from the city of Bastak in Southern Iran historically lived) was renamed "Fahidi" after the nearby Fahidi fort, stripping any references to the southern coast of Iran. The disappearance of heterogeneity from official narratives does not mean that individuals physically disappear. While the literature on the UAE's heterogeneity is small, scholars like Aisha Bilkhair and political commentators like Sultan Al Qassemi have documented the presence of Afro-Emirati and other citizens who originally migrated from Pakistan, Palestine, Jordan, Egypt, Sudan, and Syria (among others countries) prior to the formation of the state.[15] For the minorities who never received family books, "offshore citizens" has become the state's accommodation option – a way of accounting for minorities who reside in the margin between the state's imagined community and an applicant's subversive ethnicity or bloodline.

6.4 WHY OUTSOURCE NOW?

The Union of Comoros passports provide the state with a way of codifying a limbo legal status. The recipients inhabit a liminal space between citizen and noncitizen, they are neither fully included nor excluded; their cases are pending and they can feasibly be shifted into either of these seemingly mutually exclusive categories. In many cases people who received these passports have been waiting for Emirati citizenship since prior to the formation of the union since 1971 or for their entire lives. If the federal government has made people wait for citizenship for (in some cases) as much as four decades, why did it outsource passports in 2008? If the outcome essentially extends the waiting time of these cases, why not simply continue to make people wait for citizenship without introducing this additional form of foreign documentation? What explains the timing of this passport outsourcing arrangement?

I argue that three key factors explain the timing of the passport exchange, contextualizing why the UAE and Union of the Comoros adopted this policy when they did. The first factor is an internal shift in elite power that led to new leadership in the MOI in the UAE; the second factor is political entrepreneurship on behalf of Comoros Gulf Holding's CEO that linked the UAE's MOI to the presidency of the Union of the Comoros; and the third (less direct) factor is the external pressure and incentive of global passport rankings and visa-free travel.

---

[15] See Al Qassemi (2016); Bilkhair (2006).

6.4.1 Internal Shift in Elite Power

The mid-2000s marked a period of rapid institutional change in the UAE's MOI due to the rise in leadership of a new minister of interior, Sheikh Saif bin Zayed Al Nahyan. Sheikh Zayed bin Sultan Al Nahyan, the founding father and unifier of the UAE federation, passed away in November of 2004, leaving his son Sheikh Khalifa bin Zayed Al Nahyan as his successor as both amir of Abu Dhabi and president of the UAE federation. Sheikh Khalifa had already begun to take the reins in Abu Dhabi for a few years prior, due to his father's ill health. Sheikh Khalifa appointed his half brother Sheikh Saif as Minister of Interior in October 2004, marking the beginning of a multipronged campaign of institutional change. Sheikh Saif has since retained this post but was also appointed deputy prime minister of the UAE in 2009.

Focusing on the security dilemmas posed by open borders, Sheikh Saif sought to develop a more comprehensive identity management strategy that would deepen the security forces' understanding of the country's residents and strengthen border control at a time when there was growing public concern about the UAE's "demographic imbalance." One of Sheikh Saif's first initiatives was the iris scan project, which focused on border control and the tracking of visitors at the UAE's entry points. In 2004, the government began scanning the irises of all arrivals and departures in the seven international airports, three land ports, and seven seaports in the UAE (making it the largest iris scanning undertaking of its kind).[16] The goal was to ensure that deportees could not return to the UAE undetected by using different travel documents, thereby decreasing fraud at the borders.

In addition to increasing border control, Sheikh Saif also focused on how the security forces are domestically responding to the UAE's growing foreign resident population. As discussed in Chapter 3, Sheikh Saif spearheaded a "new policing concept" that shifted the scope and role of the police from criminal investigation and traffic to a more maximalist, comprehensive idea of community policing. Community policing focuses on tracking ethnic communities and embedding police officers to gain key contextual knowledge about those communities. The idea is that when police officers gain the trust of foreign communities, they will be able to manage threats preemptively as well as reactively. Community policing tracks and groups foreign residents by national origin, and each national

---

[16] The UAE's iris recognition border-crossing system was the largest system in the world when it was established in 2004, with over 2.1 million visitors being checked using this method (Daugman and Malhas 2004).

community is ranked by threat level (based on the number of crimes committed by that community).

This group-level information is gathered alongside more fine-grained information about all residents in the UAE. Specifically, Sheikh Saif introduced the Emirates Identity Authority (EIDA) to develop a national ID card system and capture biometric information about all residents. The national ID enrollment excluded anyone who did not have a family book but was not a "guest worker" in the UAE. Sheikh Saif developed a plan for the people who did not have the documentation necessary for gaining a national ID card. Specifically in 2005 (shortly after he became the minister), the MOI stopped renewing passports of people who had acquired UAE passports but could not produce proof of nationality with a family book. Then by 2008, Sheikh Saif's office spearheaded a stateless registration drive with the goal of "placing everyone in a category." This stateless drive aimed to register all individuals who did not have a family book, regardless of whether they had been previously granted an Emirati passport or naturalization decree.

The federal MOI set up several booths for registration around the country, including Uptown Mall in Dubai, Noor Al Kawthar Mall in Ajman, and Al Ta'awon Mall in Sharjah, to receive applications. Through announcements in national newspapers, the MOI announced that final decisions for granting naturalization cases would be made on a case-by-case basis after individual background checks and interviews were conducted.[17] Only people who could demonstrate their continuous residency in the UAE since 1971 were eligible to become Emirati citizens. The MOI encouraged all people without identity documents to come forward for clemency but stressed the importance of being "truthful about previous nationalities." There was a two-month window for registration, after which time all of the people who had not registered would be considered "illegal" and would be apprehended by the authorities. On the last day of the registration process, *Gulf News* announced that "intensive round the clock campaigns" would be launched to "nab violators" (Absal 2008). Major General Nasser Al Nuaimi, Director of the Interior Minister's office, announced to *Gulf News* that "officials will focus on weeding out the illegal residents" (Absal 2008). The article claimed that

---

[17] English language local news coverage of this drive includes an article published by the Emirates News Agency on September 3, 2008, entitled "MoI sets panel to close file of stateless persons" (Emirates News Agency 2008) as well as a UAE Interact article from September 8, 2008, titled "7,873 Applications Distributed to Stateless Persons" (www .uaeinteract.com/docs/7873_applications_distributed_to_stateless_persons/31876.htm, no longer available).

fifty-one of the "thousands" of stateless people were already naturalized thanks to this standardization drive.

While the standardization drive was being implemented, Sheikh Saif made public statements asserting that naturalization was a national security issue and that the MOI reserved the right to denaturalize individuals as part of its security assessment.[18] The constitution empowered the MOI to confiscate citizenship from any individual who does not respect its privileges or act in accordance with its requisites (*Emarat Alyoum* 2008). According to the clause, in order to be considered for citizenship, potential citizens from the *bidūn* population must demonstrate that they: (1) were continuously present in the UAE territory since before its independence; (2) had no linkages to any other nationality; (3) had committed no crimes or behavior that compromised the respect and integrity of the nation; and (4) were assimilated into the fabric of Emirati society. If these conditions were not met, the constitution enabled the MOI to confiscate an individual's citizenship – a right that strengthened the ministry's ability to "protect the society from any security or social threats and dangers that arise from unlawful residency and conduct in the nation" (*Emarat Alyoum* 2008). These statements laid the foundation for confiscating passports from people who were previously naturalized or issued passports.

The MOI proceeded to enact this right by confiscating passports from people who were in between legal categories because they had passports but not family books; they were recognized as citizens at the local level, but not federally. The practice of stripping citizenship was systematically applied to pending applicants who were going through the naturalization process. However, citizens with family books are not immune; the MOI has withheld identity documents from full citizens who have been accused of overthrowing the government.[19] The prerogative to strip citizenship

---

[18] These statements were made in 2008 in the newspaper *Emarat Alyoum*: "*al-wala' shart al-tajnees*" ("allegiance is a condition of naturalization") and "*al-dustur yasmah bi-saheb al-jinsiyya miman la ya'mal bi-istihqaqatiha*" ("the constitution allows for the confiscation of citizenship from those who do not abide by its requisites").

[19] During the summer of 2012, the UAE's security forces detained ninety-four individuals accused of founding a terrorist organization (*Al-Islah*) aimed at overthrowing the government. Some individuals were denaturalized and deported, others had their papers taken and could not travel, and the remainder were imprisoned. Those detained included prominent human rights lawyers, judges, and student leaders. The arrests followed the circulation of a petition that called for all UAE nationals to be allowed to vote in Federal National Council elections. At present, only 30 percent of UAE citizens are allowed to vote and only half of the assembly members are subject to the electoral process. This right does not apply to naturalized citizens. For a full report see Robertson *et al.* (2013).

rights from citizens makes their access to rights conditional upon continued political allegiance rather than an inalienable right.

In short, a transition in the leadership of the MOI was instrumental for the emergence of a new population management strategy in the UAE, one that is focused on providing the state with a comprehensive view of the population. These developments problematized the legal status of naturalization applicants and stateless populations in the country, paving the path to the government's adoption of offshore citizenship.

6.4.2 Political Entrepreneurship

The MOI acted as the main liaison for the Comoros passport exchange, aligning with Bashar Kiwan, the CEO of a (now defunct) company operating out of Kuwait and the Comoros Islands called Comoros Gulf Holding (CGH), and the presidency of the Union of the Comoros at the time (President Ahmed Abdallah Mohamed Sambi). Together, the three parties devised an informal agreement that would lead CGH to facilitate the printing of Union of Comoros passports for naturalization applicants in the UAE in exchange for Abu Dhabi's infrastructural investment in the Comoros Islands (through CGH). By outsourcing passports the UAE's federal state was able to count its own residents as "foreign residents" instead of domestic minorities, circumventing the authority of individual emirates to define the membership of their constituencies.

While the UAE's federal government had political incentives to outsource foreign passports instead of issuing Emirati passports, the Union of the Comoros had clear economic incentives for entering into this passport outsourcing agreement. Currently, 45 percent of the population lives below the poverty line, and due to limited resource endowments and small domestic markets, the economy of the Comoros Islands is highly dependent upon external sources of income, specifically foreign aid, (meager) foreign investment, and remittances. From May 2006 to May 2011, Ahmed Abdallah Mohamed Sambi held the presidency of the Union of the Comoros. During this period, Sambi worked closely with Comoros Gulf Holding, a company that monopolized investment and development on the islands, controlling major portions of the media, banking, tourism, travel, and construction industries.[20] In 2007, Sambi

---

[20] CGH's holdings included the Comoros United Company for Publishing and Distributing, which publishes a weekly newspaper (*Al Waseet*) and a daily newspaper in Arabic and French (*Al Balad*). CGH also established the *Banque Fédérale De Commerce* (BFC), the

appointed Bachar Kiwan, the CEO of CGH, to the post of Honorary Consul of Union of the Comoros in Kuwait as well as Honorary Advisor of the Union of Comoros President for the island's development and external relations with Arab countries.

It was Kiwan – born and raised in Kuwait to Syrian parents – who began an attempt to foster a lucrative source of income for the Comoros Islands while addressing Kuwait's *bidūn* "problem."[21] He attempted to broker a passport deal between the Comoros Islands and Kuwait, even flying recalcitrant members of the Comoros parliament to Kuwait. His proposal involved printing Union of Comoros passports for the Kuwaiti *bidūn* in exchange for Kuwaiti investment on the islands. This deal never came to fruition due in part to the strength of the Kuwaiti parliament and the organizational capacities and entrenched allies of the *bidūn* community in Kuwait (Abrahamian 2015; interview with former CGH employee, April 5, 2011).[22]

But the idea gained traction, with the Emiratis hearing about this proposed "solution" to statelessness. In 2008, working with Sheikh Saif and the director of his office, Nasser Al Nuaimi, Kiwan spearheaded a bilateral agreement between the MOI in Abu Dhabi and the Union of the Comoros. Under this agreement, CGH printed Union of Comoros passports for a portion of the UAE's population in exchange for foreign direct investment in infrastructural development on the islands. The names for printing were provided by the MOI, but in many cases they were purposefully changed to francophone spellings. In exchange for these passports, Abu Dhabi funded the construction of a major two-lane highway from the north to the south of the main island, Grande Comore. The road was built by Comoros Combined Group, an association between Comoros Gulf Holding and Combined Group Contracting, a Kuwait-based construction company (interview with former CGH employee,

---

only bank on the islands in alliance with Al Mawarid Bank (based in Lebanon). CGH owned the Itsandra Beach Hotel, the Comoro Combined Group (a construction arm associated with the Combined Group, a Kuwait-based construction company), and the rights to the Grande Comore Corniche (beachfront land in Moroni). CGH controlled Comoro Gulf Aviation (airline and helicopter services between islands), sea taxis (a fleet of passenger and cargo boats between islands), and Twama (a telecommunications company). Abrahamian's investigative reporting on CGH finds that the company has since become bankrupt (Abrahamian 2015).

[21] For a detailed study of the *bidūn* in Kuwait see Beaugrand (2010).

[22] Soon after the UAE gave Comoros passports to its *bidūn*, several news reports suggested that the government of Kuwait adopted a similar offshoring scheme. At the time of writing, however, there is no clear evidence that Kuwaiti *bidūn* are being issued Comoros passports.

April 5, 2011). The exchange in 2008 involved Comoros Gulf Holding and since this initial passports-for-sale scheme there have been a number of private companies that claimed to facilitate the selling economic citizenship by way of Comoros passports, providing conflicting information about eligibility criteria.[23] The economic citizenship scheme was definitively terminated by the Comoros government in May 2017.

In May 2018, the Comoros parliament led an investigation into Sambi's citizenship for sale scheme and placed him under house arrest. Sambi's successor, ex-president Ikililou Dhoinin, and ten other senior officials from both administrations have been banned from traveling. The corruption charges they face are not primarily because of his decision to sell Comoros passports to the UAE (which was sanctioned by the parliament), but rather because the Comoros parliament found that thousands of passports were sold outside of official channels via "mafia" networks and at least 100 million dollars in revenues went missing (Reuters 2018). There have been no (public) decisions by the Comoros parliament into the legality of what happened to the *bidūn* in the UAE, or clarity on whether they will be allowed to keep their Comoros passports.

6.4.3 Diffusion of International Norms and Global Mobility Incentives

A third factor that helps explain the timing of the outsourcing of passports is the emergence of new international norms for biometric travel documents (and the related incentives of global passport rankings and visa-free travel). During the same time period that the MOI issued Comoros passports to domestic minorities, it also reissued new biometric Emirati passports to all Emirati citizens. The UAE was not the only state that upgraded its identity management infrastructure and national identity documents in the mid-2000s. Between 2000 and 2010 over 107 states adopted biometric passports, including 28 states in the EU and an additional 79 countries outside it. Any state with a visa waiver program with the United States or the EU had to reissue passports with biometric chips in order to maintain the ability of its citizens to continue traveling to these states. By 2010 the International Civil Aviation Organization (ICAO) made machine-readable passports with biometric chips that contain

---

[23] One example of a different private company that used to broker economic citizenship for the Union of the Comoros is Elma Global (a residency and citizenship-by-investment firm). It has since terminated this service. See www.second-citizenship.org/second-citizenship/union-of-comoros.

digital photographs and fingerprints a key requirement for compliance with international aviation standards (Kefauver 2012). The design and features of national identity documents impact how a state's citizens are treated externally, including which borders they can cross (and at what cost). There are external incentives for adopting new international standards for travel documents – and costs to failing to do so.[24]

In the case of the UAE, the government's identity regularization initiatives yielded fruitful results for the country's position in global passport rankings. Since issuing new biometric passports, the country has moved up in global passport indices, jumping from a global ranking of 61 in 2008 to a ranking of 21 in 2019 (on the Henley Passport Index). One key reason for this elevation in rankings is the fact that the UAE has successfully adopted all of the convergence criteria needed for gaining visa-free travel to the Schengen area, becoming the first and only Arab country to sign a Schengen visa waiver in 2015.[25] The key factors that allowed the UAE to successfully negotiate this waiver included the fact that the UAE government adopted all the travel document security requirements (biometric passports) and it does not produce large numbers of irregular migrants who are likely to seek jobs in Europe. According to the committee notes for the EU plenary session that voted on this waiver, the UAE is a good fit because "With regard to mobility, the UAE does not present any risk of clandestine immigration or threat to public policy or security, and it has supplied the European Institutions with the necessary evidence to this effect. In addition, the UAE issues biometric passports to its citizens (European Parliament Legislative Observatory 2015).

This case shows how a state can gain access to new geographic spaces by increasing the quantity and kind of data that is collected about its citizens and tightening controls on how passports are issued and to whom. Contractions in passport issuances can thus pave the way for states to move their citizens "up" in the global hierarchy of mobility controls.

---

[24] For example, many Palestinians with Palestinian Authority (PLO) travel documents are unable to travel after this upgrade to new machine-readable passports.

[25] These passport rankings are based on how many countries passport holders can travel to without a visa; the more countries a passport holder can travel to the higher the rank. See www.henleypassportindex.com/global-ranking. The short-term Schengen visa waiver creates a precipitous increase for Emirati passport holders by allowing them to travel to an additional thirty-four countries without a visa: Austria, Belgium, Denmark, Sweden, Malta, Estonia, Finland, France, Germany, Poland, Lithuania, Latvia, Greece, Iceland, Italy, Slovakia, the Czech Republic, Switzerland, Luxembourg, the Netherlands, Hungary, Slovenia, Croatia, Bulgaria, Romania, Liechtenstein, Cyprus, Norway, Portugal, Spain, the Vatican, Andorra, San Marino, and Monaco.

The UAE applied international norms by "upgrading" its passports to biometric travel documents, and this process of reissuing national identity documents created a critical juncture that enabled the state to reset the boundaries of who is included and excluded in the national body politic. Existing studies predict that the diffusion of international norms will lead to more liberal incorporation policies.[26] While this sets the expectation that liberal democratic states will pressure authoritarian states to adopt more inclusive standards, this case shows the opposite. The UAE's ability to gain a visa waiver for Schengen came from its redrawing of the boundaries of the citizenry in a more stringent manner. The identity regularization drive and issuance of new national passports effectively turned some former UAE passport holders into "foreign residents" from the Comoros (with less mobility than they had previously), while increasing the mobility of those who were reissued Emirati passports at the same time. These newly recertified "true" citizens gained visa-free access to Schengen (and therefore greater mobility than before). The identity regularization drive thus had dual effects on the population: it led to the loss of citizenship rights and privileges for one subset of the population, while increasing the privileges and mobility of another subset of the population.

External actors can create critical junctures in citizenship and incorporation policies by pressuring national authorities to reissue travel documents. These external pressures can incentivize national authorities to define the boundaries in a more stringent, rather than more inclusive, manner. Convergence on security norms supersedes any convergence on inclusive citizenship and migration policies. It is telling that the UAE signed two agreements with the EU on the same day, December 15, 2015 – a short-stay visa waiver and strategic cooperation between the UAE security forces and Europol on fighting serious crimes and terrorism.[27]

---

[26] Gurowitz (1999) argues that the domestic implementation of international norms in immigration policies is leading to a greater liberalization of citizenship laws and inclusion of minorities. Others argue that states are constrained by the international human rights discourse surrounding immigrant rights, and are pressured into adopting more inclusionary and liberal policies. Sassen (1996) argues that the emergence of an international human rights regime has curbed state sovereignty over citizenship and immigrant decisions. Soysal (1995) argues that the postwar discourse on rights endows rights to individuals rather than citizens, leading to an international trend of granting rights to noncitizens. Meanwhile, Jacobson (1996) also argues that international human rights standards are key tools for immigrants to make claims on states and that citizenship has been devalued.

[27] See minutes on European Parliamentary Vote 4.10 (*European Parliamentary Vote 4.10. EU-United Arab Emirates Agreement on the Short-Stay Visa Waiver *** (Rule 150)* http://www.europarl.europa.eu/sides/getDoc.do?pubRef=-//EP//TEXT+PV+20151215+ITEM-004-10+DOC+XML+V0//EN&language=EN) and minutes on European Parliamentary Vote

The Schengen agreement presents one concrete external incentive for reissuing national IDs. This is not to suggest that adopting the convergence criteria for Schengen was the sole or most important motivation for outsourcing passports. But the Schengen visa waiver deal helps explain the timing of the outsourcing agreement. It also shows that the UAE authorities were not operating in isolation and that the MOI's efforts to upgrade its identity management system are in line with the external pressures that many other states faced in the mid-2000s.

6.5 PASSPORTS FOR SALE

In order to contextualize the offshore citizens case, this section compares this case of outsourcing to other citizenship for sale schemes. This case of offshore citizens is novel because it involves a government issuing passports from a foreign state to its own residents without their consent. But the precedent of outsourcing passports had already been established with the emergence of a lucrative citizenship-by-investment industry. Individuals can acquire passports from "offshore" sites without residing there, but citizenship without residency is generally an option open only to wealthy elites seeking to evade taxation or other forms of state expropriation associated with their existing nationalities. National citizenships are bought and sold, usually through private firms who consult their clients on "citizenship planning" as a part of their wealth management strategies.[28]

The prime example of this is the citizenship-by-investment scheme of St. Kitts and Nevis in the Caribbean.[29] While St. Kitts and Nevis has the longest-running citizenship-by-investment program, Dominica, Antigua, and Barbuda, and even Austria (unofficially), have also implemented

---

4.20 (*European Parliamentary Vote 4.20. Strategic Cooperation in the Fight against Serious Crime and Terrorism between the United Arab Emirates and Europol* * (Vote) www .europarl.europa.eu/doceo/document/A-8-2015-0351_EN.html).

[28] The two largest multinational firms in this industry are Arton Capital and Henley and Partners, with a growing number of new firms emerging in Shanghai, Singapore, and Dubai. For more on the citizenship-by-investment industry see the investigative reporting of Abrahamian (2015) and the scholarship of Shachar 2017, 2018.

[29] The program was designed to increase state revenues by allowing foreigners to shield their wealth in an offshore enclave. In order to qualify, an individual must spend at least 250,000 USD on investment projects in the islands. The government of St. Kitts and Nevis first devised the scheme to keep the economy afloat when the major sugarcane exporter faced an economic crisis after the price of sugar commodities fell in the early 1980s. A St. Kitts and Nevis passport gives the holder legal belonging to a state that has zero personal income tax, allows multiple citizenships, and affords its citizens visa-free access to 152 countries and territories.

versions of citizenship through investment schemes without prior residence requirements (see Table 6.1).[30] Other states have also adopted variations on this arrangement (with residency requirements): Hong Kong and Singapore both have residency-by-investment programs (without citizenship) and Australia and the United States offer investor visas that create expedited tracks to residency (and eventually citizenship) for foreign investors and their families. In all of these cases, individual applicants seek new national citizenships as a means of avoiding the jurisdiction of the states to which they legally belonged, either to minimize taxation or maximize their global mobility.

Though states benefit from additional revenue streams, in all of these cases the individual involved is the driver of his or her status change to a new jurisdictional authority. What is different about this case of offshore citizens is that (1) a state outsourced the naturalization cases of its own residents without their consent and (2) the new national passports led the recipients to have less mobility and privileges, not more. The Comoros passport holders in the UAE did not apply for a new citizenship; they were applying for Emirati citizenship. Moreover, instead of increasing their income or global mobility, this new juridical status did the opposite, placing them in a legal category with lower employment prospects and far less mobility – now even requiring a visa to continue residing in the same country.

One Union of Comoros website advertising the sale of economic citizenship revealed that stateless individuals are not eligible for passports under the citizenship-by-investment program.[31] This formal exclusion of

---

[30] The list of schemes presented in Table 6.1 provided for illustrative purposes and is not exhaustive. The Austrian government contests the idea that citizenship-by-investment is possible (Abrahamian 2012). However, Henley and Partners has represented successful cases in Austria. The law firm's website explains that the Austrian provision is applied on a case-by-case basis and applicants are required to invest "actively" in Austrian economy. Active investments require joint ventures or direct investments in businesses that create jobs or generate new export sales. www.henleyglobal.com/citizenship-austria-overview.

[31] Original Comoros Citizenship website: www.comoros-government-citizenship.com/citizen ship-by-investment-program (this resource is no longer available due to the termination of this program). Somewhat conflictingly, a brochure advertising the Comoros Economic Citizenship Program issued by a Dubai-based company called Citizenship Services Group states, "The UAE governments of Abu Dhabi and Dubai signed an agreement with the Comoros Islands in 2009 entitling *paperless residents* of 15 years in the UAE to Comoros Citizenship" (emphasis added) (brochure on file with author, downloaded from www .citizenshipservicesgroup.com, the company's website, which is defunct as of October 2016); another purveyor of Comoros citizenship, Cyprus-based Multitravel Consultants, lists in its brochure "nationalities restricted from participation." Among these are all Middle East countries, including *bidūn* from the UAE and Kuwait. MultiTravel Consultants Inc., Comoros Citizenship Programme brochure (2015) (on file with author).

TABLE 6.1 *Citizenship-by-investment schemes*

Country	St. Kitts and Nevis	Dominica	Antigua and Barbuda	Austria
Process	Official scheme est. in 1984	Official scheme est. in 1993	Bill for official scheme passed in March 2013	Unofficial channel through clause 10 (6) in Austrian Citizenship Act
Fee	Path 1: 250,000 USD to sugar industry diversification program Path 2: 400,000 USD+ investment in real estate and development	Minimum investment of 100,000 USD	Path 1: 250,000 USD to National Development Fund Path 2: 400,000 USD real estate development Path 3: 1.5 million USD business investment (gov't-approved company) Application fees 57,500 USD	Rendering "exceptional services in the interest of the Republic" = minimum of 10 million USD in business investments
Benefits	1. No taxes on capital gains, net wealth, personal income, inheritance, or gifts 2. Multiple citizenship allowance	1. No taxes on capital gains, inheritance, or personal income 2. Multiple citizenship allowance	1. No taxes on capital gains or inheritance 2. Personal income tax of 10–25% was reintroduced in 2005; applies only to locally sourced income	1. 50% personal income tax (only applicable to Austrian citizens who actually reside in Austria)

(continued)

TABLE 6.1 *(continued)*

Country	St. Kitts and Nevis	Dominica	Antigua and Barbuda	Austria
	3. Visa-free access to 152 countries	3. Visa-free access to 137 countries 4. Can apply from outside country if pay for three interviewers to fly to applicant for the interview	3. Visa-free access to 150 countries (including UK, France, Canada)	1. Schengen-area mobility and visa-free access to 185 countries

the *bidūn* from individual applications suggests that this case was based on a bilateral state agreement rather than individual investors.[32] Since individuals interviewed for this book and other minorities in the UAE cannot apply directly to the Union of the Comoros, the burden of processing applications (and therefore sovereignty over determining who would receive these passports) does not fall to the Union of the Comoros, but is instead conducted internally in the UAE by the MOI.

Moreover, the text of the economic citizenship law itself hints at the fact that the program is primarily a state-to-state outsourcing deal rather than an individual investment scheme. In its last substantive article, absent any prior mention of institutional partnerships or international agreements, it is stated, "Comoros shall make arrangements with States or public or private institutions for the promotion and implementation of economic investment programs" (Assemblée de l'Union 2008).

The key difference between "offshore citizens" and citizenship-by-investment schemes is the question of consent. While individuals apply for their new citizenship status under citizenship-by-investment schemes, in the case of "offshore citizens," passport recipients report feeling that they had little choice in the matter. There are conflicting accounts of how these passports were issued. Early recipients report that they went through the MOI in Abu Dhabi, while interviewees who received passports after 2009 explain that they went through representatives of the Union of the Comoros in Abu Dhabi. One of these individuals, Mohammed, explained how his Union of Comoros passport was issued to him in Abu Dhabi. He explained:

Can you see now how it works? You are expecting to get your Emirati passport, and then you are shocked. "What? What is this? What country is this?" I have never even heard of this country. It is not my country. Even my name was spelled wrong. It was written in a French way. But what can you do? You could say no, but it is the Ministry of the Interior, you are scared that then you would be held there for days until you were prepared to accept it. Finally you say thank you, this is my passport, just so you can leave. (Interview with Mohammed, June 6, 2011)

[32] Evidence in support of the fact that this agreement was brokered by two states rather than individuals be found in the publications of two reputable sources. The World Bank (2015) at page 4, fn. 4: "The [economic citizenship program] allows Comoros to offer citizenship to foreigners who reside in partner countries. The partner government selects the candidates following a background check conducted by the partner government. In exchange, Comoros receives a fee for each passport issued. In recent years revenue from the program has become significant in relation to Comoros' GDP." International Monetary Fund (2015) at page 35, fn. 3: "The ECP refers to a 2008 arrangement whereby the government sells passports to certain foreigners under bilateral agreement with certain countries."

In such cases, the MOI issued the new passport and UAE residency permit at the same time. However, the majority of interviewees reported that the MOI withheld their passports and then instructed them to apply for new passports at a two-story villa in Abu Dhabi that served as the Union of Comoros consulate. They were told to then return to the MOI to apply for their new residency permits. In either case, the Comoros passport recipients in the UAE did not have the same level of consent as other individuals who have benefited from citizenship-by-investment schemes. While the UAE and Union of the Comoros are not the first to be involved in the selling of citizenship documents, citizenship for individual purchase is a very different type of arrangement, driven by the resources and choices of rich individuals rather than the exclusionary vision of a powerful state.

6.6 THE IMPACT OF COMOROS VERSUS EMIRATI PASSPORTS

The final section of this chapter examines the impact of the Union of Comoros passports on UAE residents. In addition to being barred from accessing any of the benefits associated with Emirati citizenship, the Union of Comoros passport recipients have lower employment prospects and far less mobility. Because they are now considered expatriate workers, they must pay for healthcare out of pocket, which can be prohibitively expensive. The passport recipients have the same Arabic-language public schooling that makes it challenging for Emiratis to compete in a private sector dominated by English speakers. However, they do not qualify for the nationalization quotas that are in place to ensure the participation of citizens in the labor force. As a result, some of the Union of Comoros passport recipients have already lost their jobs, while others report attempting to hide this new citizenship status from their employers, fearing that they will lose their jobs if their employers can no longer count them as Emirati citizens. Some continue to remain in poorly paid positions for fear that they would not be able to get anything else if they quit. Several interviewees have reported that their employers abuse their situation, lowering wages or threatening them with dismissal because they know that they would be unemployable if dismissed.

Moreover, recipients now require a visa to legally reside in the country of their birth (or long-term residence), becoming financially and legally dependent upon national sponsors (*kafīls*) in order to maintain legal residency. Those who are married to foreign spouses can no longer sponsor them, having to depend upon friends and family members to act as sponsors and fearing deportation and the breakup of their families. When guest workers in the UAE reach sixty-five years of age, they cannot renew their own visas; they can only be sponsored as family members of other migrant workers. The Comoros passport recipients who are getting older report experiencing significant anxiety about this specter of deportation. They also need more care and support than their children can provide.[33]

Comoros passport recipients have also lost the ability to move and work freely within the Gulf Cooperation Council (GCC), and require many more visas than needed before in order to travel to destinations that are freely accessible to Emirati citizens. Despite an understanding among the interior ministries in the Gulf that these passports have been issued to domestic minorities in the UAE, the passport holders have also experienced difficulty entering other GCC states, even though as holders of a GCC country residency permit they should be allowed to freely enter the other six constituent states. In practice, interviewees who had previously visited Oman, Bahrain, and Saudi Arabia with their Emirati passports have since been denied entry at the border with their Union of Comoros passports. One reason provided for these denials is the assessment that these passports have been issued to Iranians and that they have become synonymous with black-market passports that could fall into the hands of terrorists (interview with immigration official in Bahrain, January 5, 2015). Since the Union of the Comoros does not provide diplomatic protection or acknowledge these populations, external security forces have no way of vetting who these passports have been issued to.

Moreover, in addition to having clear disadvantages in comparison to Emirati citizenship, these passports have rendered the recipients effectively stateless. The passport recipients should be considered as stateless for the following reasons. First, as previously discussed, they are unable to actually reside in the Comoros Islands. Second, they lack consular protection from Comoros embassies and consulates abroad. The Comoros consulates in Chicago and Manchester confirmed in the spring of 2016 that Emirates-based Comoros passport holders are not entitled to diplomatic protection or consular services when they travel abroad. In a phone exchange with an interviewee, the Honorary Consul of the Union of the Comoros in Chicago, Mr. Charif Hachim (CH) explained that he could not replace a misplaced

---

[33] At the time of publication there is no indication that Comoros passport holders over the age of sixty-five have been expelled if they could not find sponsors. Several interviewees with these passports have been able to renew their visas over the age of sixty-five. The UAE government currently appears to be overlooking the age restrictions that apply to other guest workers but it is not clear to what extent this will continue.

Union of Comoros passport if it was issued in the UAE. He instructed the interviewee to go to either the UAE or to the Ministry of Foreign Affairs in Moroni, Comoros Islands. As Mr. Hachim explained:

Now, people who may have lost their passport or whose passport has expired ... if they are Comorian born OK, that's a different matter, New York would be able to help them ... if you acquired your passports through the Beduin program with the UAE there is nothing that can be done [unintelligible] because these have been [unintelligible] in a different manner ... OK ... it's a very delicate problem ... I mean program ... so it has to be handled properly by the authorities ... (Phone conversation with passport recipient and Yoana Kuzmova (legal fellow at Boston University), March 4, 2016)

In other words, neither the UAE nor the Union of the Comoros claim these passport holders as citizens and neither government takes responsibility for providing diplomatic protection for these individuals.

Finally, the UNHCR statelessness unit acknowledges that it is aware of these passports and considers the recipients to be effectively stateless. In an exchange with the International Human Rights Clinic at Boston University, Melanie Khanna, the chief of the UNHCR's statelessness unit in Geneva, explained the following: "You have also raised concerns about the Comoros passport and asked for UNHCR's policy on this matter. We recognize that so called passports of convenience that do not convey full nationality rights are not an appropriate solution for stateless persons. To the extent this population remains stateless they remain persons of concern to UNHCR under our statelessness mandate."[34]

These Union of Comoros Islands passports create a challenge for the recipients, because even though the recipients are effectively stateless, it is difficult to prove statelessness by the letter of the law when they also carry national passports. If citizenship is conferred through documentation, then what the arrangement of "offshore citizens" achieves is the codification and formalization of an ambiguous and precarious citizenship status.

6.7 CONCLUDING REMARKS

In this chapter, I explain the case of "offshore citizens" – the UAE's outsourcing of passports from the Union of the Comoros to count its

---

[34] Melanie Khanna and UNHCR Statelessness Unit, "Re: Statelessness," May 23, 2017 (email correspondence with Kuzmova (legal fellow), on file with author). These comments do not reflect official UNHCR policy. See methodological appendix for an explanation of Kuzmova's role as a legal fellow at Boston University.

own domestic minorities as foreign residents. I argue that Abu Dhabi adopted this arrangement not for the purposes of incorporation (citizenship and secure residency), nor expulsion (deportation and nonresidency), but rather to codify the conditional inclusion of a population with contingent and revocable residency rights. By issuing foreign passports to domestic minorities, Abu Dhabi is able to evade the national dilemma (competing definitions of citizenship across the federation) while addressing its security dilemma (eliminating irregular legal statuses and placing everyone in a category).

This chapter examines the expected outcomes of identity regularization drives, showing how the case of offshore citizens compares to how other states respond to irregular populations during identity management upgrades. It addresses alternative explanations for the UAE's outsourcing of national identity documents, and then discusses the factors that explain the timing of this exchange in greater detail. Showing how this is an extreme but not anomalous case, the chapter then examines how both the problem the UAE faced (eradicating irregular statuses) and the solution it developed (outsourcing passports) compare to other cases. Finally, the chapter concludes by examining the impact of passport outsourcing on the individuals who received these passports, providing a side-by-side comparison of Emirati and Comoros passports.

This arrangement of "offshore citizens" may be the particular articulation of how the UAE and Union of the Comoros have created a codified ambiguous legal status, and the specific contours of this arrangement are shaped by contextual factors related to these cases. However, in essence, the outcome of this arrangement is the creation of a conditional and ambiguous legal status, and that outcome is not specific to the UAE or its state formation process. Much like the Three-Fifths compromise in the United States,[35] the specific articulation matters less than what a legal maneuver does – that is, shift part of the population into a legal gray zone so that people "count less" than what they are, whether what is being counted is voting rights or welfare benefits. Such conditional and temporary legal statuses provide states with a means of evading and postponing larger political impasses about the boundaries of the national body,

---

[35] The Three-Fifths Compromise was established between the southern states and northern states during the 1787 US Constitutional Convention. The national dilemma in this case was how slaves would be counted when determining the state's population for the House of Representatives and taxation purposes.

especially when it comes to the incorporation of minorities, labor, or refugees. The codification of legal status is contentious because it always raises questions about the boundaries of the national body politic – which inevitably raises questions about who rules and how power should be distributed.

7

Conclusion

Interviewer: "So ... after all of this, how would you answer the question – 'where are you *really* from?'"
Mansour: [Laughs spontaneously and uncontrollably]
Interview with Mansour, October 22, 2012

Mansour – who was seventy-nine years old when I conducted this interview – has spent most of his life waiting for citizenship and a path to inclusion – first in Uganda, then in the UAE, and then again in the United States. Having been expelled from Uganda by Idi Amin in 1972, his first experience with the loss of citizenship was due to targeted exclusion by a state authority for not being "African" enough for the new nation-state. The Red Cross and the UNHCR resettled Mansour and his family to Abu Dhabi in 1973. There Mansour had a second experience with being denied citizenship; this time he was never individually targeted for expulsion; his case was simply constantly postponed. He lived in Abu Dhabi for over forty years – but the federal government's identity regularization drive led to a denial of his citizenship claim and a referral of his case to the UNHCR yet again. In 2009 he was resettled by the UNHCR a second time, this time to the United States. As his community has been shifted from one location to another, from one legal category to another, the constant thread that can be traced, across national contexts and over generations, is that of a life spent waiting.

By having a conditional and temporary status for a protracted period, Mansour inhabited an ambiguous legal status for most of his adult life – caught between legal categories. As he waited to get the proper citizenship documents in the UAE over the years, his ambiguous status didn't change, but the state around him did, and the gradual forces of centralization and boundary enforcement made it increasingly difficult for him to live and work in the UAE. Mansour's second path to statelessness was less formal, less violent, and more protracted, but the outcome was effectively the same: his legal status did not provide him with secure membership or legal protection by the state in which he resided.

Who is Mansour? Where is he *really* from? What may appear, at face value, to be an "empirical" question is actually a political determination – one that is deeply bounded by the ways that modern states use time to construct and police national boundaries. One might concede that the formal acquisition of citizenship is political, in the sense that it is about belonging to a modern state. But the reader might still like to know, in terms of bloodline, what is Mansour's most dominant ethnic origin that might be grafted onto a national origin? What is he "originally"? Is he an Arab? Is he South Asian? Is he African? For Mansour the answer to the question of national origin is entirely dependent upon timing – one cannot pinpoint a "true" origin because his ethnic lineage reflects the political economy of the Indian Ocean. Populations from across three continents circulated for centuries prior to the wave of postcolonial state formation that swept the Indian subcontinent, Persian Gulf, and East Africa between World War II and the early 1970s.

Mansour's ethnic composition and mixed descent reflects this history of interconnectedness. He was born and raised in Uganda, but believes his ancestors moved from Baluchistan to East Africa with the Omani Empire prior to the nineteenth century. He spent over forty years living in Abu Dhabi and now close to ten years in the United States. To get Mansour back to his Baluchi "origin" we would have to trace his descendants over 150 years. Why choose that moment in time to define the truth about someone's national origin – why not before or after? If we could identify the precise village of his ancestors, would the question of his national origin be solved – would he "properly" be Pakistani, Iranian, or Afghan? If Mansour's family was in Abu Dhabi in 1971 instead of 1973 – would they have Emirati citizenship now? Or would the ruling elites in Abu Dhabi still have denied these cases for not being Arab enough? How does one distinguish the Arab from the non-Arab? In the case of the UAE it was a political pact from 1925. If Mansour's family were in the UAE in 1925 instead of Uganda – would they have been considered Arab enough then? Or would the mix of African, Arab, and South Asian bloodlines still have prevented their entry into the UAE's citizenry?

Mansour's story shows how integral the use of time is to the way political entities build and police national boundaries. First, the UAE constitution (like other constitutions) uses a countdown temporal dead-line (1925) to determine who is a native citizen – what is being traced is a snapshot of a resident population at a particular point in time. In addition to being partial to the dominant Arab group at the expense of the non-Arab communities of the Trucial State shoreline, this snapshot also freezes a community as being "native" and all others who come after as "foreign." Second, time is also integral to the way that federal authorities police national boundaries in the UAE; the use of delays shows that citizenship can be denied – not only through expulsions, but also through the more subtle power of bureaucratic delays. What matters is not how much time a person has resided in a state, but rather how that time is counted.

I return to Mansour in this book's conclusion because he asked a question that is central to this book when he reflected on his experiences waiting for citizenship: "Why don't you say 'yes' or 'no'?" Why did the UAE government postpone his – and other naturalization cases – for so long? Though he continues to miss and yearn for the UAE, Mansour is relatively privileged in comparison to the Asian-Ugandan group in Dubai or other minorities who now have Union of Comoros passports because he has been resettled to the United States and is no longer waiting for Emirati citizenship. For everyone else, the waiting continues, but under a more formalized status of permanent temporariness.

One may argue that unlike other stateless populations, at least the Union of Comoros passport holders in the UAE have passports and can therefore leave the UAE. Foreign passports could be an exit strategy – their ticket out of the waiting line for Emirati citizenship. But who will accept them? The bearers of these passports are met with suspicion by other authorities who do not know how to process or vet documents that are detached from any sovereign authority. These Union of Comoros passports provide no diplomatic protection from the Union of the Comoros or a right to reside there. This case of offshore citizens has codified foreign residency into a citizenship status, shuffling this population from being contested citizens into incontrovertible aliens.

7.1 COMPARATIVE IMPLICATIONS AND FUTURE RESEARCH

The dominant political theories of citizenship tend to recognize and endorse clear distinctions between citizens and aliens; either one has citizenship or one does not. The existing literature has sought to explain these settled outcomes – why states choose to include or exclude minorities and new migrants. Scholarship has shown that policy makers differentiate between groups that they target for inclusion or exclusion based on strategic calculations, such as a state's need for labor or military conscription (Weil 2001), or national security threats, especially when it comes to the perceived connection between minority groups and foreign allies or enemies (Greenhill 2010; Mylonas 2013; Weiner 1992). Others have argued that whether a group is included or excluded is based on the political ideologies of ruling elites (Browning and Matthäus 2004) or long-standing ideas about nationhood and political culture (Brubaker 1992). Another subset of the literature focuses more on the attributes of the group than the ideas of ruling elites, arguing that the likelihood a group will be included or excluded is largely determined by the salience of differences between the dominant and minority group (such as ethnic, religious, or linguistic attributes) (Geertz 1963; Gurr 1993; Horowitz 1985; Kaufman 2001). Yet another contribution to the literature has been an attention to the historical trajectory of group interactions; past interactions between the dominant and minority groups can determine whether that minority group will be included or excluded (Petersen 2001, 2002). This study shows that at different times all of these factors played a role in why elites in Abu Dhabi excluded some domestic minorities from full citizenship. This case contributes to this literature by showing that groups can be excluded because of rivalries between ruling elites and their competing visions of the citizenry.

All of these explanations capture important dynamics of the politics of inclusion or exclusion. My contribution is less about explaining *why* groups are targeted for exclusion, and more about showing *how* that exclusion occurs. While a robust literature has illuminated the variety of reasons why groups might be included in a citizenry or expelled from it, the outcomes of inclusion and exclusion have largely been treated as a binomial variable. Mylonas (2013) makes the theoretical contribution of showing that instead of understanding inclusion and exclusion as a dichotomy, this dynamic is best captured as a categorical variable of assimilation (erasing group differences through full inclusion), accommodation (inclusion of a group but with the acknowledgment of minority group differences and special rights), and exclusion. But exclusion has overwhelmingly been treated as the outcome of being expelled from a territory. This case shows how exclusion can occur even while residency is sanctioned.

While a variety of alternative explanations have been provided for explaining settled citizenship outcomes, much less attention has gone into explaining pending legal statuses – that is, the suspension of any citizenship outcome. This book contributes to this literature by showing that in addition to being fully included or excluded, the status of certain groups can be also suspended and postponed, creating a liminal zone of individuals who are not citizens, but are not aliens either. Not all populations are fully included or expelled by states; many are granted temporary and circumscribed authorization to reside in the territory, often for protracted periods.

The UAE provides an important case study of limbo statuses. This book examines the emergence, consolidation, and maintenance of migration and citizenship policies in the UAE to argue that states adopt conditional and temporary statuses in order to evade larger dilemmas about the boundaries of the national body. These dilemmas emerge when there is a contestation among domestic actors over the incorporation of ethnic minorities, refugees, or labor. In such cases, states often find it more politically expedient to postpone the larger questions of belonging and address the more immediate issues of identity management. While temporary and conditional statuses provide state actors with ad hoc solutions to larger national dilemmas, these statuses can also place individuals in an ambiguous zone of legal belonging.

In an effort to place the UAE in comparative context, this book examines other examples of limbo statuses and develops the concept of *precarious citizenship* to refer to people who are unable to gain access to secure citizenship rights and instead inhabit ad hoc conditional and temporary legal statuses for protracted periods. This study provides a typology of four types of precarious statuses:

(1) individuals who cannot gain national identity documents and effectively become stateless;
(2) individuals who may have one state's identity documents but who lack legal status in the state of their residence and thus become "illegal";
(3) individuals with temporary humanitarian protected statuses;
(4) individuals with temporary employment authorization.

The secondary literature on citizenship and migration clearly shows that the UAE is not alone in adopting temporary and conditional legal statuses; incidences of these types of precarious citizenship statuses have emerged across regime types and world regions. While no one has aggregated these various "limbo" populations into one category, there is a growing literature that is documenting how specific groups of domestic minorities and migrants experience precarious citizenship.

The case of offshore citizens is unique in that it codifies "temporary foreign residency" into a citizenship status, but the UAE is not alone in creating ambiguous and temporary legal statuses for its residents. Recent scholarship has questioned this citizen/noncitizen binary to demonstrate the emergence of "in-between" and ambiguous legal statuses. This literature reveals that ambiguous legal statuses are proliferating in a number of ways. First, "in-between" statuses emerge as states develop temporary statuses to accommodate flows of labor migrants or refugees. The modus operandi of the global order is to adopt ad hoc and temporary solutions to manage unsolved questions of belonging. Postponement is the increasingly dominant response adopted by nation states and international organizations like the UNHCR to deal with displaced populations. Most states have provisions for temporary work authorization and temporary humanitarian protection, and the literature shows that not only is this practice of temporary authorization common, but that it also leads to protracted settlement (Akram and Syring 2014). This means that temporary authorization does not necessarily lead to temporary residency; more often than not it leads to the creation of groups of residents who have circumscribed and revocable rights for protracted time periods. For example, in her work on El Salvadorans with temporary protected status (TPS) in the United States, Menjivar shows that they inhabit a space of "legal liminality." This "liminal legality" is "characterized by its ambiguity, as it is neither an undocumented status nor a documented one, but may have the characteristics of both" (2006: 1008). Individuals on TPS have an ambiguous legal status (neither "legal" nor "illegal"), because at times they are treated as refugees and granted temporary relief from deportation, whereas at other times they are not allowed to renew their permits, becoming "illegal" immigrants again (as has recently occurred with President Trump's removal of El Salvador from the TPS list).

Ambiguous legal statuses are also an outcome of the growing administrative power of modern states, especially with the adoption of new technologies in identity management. In their recent edited volume *Citizenship in Question* (2017), Lawrance and Stevens focus on a wide range of populations who are misrecognized by their states and labeled as aliens. From Argentina to Australia, Togo to Thailand, they show how states question the citizenship status of their citizens, rendering their own citizens stateless, or deporting them as foreigners. Sadiq's chapter on India and Malaysia and Flaim's chapter on Thailand "reveal that the very administrative regimes implemented to integrate unenumerated individuals into the state bureaucracy are actually removing them from political society and the welfare state altogether. Only after one is expected to have a piece of paper can one be judged for not having it" (Stevens 2017: 4). In other words, the growing entrenchment of state institutions and the emphasis on fraud and particular kinds of evidence needed to "prove" citizenship render those without access to documentation outside of the national body politic and in a liminal space between the citizen and alien.

This case study raises key questions about the conditions that drive states to adopt temporary and conditional statuses. While this book is comparative (subnationally and cross-temporally) it does not provide a comprehensive cross-national assessment of limbo statuses and precarious citizenship. In the absence of a quantitative assessment of the sizes of these populations across political systems and regions and a temporal understanding of when they emerge in each case, it is not possible to isolate scope conditions and generate a theory about when ruling elites are likely to adopt conditional and temporary statuses versus when they might fully incorporate or exclude minority and migrant populations. Future research may build on this case study by quantifying the sizes of limbo populations and examining the legal and historical trajectory of the development of these statuses in large migrant-receiving states.

The dilemma of who will be part of the national body politic is the oldest and most fundamental question in processes of national determination. This book builds upon a long tradition of literature on nationalism that shows how nations are not discovered but built. Homogenous nations have never existed – "native" citizens have to be carved out from existing resident populations who are always more heterogeneous than official nationalisms acknowledge. The very same process that transforms one group of residents into citizens can turn other groups into aliens and yet another subset of the population into limbo populations. Much of this book's discussion revolves around people caught in limbo in order to make the larger contribution of showing that ambiguous legal statuses are integral to the consolidation and maintenance of modern citizenship regimes. It is not only that the "alien" elements solidify the boundaries of a national body politic and the distributions of power within it. It is that the national boundary itself is never a clean line between citizens and aliens – there are gray zones of ambiguous and conditional inclusion that relegate certain populations to "limbo" legal statuses.

If citizenship represents the relationship between individuals and the modern state, then for the individuals who have ambiguous legal statuses, citizenship is known only through its absence. This absence is not experienced as an abandonment of state power, but rather an ever-increasing ensnarement and dependency upon the state. In the words of Mansour, that ensnarement is summed up by the phrase "come tomorrow" and the suspension of time this command entails. "Come tomorrow," until the tight threads of rational chronological time unravel. "Come tomorrow," until "tomorrow" ceases to have the parameters of minutes or hours, its seams expanding from days, to weeks, to months, to years, to decades. "Come tomorrow," until time is experienced as an endless and vast space of suspended duration. Just "come tomorrow," even though tomorrow will never come.

Methodological Appendix

Political, legal, and ethical considerations have dominated the efforts
I have put into this research over the past eight years. These considerations
shaped the book's methodology, which combines interview and archival
methods (in English and Arabic) with legal advocacy. I developed this
three-pronged approach because – in addition to the fact that naturalization policies are considered a realm of national security in the UAE – the
Arab Spring protests of 2011 had a chilling effect on the work. I feared
putting both my informants and myself at risk and struggled with questions of informed consent, having conducted the majority of the initial
interviews in Dubai and Abu Dhabi from 2009 to 2011 in a political
environment that was decidedly less heated.

Informed consent can only be granted on the basis of a participant
having full knowledge of the possible consequences of the research. But
the calculation of risks is situational, and the political environment in the
UAE shifted critically in 2011, changing the potential risks to participants.
The UAE did not experience any large-scale protests, but as protests
spread across other Arab states, the government initiated preemptive
arrests of activists and academics, especially after an online petition for
reform was circulated in March 2011. In the aftermath, the "UAE 94"
mass trial led to arrests and the withdrawal of citizenship from those
whose allegiance was questioned. The government's ongoing practice of
withdrawing citizenship from those whose nationality status was previously perceived as secure has been particularly worrisome for my informants who have spent their lives in limbo waiting for full citizenship.

In response, I scrubbed the manuscript of much of the ethnographic materials that I had collected for my dissertation (which also used degendered and anonymized data) and instead incorporated new archival records to tell the story of waiting for citizenship. Since starting this process in 2013, I have collected, read, translated (from Arabic), sorted, and coded close to 2,000 additional documents to develop this manuscript.

Additionally, a legal clinic accompanies this book. Over the course of the years of working with my informants, I learned that more than any monetary gain, what my interviewees wanted was an end to the limbo of waiting for citizenship. I began working toward this goal by setting up a legal initiative on statelessness. Yoana Kuzmova (JD/MA) has largely spearheaded these cases with the support of Professor Susan Akram's International Human Rights Clinic at Boston University's School of Law. From 2016 to 2019, Kuzmova and several law students have focused on exploring legal options for the *de facto* stateless persons who carry Comoros passports.

IN-DEPTH INTERVIEWS

This book draws on extensive qualitative research, including 180 interviews conducted from 2009 to 2016. Of these interviews, 123 were conducted from 2009 to 2011, and 57 were conducted between 2012 and 2016 (35 of these were follow-up, 22 were with new interviewees). In total 145 unique individuals were interviewed. The interviews were designed to examine how the citizen/noncitizen boundary of the UAE is enforced from the top down and experienced from the bottom up.

The majority of the ethnographic work was concentrated from 2009 to 2011, when I conducted 123 interviews in Dubai and Abu Dhabi for my dissertation fieldwork in Arabic and in English. Of these initial interviews, sixty-eight were conducted with applicants who had experience with the process of applying for naturalization in the UAE. Six of these applicants were from Abu Dhabi, twenty-nine of the applicants were from Dubai, eighteen were from Sharjah, ten were from Ras al Khaimah, and five were from Ajman. Fourteen were born elsewhere but had arrived in the UAE prior to the formation of the state in 1971, and the remaining fifty-four were born in the UAE. Twenty-three of the sixty-eight naturalization applicants had Emirati mothers. The questions posed to naturalization applicants focused on the following points: where the applicants were born and how long they had been in the UAE, whether any of their family members had UAE citizenship, whether they were employed (and in which fields), whether they had any alternative citizenships, what nationality they identified with the most, whether they received any public resources (including healthcare or education), how long they had spent applying and waiting for citizenship, what the process entailed (including how many times they had been interviewed by the Ministry of Interior), what identity documents they carried (and how often and when they were able to renew them), and how they thought their lives would be different if they were able to gain UAE citizenship.

In addition to those undergoing the naturalization process, between 2009 and 2011 I also conducted thirty-eight interviews with individuals involved with enforcing the citizen/noncitizen boundary in the UAE. This included three interviews with civil servants in the MOI's naturalization and residency departments about naturalization processes, three interviews with lawyers about why they thought the courts lacked jurisdiction in this arena, fourteen interviews with police officers in Abu Dhabi and Dubai about enforcing residency status, fifteen interviews with security consultants in Abu Dhabi and Dubai about the management of open borders and adoption of new population management technologies, and three interviews with people from the private sector who were privy to Comoros Gulf Holding's passport deal between the Comoros Islands and UAE.

To get a sense of the history that was not available in writing, I also conducted seventeen interviews with Emirati and other Gulf Arab social science professors about the formation of the UAE state and the differences between incorporation practices of different emirates, the historical differences between the ethnic composition of different emirates, the significance of different factors on the demographic makeup of the country (including policies, wars, and labor migration), the reasons for the presence of *bidūn* (stateless) populations in the country, as well as their personal views on naturalization policies and the role of allegiance in citizenship acquisition.

In addition to these initial 123 interviews, fifty-seven interviews have been conducted from 2012 to 2016. Of these, thirty-five were follow-up phone interviews with naturalization applicants who were originally interviewed between 2009 and 2011. My goal was to verify whether there was any change in status, especially among cases of individuals whose mothers were Emirati, since a law allowing Emirati women to transfer their citizenship to their children was enacted in 2011. At the time of publication none of the twenty-three applicants with Emirati mothers have received Emirati citizenship and instead continue to hold Union of Comoros passports.

ARCHIVAL RESEARCH

The ethnographic research was combined with an analysis of approximately 3,200 archival documents to allow for multiple forms of verification while maintaining the anonymity of interviewees. These consulted documents are in Arabic, English, and French and include local newspaper articles, security directives, police studies, magazines, and educational materials produced by the MOI, the British Archives of the Emirates (1938–1971), UNHCR records, letters between ministries on behalf of citizenship applicants, letters from applicants to international organizations, and Comorian and Emirati identity documents. The two largest sources of these primary archival materials are the British records of the Emirates and approximately two thousand documents from a previously unused archive about refugees who arrived in Dubai during the early stages of the UAE's state formation.

The British Archives of the Emirates

The British archives of the Emirates are contained in the *Records of the Emirates*, a comprehensive selection of archived British government documents which details the history of the UAE from 1820 to 1971. The following list gives details of the volumes consulted in this book.

Records of the Emirates: Primary Documents 1820–1958, 12 vols. (Farnham Common: Archive Editions, 1990)

- Vols. 1–10 edited by Penelope Tuson.
- Vols. 11–12 have the subtitle *Primary Documents 1820–1960*.
- Vol. 10 comprises eleven folded maps and tables.
- Volume 9: 1947–1958

Records of the Emirates: Primary Documents 1820–1960, 12 vols. (Penelope Tuson ed., Cambridge Archive Editions, 1992)

- Volume 11: 1958–1959

Records of the Emirates 1961–1965, 12 vols. (Anita L. P. Burdett ed., Farnham Common: Archive Editions, 1997)

- Volume 1: 1961
- Volume 2: 1962

- Volume 3: 1963
- Volume 4: 1964
- Volume 5: 1965

Records of the Emirates 1966–1971, 6 vols. (Anita L. P. Burdett ed., Cambridge Archive Editions, 2002)

- Volume 1: 1966
- Volume 2: 1967
- Volume 3: 1968
- Volume 4: 1969
- Volume 5: 1970
- Volume 6: 1971

The British archives of the Emirates were consulted to determine how the citizen/noncitizen boundary was defined historically, as well as how its enforcement infrastructure was erected. The archival analysis focused on the interests of the different emirates in the formation of the citizenship policy of the union, questions of competing tribal allegiance, and the security and commercial concerns of the different emirates. The documents also demonstrated the role played by oil concessions, the formation of a policing infrastructure at the shoreline and interior, and the formalization of the citizenship and immigration policies as the UAE gained its independence from the British.

The consulted records include primary materials on:

- the Abu Dhabi–Dubai War (1947–1948)
- the Abu Dhabi–Dubai boundary dispute (1949–1952)
- discussions on Abu Dhabi's and Dubai's internal affairs (1954, 1955)
- discussions on interstate boundaries (1956–1958)
- discussions of the Trucial States Council: economic and political federation (1958–1959)
- discussions on internal frontiers (1958–1959)
- discussions on Dubai's succession following the death of Sheikh Saeed bin Maktoum and accession of Sheikh Rashid (1958)
- the development of the oil industry and discussions on oil concessions (1959; 1961; 1965; 1966)
- the budgets and plans for Dubai and Abu Dhabi police (1959)
- notes on interior affairs (including "imbalance" between states, frontier issues, and "tribal friction," and fears about communism) (1961; 1962; 1963; 1964; 1965; 1969)

- notes on labor and social affairs (including discussions about slavery and labor strikes) (1961; 1962; 1963)
- affairs of the royal *diwans* (high governmental bodies) (1965; 1966)
- the Council of Ministers (Trucial States Council and related bodies) (1965)
- discussions on external affairs (including relations with Great Britain and the Arab League) (1965)
- discussions on inter-Arab relations (including the questions of Yemeni immigrants and Arab Manga refugees from Zanzibar) (1965)
- discussions on internal affairs, including intelligence organization, counter-subversion planning and general administration (1966; 1967)
- discussions on legal affairs (including visas and "illegal" immigration) (1966; 1967; 1969)
- regional and intra-Gulf relations (including conflicts between Dubai and Abu Dhabi; conflicts between Abu Dhabi and Muscat; conflicting interests on tribal matters between Ras al Khaimah, Abu Dhabi, and Muscat; and Gulf states' attitudes to the "Palestinian Problem") (1967; 1969)
- discussions on the creation of a Federation of Gulf States (including the initial proposal of a "union of nine") (1968; 1969; 1970; 1971)
- establishment and improvement of local security forces and intelligence (1971)
- internal governance and control: transfer of residual responsibilities for visas and immigration to the Trucial States Council (1971).

Displaced Persons Archive

This book incorporates close to 2,000 additional documents from a previously unused archive about displaced persons arriving in the Dubai ports from 1967 to 2013. This archive originated as the records of Mr. William R. Duff (aka Bill), a prominent British advisor to Sheikh Rashid bin Saeed Al Maktoum (the ruler of Dubai from 1958 to 1990). Duff collected these documents for a subdivision of the *diwan* (ruler's office) called the Ugandan Refugee Liaison Office. Duff entrusted the records of this office to a trusted member of the Dubai ruler's office (who is now deceased) for the purposes of allowing the refugees to continue working toward resolving their cases. Over the course of three years of sorting and coding from 2013 to 2016, these documents have been summarized, translated (when necessary), chronicled into a comprehensive timeline, and indexed for content. The archives largely focus on Zanzibari and Asian-Ugandan refugees, tracing the Dubai ruler's office's efforts to help them either gain Emirati citizenship or resettle elsewhere over the course of almost half a century. The analysis of the distribution of records provides a basis for evaluating the impact of waiting for citizenship on different aspects of peoples' lives without using personal narratives that may uniquely identify individuals.

ESTABLISHING A LEGAL STATELESSNESS INITIATIVE ALONGSIDE THE BOOK

Since 2016, Yoana Kuzmova (JD/MA) and I have worked with Professor Susan Akram's International Human Rights Clinic at Boston University's School of Law to better understand the legality of these passports and advocate on behalf of stateless populations. To our knowledge, the UAE is the first country to have "offshored" its stateless population by arranging its own residents to acquire the passports of the Union of the Comoros. Our initiative is currently exploring legal options for Emirates-based Comoros passport holders, specifically with those who have previously held UAE passports (rather than other documents), but were reclassified as "foreign residents" and issued passports from the Union of the Comoros in 2008.

It should be noted that the dynamics of waiting has meant that there is not an unequivocal and uniform push for resettlement by the individuals who we have been in contact with. At times the desperation of waiting motivates some of our informants to ask us to explore any possible options for resettlement. But when they hear news or rumors about the successful naturalization of similarly situated individuals, they often want us to halt this work and wait to see what will happen. This is heightened by the fact that the UNHCR in Abu Dhabi frequently signals that resettlement is not an option for stateless populations and it is only a matter of time before they will be incorporated by the federal state. Without exception, every single one of the individuals interviewed has expressed the desire to remain in the UAE and become a UAE citizen over resettling to any (European or North American) context. This uncertainty and oscillation of objectives has made it challenging to develop a coherent legal strategy – a fact that is exacerbated by the widespread acceptance that states like the UAE and the Union of the Comoros have the sovereign prerogative to define the boundaries of their own citizenries.

References

Abdullah, Mohamed Murad. 1996. *Juvenile Delinquency Indicators*, trans. Mohamed Abdel-Rahman. Police Studies No. 54. Dubai: Dubai Police General Headquarters Research and Studies Centre.

Abrahamian, Atossa Araxia. 2012. "Special Report: Passports ... for a Price." *Reuters*, February 12. www.reuters.com/article/us-passport-idUSTRE 81B05A20120212.

2015. *The Cosmopolites: The Coming of the Global Citizen*. New York: Columbia Global Reports.

Absal, Rayeesa. 2008. "Stateless People's Registration to End." *Gulf News*, November 5.

Achiume, Tendayi E., Alexander Aleinikoff, James Cavallaro, Vincent Chetail, Robert Cryer, Gearoid O Cuinn, Tom J. Dannenbaum, et al. 2017. *The Situation in Nauru and Manus Island: Liability for Crimes against Humanity in the Detention of Refugees and Asylum Seekers*. www-cdn.law.stanford.edu/wp-content/uploads/2017/02/Communiqu%C3%A9-to-Office-Prosecutor-IntlCrimCt-Art15RomeStat-14Feb2017.pdf.

Ahlin, Christian, and Pinaki Bose. 2007. "Bribery, Inefficiency, and Bureaucratic Delay." *Journal of Development Economics* 84 (1): 465–486.

Ahmad, Attiya. 2012. "Beyond Labor: Foreign Residents in the Persian Gulf." In *Migrant Labor in the Persian Gulf*, edited by Mehran Kamrava and Zahra Babar, 21–40. New York: Columbia University Press.

Akram, Susan, and Tom Syring, eds. 2014. *Still Waiting for Tomorrow: The Law and Politics of Unresolved Refugee Crises*. Newcastle upon Tyne: Cambridge Scholars Publishing.

Al Ameeri, Saeed Mohammad. 2004. "The Baloch in the Arabian Gulf States." In *The Baloch and Their Neighbours*, edited by Carina Jahani and Agnes Korn, 237–245. Wiesbaden: Dr. Ludwig Reichert Verlag.

Al Jandaly, Bassma. 2008. "Emirati Passports Not Enough for IDs." *GulfNews*, October 27. www.pressreader.com/uae/gulf-news/20081027/281573761526033.

Al Qassemi, Sultan. 2010. "Book That Proves Some Emiratis Are More Equal than Others." *The National*, February 7. www.thenational.ae/uae/book-that-proves-some-emiratis-are-more-equal-than-others-1.524231.

2016. "United Arab Emigrants: Stories of Pioneer Arab Migrants Who Became Emirati." *Medium*, July 26. https://medium.com/@SultanAlQassemi/united-arab-emigrants-92314e7f3eca.

Al Dailami, Ahmed. 2014. "Crude Nations: Histories of Oil, State, and Society in the Arab Gulf." PhD Dissertation, Faculty of History, University of Oxford.

Al-Fahim, Mohamed. 1995. *From Rags to Riches: A Story of Abu Dhabi*. London: The London Centre for Arab Studies.

Al Khouri, Ali. 2010. *"The Challenge of Identity in a Changing World: The Case of GCC Countries."* In *Proceedings of the 21st-Century Gulf: The Challenge of Identity*, June 30–July 3, 1–7. Exeter, UK: University of Exeter.

Allen, Calvin. 1981. "The Indian Merchant Community of Masquat." *School of Oriental and African Studies* 44 (1): 39–53.

Al-Muhairi, Butti Sultan Butti Ali. 1996. "The Development of the UAE Legal System and Unification with the Judicial System." *Arab Law Quaterly* 11 (2): 116–160.

Al-Qasimi, Sultan. 1986. *The Myth of Arab Piracy in the Gulf*. New York and London: Croom Helm.

Al-Sayegh, Fatma. 1998. "Merchants' Role in a Changing Society: The Case of Dubai, 1900–1990." *Middle Eastern Studies* 34 (1, January): 87–102.

Amnesty International. 2015. *"Without Paper, I Am No One" – Stateless People in the Dominican Republic*. London: Amnesty International. https://www.amnesty.org/en/documents/amr27/2755/2015/en/.

2016. *"Where Are We Going to Live?" Migration and Statelessness in Haiti and the Dominican Republic*. AMR 36/4105/2016. Amnesty International. www.amnesty.org/en/documents/document/?indexNumber=amr36%2f4105%2f2016&language=en.

Anderson, Benedict. 2006. *Imagined Communities: Reflections on the Origin and Spread of Nationalism*. 3rd revised ed. London: Verso.

Anderson, Bridget. 2018. "About Time Too: Precarity and Life Stage in Labour Migration." Presented at "Labor Migration: Global and Comparative Dimensions" Workshop, Max Planck Institute, University of Göttingen, Germany, May 18.

Andersson, Ruben. 2014. *Illegality, Inc.* California Series in Public Anthropology. Berkeley, CA: University of California Press.

Andonova, Liliana B. 2004. *Transnational Politics of the Environment: The European Union and Environmental Policy in Central and Eastern Europe*. Cambridge, MA: MIT Press.

Arendt, Hannah. 1976. *The Origins of Totalitarianism*. New York: Harcourt Brace Jovanovich.

Assemblée de l'Union. 2008. *Loi relative à la citoyenneté économique en Union des Comores (Law Concerning Economic Citizenship for the Union of the Comoros)*. www.refworld.org/pdfid/4c582c692.pdf

Auyero, Javier. 2012. *Patients of the State*. Durham, NC: Duke University Press.

Avaro, Dante. 2014. "Citizen Traceability: Surveillance à la Argentina." *Journal of Power, Politics & Governance* 2 (3–4): 93–113.

Baldwin-Edwards, Martin. 2011. *Labour Immigration and Labour Markets in the GCC Countries: National Patterns and Trends*. Research Paper, Kuwait

Programme on Development, Governance and Globalisation in the Gulf States. London School of Economics and Political Science.

Barbero, Iker. 2012. "Orientalising Citizenship: The Legitimation of Immigration Regimes in the European Union." *Citizenship Studies* 16 (5–6): 751–768.

Bauböck, Rainer. 2017. "Democratic Representation in Mobile Societies." In *Multicultural Governance in a Mobile World*, edited by Anna Triandafyllidou, 283–306. Edinburgh: Edinburgh University Press.

Bearce, David H., and Jennifer A. Laks Hutnick. 2011. "Toward an Alternative Explanation for the Resource Curse: Natural Resources, Immigration, and Democratization." *Comparative Political Studies* 44 (6): 689–718.

Beaugrand, Claire. 2010. "Statelessness and Transnationalism in Northern Arabia: Biduns and State Building in Kuwait, 1959–2009." London School of Economics and Political Science. ProQuest Dissertations Publishing.

Beckett, Samuel. 1955. *Waiting for Godot: A Tragicomedy in Two Acts*. London: Faber and Faber.

Bergeron, Claire. 2014. "Temporary Protected Status after 25 Years: Addressing the Challenge of Long-Term 'Temporary' Residents and Strengthening a Centerpiece of US Humanitarian Protection." *Journal on Migration and Human Security* 2 (1): 22–43.

Berkeley, Bill. 2009. "Stateless People, Violent States." *World Policy Journal* 26 (1): 3–15.

Bilkhair, Aisha. 2006. *Afro-Emarati: A Unique Historical Experience*. The Slave Route research publication, United Nations Educational, Scientific and Cultural Organization.

Birks, J. S., and Sinclair, C. A. 1980. *Arab Manpower: The Crisis of Development*. New York: St Martin's Press.

Bishara, Fahad. 2012. "A Sea of Debt: Histories of Commerce and Obligation in the Indian Ocean, c. 1850–1940." PhD Dissertation, Faculty of History, Duke University, Durham, NC.

Blitz, Brad. 2006. "Statelessness and the Social (De)Construction of Citizenship: Political Restructuring and Ethnic Discrimination in Slovenia." *Journal of Human Rights* 5 (4): 453–479.

Bloom, T. 2015. "The Business of Migration Control: Delegating Migration Control Functions to Private Actors." *Global Policy* 6 (2): 151–157.

Blyth, Mark, and Varghese, Robin. 1999. "The State of the Discipline in American Political Science: Be Careful What You Wish For?" *British Journal of Politics and International Relations* 1 (3): 345–365.

Bose, Gautam. 2004. "Bureaucratic Delays and Bribe-Taking." *Journal of Economic Behavior & Organization* 54 (3): 313–320.

Bose, Sugata. 2006. *A Hundred Horizons: The Indian Ocean in the Age of Global Empire*. Cambridge, MA: Harvard University Press.

Bristol Rhys, Jane. 2010. "A Lexicon of Migrants in the United Arab Emirates." In *Viewpoints Special Edition: Migration and the Gulf*, February, 24–26. Washington, DC: Middle East Institute.

Brown, Eleanor Marie Lawrence. 2010. "What the US Can Learn from the Gulf States About Immigration: Visa Bonds and a Novel Proposal for Financing

Them." In *Viewpoints Special Edition: Migration and the Gulf*, February, 87–92. Washington, DC: Middle East Institute.

Browning, Christopher R., and Jürgen Matthäus. 2004. *The Origins of the Final Solution: The Evolution of Nazi Jewish Policy, September 1993– March 1942*. London: William Heinemann.

Brubaker, Rogers. 1992. *Citizenship and Nationhood in France and Germany*. Cambridge, MA: Harvard University Press.

Butt, Gerald. 2001. "Oil and Gas in the UAE." In *United Arab Emirates: A New Perspective*, edited by Ibrahim Al Abed and Peter Hellyer. London: Trident Press Ltd. www.badrinvestments.com/wp-content/uploads/2012/06/oil-and-gas-in-UAE-DA.pdf

Castillo, Mariano. 2016. "Faces of a Divided Island." *CNN*, April 13. www.cnn.com/2016/04/12/world/dominican-republic-haiti-immigration/index.html.

Castles, Stephen. 1986. "The Guest-Worker in Western Europe: An Obituary." *International Migration Review* 20 (4): 761–778.

Chalcraft, John. 2010. *Monarchy, Migration and Hegemony in the Arabian Peninsula*. Research Paper, Kuwait Programme on Development, Governance and Globalisation in the Gulf States. London: London School of Economics and Political Science.

2011. "Migration and Popular Protest in the Arabian Peninsula and the Gulf in the 1950s and 1960s." *International Labor and Working-Class History*, 79: 28–47.

Chauvin, Sebastien, and Blanca Garcés-Mascareñas. 2012. "Beyond Informal Citizenship: The New Moral Economy of Migrant Illegality." *International Political Sociology* 6 (3): 241–259.

Chavez, Linda. 1991. *Out of the Barrio: Toward a New Politics of Hispanic Assimilation*. New York: Basic Books.

Chin, Christine B. N. 1998. *In Service and Servitude: Foreign Female Domestic Workers and the Malaysian "Modernity" Project*. New York: Columbia University Press.

Chung, Erin. 2006. *Immigration and Citizenship in Japan*. Cambridge, UK and New York: Cambridge University Press.

Clarence-Smith, W. G. 1989. *The Economics of the Indian Ocean Slave Trade in the Nineteenth Century*. London and Totowa, NJ: Frank Cass.

Cohen, Elizabeth F. 2009. *Semi-Citizenship in Democratic Politics*. Cambridge University Press.

Cohen, Elizabeth F. 2018. *The Political Value of Time: Citizenship, Duration, and Democratic Justice*. Cambridge University Press.

Colton, Nora Ann. 2010. "The International Political Economy of Gulf Migration." In *Viewpoints Special Edition: Migration and the Gulf*, February, 34–36. Washington, DC: Middle East Institute.

Coutin, Susan Bibler. 2000. *Legalizing Moves: Salvadoran Immigrants' Struggle for US Residency*. Ann Arbor, MI: University of Michigan Press.

Dahan, Mariana. 2015. *Identification for Development (ID4D) Integration Approach Study*. Report No. 98383. Washington, DC: The World Bank. http://docplayer.net/35602110-Study-conference-edition.html.

Dajani, Haneen. 2010. "Camera Network to Keep the Capital under Observation." *The National*, March 3.

Das Gupta, Ashin. 2004. *India and the Indian Ocean World: Trade and Politics*. New Delhi: Oxford University Press.

Daugman, John, and Imad Malhas. 2004. "Iris Recognition Border-Crossing System in the UAE." *International Airport Review* 8 (2). www.cl.cam.ac.uk /~jgd1000/UAEdeployment.pdf.

Davidson, Christopher M. 2005. *The United Arab Emirates: A Study in Survival*. Boulder, CO: Lynne Rienner Publishers, Inc.

2008. *Dubai: The Vulnerability of Success*. New York: Columbia University Press.

De Bel-Air, Françoise. 2015. "A Note on Syrian Refugees in the Gulf: Attempting to Assess Data and Policies." Explanatory Note No. 11. GLMM Gulf Labor Markets and Migration.

De Genova, Nicholas, and Nathalie Peutz, eds. 2010. *The Deportation Regime: Sovereignty, Space, and the Freedom of Movement*. Durham, NC: Duke University Press.

Degorge, Barbara. 2006. "Modern Day Slavery in the United Arab Emirates." *The European Legacy* 11 (6): 657–666. https://doi.org/10.1080/108487706 00918307.

Dito, Mohammed. 2008. "GCC Labour Migration Governance" (UN/POP/ EGM-MIG/2008/7). Presented at the United Nations Expert Group Meeting on International Migration and Development in Asia and the Pacific, Bangkok, Thailand, June 20–21.

Dresch, Paul, and James Piscatori. 2005. *Monarchies and Nations: Globalisation and Identity in the Arab States of the Gulf*. Vol. 52, Library of Modern Middle East Studies. London: I. B. Tauris.

Dunmore, Charlie. 2014. "Born in Exile, Syrian Children Face Threat of Statelessness." UNHCR. www.unhcr.org/news/latest/2014/11/54589fb16/b orn-exile-syrian-children-face-threat-statelessness.html.

Eckstein, H. 1975. "Case Studies and Theory in Political Science." In *Handbook of Political Science*, edited by F. Greenstein and N. Polsby. Vol. 7, 94–137. Reading, MA: Addison-Wesley Press.

Economic Times. 2007. "UAE's Handouts Ruin Dream of an Emirati-Run Economy." October 5. https://economictimes.indiatimes.com/news/interna tional/uaes-handouts-ruin-dream-of-an-emirati-run-economy/articleshow/2 430754.cms.

Economist Intelligence Unit. 2009. *The GCC in 2020: The Gulf and Its People*. London: Economist Intelligence Unit. http://graphics.eiu.com/upload/eb/Gul f2020part2.pdf.

Ehrenreich, Barbara, and Arlie Russell Hochschild, eds. 2004. *Global Woman: Nannies, Maids, and Sex Workers in the New Economy*. 1st ed. New York: Holt Paperbacks.

Emarat Alyoum. 2008. "*Saif Bin Zayed: Al-Dustur Yasmah Bi-Saheb Al-Jinsiyya Miman La Ya'mal Bi-Istihqaqatiha* (Saif Bin Zayed: The Constitution Allows for the Confiscation of Citizenship from Those Who Do Not Abide by Its Requisites)," September 25.

Emirates News Agency. 2008. "MoI Sets Panel to Close File of Stateless Persons," September 3. http://wam.ae/en/details/1395228180581.

Esim, Simel, and Monica Smith. 2004. *Gender and Migration in Arab States: The Case of Domestic Workers*. Beirut: International Labour Organization. http s://www.ilo.org/beirut/publications/WCMS_204013/lang–en/index.htm.

European Parliament Legislative Observatory. 2015. Committee Report Tabled for Plenary, 1st Reading/Single Reading. www.europarl.europa.eu/oeil/pop ups/summary.do?id=1411612&t=e&l=en.

Fargues, Philippe. 2011. "Immigration without Inclusion: Non-Nationals in Nation-Building in the Gulf States." *Asian and Pacific Migration Journal* 20 (3–4), 273–292. http://cadmus.eui.eu//handle/1814/20565.

Fargues, Philippe, and Imco Brouwer. 2011. "GCC Demography and Immigration: Challenges and Policies." http://philippefargues.com/wp-content/uploads/201 6/12/33-Fargues-Brouwer-2012-GCC-Demography.pdf.

Federal Law No. 17 for 1972 Concerning Nationality, Passports and Amendments Thereof. www.refworld.org/pdfid/3fba182do.pdf.

Federal Authority for Identity and Citizenship. 2018. "Laws and Legislation." www.id.gov.ae/en/emirates-id/laws-and-legislation.aspx.

Federal National Council. 2010. *United Arab Emirates Constitution: By-Law of the Federal National Council*. www.wipo.int/edocs/lexdocs/laws/en/ae/a e031en.pdf.

Feldblum, Chai R. 1997. "The Moral Rhetoric of Legislation." (Response to article by Thomas B. Stoddard in the same issue, p. 967). *New York University Law Review* 72 (5): 992–1008.

Fitzgerald, David Scott. 2017. "The History of Racialized Citizenship." In *The Oxford Handbook of Citizenship*, edited by Ayelet Shachar, Rainer Bauböck, Irene Bloemraad, and Maarten Vink, 103–129. Oxford, UK: Oxford University Press.

Flaim, Amanda. 2017. "Problems of Evidence, Evidence of Problems: Expanding Citizenship and Reproducing Statelessness among Highlanders in Northern Thailand." In *Citizenship in Question: Evidentiary Birthright and Statelessness*, edited by Benjamin N. Lawrance and Jacqueline Stevens, 147–164. Durham, NC: Duke University Press.

Fouad, Daad. 1999. *Demographic Indicators and Family Social Security: Effects and Consequences*. Police Studies 92. Dubai: Dubai Police General Headquarters Research and Studies Centre.

Frelick, Bill. 2014. "Unlocking Protracted Refugee Situations: Lessons from Four Asian Cases." In *Still Waiting for Tomorrow: The Law and Politics of Unresolved Refugee Crises*, edited by Susan Akram and Tom Syring, 169–193. Newcastle upon Tyne: Cambridge Scholars Publishing.

Frelick, Bill, and Barbara Kohnen. 1995. "Filling the Gap: Temporary Protected Status." *Journal of Refugee Studies* 8 (4): 339–363.

Gardner, Andrew M. 2008. "Strategic Transnationalism: The Indian Diasporic Elite in Contemporary Bahrain." *City & Society* 20 (1): 54–78.

Geertz, Clifford. 1963. "The Integrative Revolution: Primordial Sentiments and Politics in the New States." In *Old Societies and New States: The Quest for*

Modernity in Asia and Africa, edited by Clifford Geertz, 255–310. New York: Free Press of Glencoe.

Gelb, Alan, and Julia Clark. 2013. "Identification for Development: The Biometrics Revolution." Working Paper 315. Washington, DC: Center for Global Development.

Gibney, Matthew. 2009. "Statelessness and the Right to Citizenship." *Forced Migration Review* 32: 50–51.

Goodman, Sara Wallace. 2014. *Immigration and Membership Politics in Western Europe*. Cambridge University Press.

Greenhill, Kelly M. 2010. *Weapons of Mass Migration: Forced Displacement, Coercion, and Foreign Policy*. Cornell Studies in Security Affairs. Ithaca, NY: Cornell University Press.

Gulf Labor Markets and Migration (GLMM). 2015. "Saudi-Arabia: Population Estimates by Nationality (Saudi / Non-Saudi) (Mid-Year Estimates, 1974–2015)." September 24. http://gulfmigration.org/saudi-arabia-population-estimates-nationality-saudi-non-saudi-mid-year-estimates-1974-2015.

Gulf News. 2008. "Saif Recommends 25 Ministry Employees for UAE Citizenship." *Gulf News*, July 22. http://gulfnews.com/business/visas/saif-recommends-25-ministry-employees-for-uae-citizenship-1.119527 (no longer available).

Gurowitz, Amy. 1999. "Mobilizing International Norms: Domestic Actors, Immigrants, and the Japanese State." *World Politics* 51 (3): 423–445.

Gurr, Ted. 1993. *Minorities at Risk: A Global View of Ethnopolitical Conflicts*. Washington, DC: United States Institute of Peace.

Hall, Camilla, and Michael Peel. 2012. "UAE's Stateless Acquire Foreign Passports." *Financial Times*, June 4. www.ft.com/content/8abfc14a-a8aa-11e1-be59-00144feabdc0.

Hall, Peter, and Rosemary Taylor. 1996. "Political Science and the Three New Institutionalisms." *Political Studies* 44 (5): 936–957.

Hammar, Tomas. 1990. *Democracy and the Nation State: Aliens, Denizens, and Citizens in a World of International Migration*. Research in Ethnic Relations Series. Aldershot: Gower Publishing Ltd.

Hancock, Ange-Marie. 2004. *The Politics of Disgust: The Public Identity of the Welfare Queen*. New York University Press.

Harris, Joseph. 2013. "Uneven Inclusion: Consequences of Universal Healthcare in Thailand." *Citizenship Studies* 17 (1): 111–127.

Hawley, David. 1970. *The Trucial States*. London: Allen and Unwin.

Heard-Bey, Frauke. 1982. *From Trucial States to United Arab Emirates: A Society in Transition*. New York and London: Longman.

Heeg, Jennifer. 2011. "Gender, International Trafficking Norms and Gulf Migration." Paper presented at the annual meeting of the International Studies Association Annual Conference "Global Governance: Political Authority in Transition," Le Centre Sheraton Montreal Hotel, Montreal, Canada, March 16. http://citation.allacademic.com//meta/p_mla_apa_research_citation/5/0/2/9/0/pages502906/p502906-1.php.

Held, David. 1995. *Democracy and the Global Order: From the Modern State to Cosmpolitan Governance*. Cambridge University Press.

Helmke, Gretchen, and Steven Levitsky. 2004. "Informal Institutions and Comparative Politics: A Research Agenda." *Perspectives on Politics* 2 (4): 725–740.

Hesse, Barnor. 2004. "Im/Plausible Deniability: Racism's Conceptual Double Bind." *Social Identities* 10 (1): 9–29.

Heyman, J. M. 2004. "The Anthropology of Power-Wielding Bureaucracies." *Human Organization* 63 (4): 487–500.

Ho, Enseng. 2004. "Empire through Diasporic Eyes: A View from the Other Boat." *Comparative Studies in Society and History* 46 (2): 210–246.

2006. *The Graves of Tarim: Geneaology and Mobility across the Indian Ocean.* Berkeley, CA: University of California Press.

Holston, James, ed. 1998. *Cities and Citizenship.* Durham, NC: Duke University Press.

2008. *Insurgent Citizenship: Disjunctions of Democracy and Modernity in Brazil.* Princeton, NJ: Princeton University Press.

Honig, Bonnie. 2003. *Democracy and the Foreigner.* Princeton, NJ: Princeton University Press.

Hopper, Mathew. 2015. *Slaves of One Master: Globalization and Slavery in Arabia in the Age of Empire.* Ithica, NY:Yale University Press.

Horowitz, Donald. 1985. *Ethnic Groups in Conflict.* Berkeley, CA: University of California Press.

Human Rights Watch. 2006. "Building Towers, Cheating Workers: Exploitation of Migrant Construction Workers in the United Arab Emirates." Volume 18, No. 8(E). https://www.hrw.org/sites/default/files/reports/uae1106webw cover.pdf.

(2015). "Concerns and Recommendations on Kuwait Submitted to the UN Human Rights Committee in Advance of its Pre-Sessional Review," August 7. http://tbinternet.ohchr.org/Treaties/CCPR/Shared%20Document s/KWT/INT_CCPR_ICO_KWT_21314_E.pdf.

International Monetary Fund. 2015. *Union of the Comoros : Staff Report for the 2014 Article IV Consultation.* Country Report 15/34. Washington, DC: International Monetary Fund. https://www.imf.org/en/Publications/CR/Issu es/2016/12/31/Union-of-the-Comoros-Staff-Report-for-the-2014-Article-I V-Consultation-42701.

International Monetary Fund. 2016. *Union of Comoros: Selected Issues.* IMF Country Report 16/394. Washington, DC: International Monetary Fund. www.imf.org/external/pubs/ft/scr/2016/cr16394.pdf.

Ismail, Netty Idayu, and Filipe Pacheco. 2018. "UAE Raises the Stakes to Stop Foreigners From Leaving Dubai." *Bloomberg,* May 22.

Jacobson, David. 1996. *Rights across Borders: Immigration and the Decline of Citizenship.* Baltimore, MD: John Hopkins University Press.

Jamal, Manal A. 2015. "The 'Tiering' of Citizenship and Residency and the 'Hierarchization' of Migrant Communities: The United Arab Emirates in Historical Context." *International Migration Review* 49 (3): 601–632.

Janahi, Carina. 2014. "The Baloch as an Ethnic Group in the Persian Gulf Region" *The Persian Gulf in Modern Times.* Edited by Lawrence Potter. 267–297. New York: Palgrave McMillan.

Janakiraman, Narayan, Robert J. Meyer, and Stephen J. Hoch. 2011. "The Psychology of Decisions to Abandon Waits for Service." *Journal of Marketing Research* 48 (6): 970.

Jenkins, J., and S. Schmeidl. 1995. "Flight from Violence: The Origins and Implications of the World Refugee Crisis." *Sociological Focus* 28: 63–82.

Jones, Calvert. 2015. "Seeing Like an Autocrat: Liberal Social Engineering in an Illiberal State." *Perspectives on Politics* 13 (1): 24–41.

2017. *Bedouins into Bourgeois: Remaking Citizens for Globalization.* Cambridge University Press.

Joppke, Christian. 2017. "Citizenship in Immigration States." In *The Oxford Handbook of Citizenship*, edited by Ayelet Shachar, Rainer Bauböck, Irene Bloemraad, and Marteen Vink, 385–406. Oxford: Oxford University Press.

Kaabour, Mahmoud. 2009. "In This Country We Are Often Strangers Together." *The National*, July 18. https://www.thenational.ae/uae/in-this-country-we-a re-often-strangers-together-1.535389.

Kahn, Jeffrey. 2018. *Islands of Sovereignty: Haitian Migration and the Borders of Empire.* University of Chicago Press.

Kapiszewski, Andrzej, and United Nations Department of Economic and Social Affairs, Population Division. 2006. "Arab Versus Asian Migrant Workers in the GCC Countries." UN/POP/EGM/2006/02. United Nations Expert Group Meeting on International Migration and Development in the Arab Region, Beirut.

Karsh, Efraim, and Inari Karsh. 1996. "Reflections on Arab Nationalism: Review Article." *Middle Eastern Studies* 32 (4): 367–392.

Kasimis, Demetra. 2013. "The Tragedy of Blood-Based Membership: Secrecy and the Politics of Immigration in Euripides's Ion." *Political Theory* 41 (2): 231–256.

Kaufman, Stuart J. 2001. *Modern Hatreds: The Symbolic Politics of Ethnic War.* Ithica, NY: Cornell University Press.

Keane, David, and Nicholas McGeehan. 2008. "Enforcing Migrant Workers' Rights in the United Arab Emirates." *International Journal on Minority and Group Rights* 15: 81–116.

Kefauver, Barry. 2012. *International ePassport Standards and Implementation: Maybe You Want One, But Are You Ready?* Eighth Symposium and Exhibition on ICAO MRDTs, Biometrics and Security Standards, ICAO Headquarters, Montreal, Canada, October 10. www.icao.int/Meetings/mrt d-symposium-2012/Documents/11_am_Kefauver.pdf.

Khaleej Times. 2008. "Stateless Person to Get UAE Citizenship on 'Clean Record.'" July 10. www.khaleejtimes.com/nation/general/stateless-person-to-get-uae-citizenship-on-clean-record.

Khalifa, Ali. 1979. *The United Arab Emirates: Unity in Fragmentation.* Boulder, CO and London: Westview and Croom Helm.

Kingdom of Bahrain. 2006. *Act No. 19 with Regard to the Regulation of the Labour Market.* http://lmra.bh/portal/files/cms/shared/file/law-no19-year20 06-english.pdf.

Koopmans, Rudd, and Paul Statham, eds. 2000. *Challenging Immigration and Ethnic Relations Politics: Comparative European Perspectives.* New York: Oxford University Press.

Kumar, Anil. 2012. "The Price of Illegal Maids." *999*, March.

Larson, Richard C. 1987. "Perspectives on Queues: Social Justice and the Psychology of Queueing." *Operations Research* 35 (6): 895–905.

Laubenthal, Barbara. 2011. "The Negotiation of Irregular Migrants' Right to Education in Germany: A Challenge to the Nation-State." *Ethnic and Racial Studies* 34 (8): 1357–1373.

Lauth, Hans-Joachim. 2000. "Informal Institutions and Democracy." *Democratization* 7 (4): 21–50.

Lawrance, Benjamin N. 2017. "Statelessness-in-Question: Expert Testimony and the Evidentiary Burden of Statelessness." In *Citizenship in Question: Evidentiary Birthright and Statelessness*, edited by Benjamin N. Lawrance and Jacqueline Stevens, 60–80. Durham, NC: Duke University Press.

Lawrance, Benjamin N., and Jacqueline Stevens. 2017. *Citizenship in Question: Evidentiary Birthright and Statelessness*. Durham, NC: Duke University Press.

Leclerc, France, Bernd H. Schmitt, and Laurette Dubé. 1995. "Waiting Time and Decision Making: Is Time like Money?" *Journal of Consumer Research* 22 (1): 110–119.

Lesch, Ann Mosely, and Ian Lustick. 2005. *Exile and Return: Predicaments of Palestinians and Jews*. Philadelphia: University of Pennsylvania Press.

Levinson, Amanda. 2005. *The Regularisation of Unauthorised Migrants: Literature Survey and Country Case Studies* (Report). Centre on Migration, Policy and Society, University of Oxford. www.compas.ox.ac.uk/wp-content /uploads/ER-2005-Regularisation_Unauthorized_Literature.pdf

Levy, Jack S. 2008. "Case Studies: Types, Designs, and Logics of Inference." *Conflict Management and Peace Science* 25 (1): 1–18.

Lewis, Nell. 2018. "Who Stands to Benefit from the UAE's Visa and Investment Rules?" *CNN*, June 17. https://edition.cnn.com/2018/06/17/middleeast/uae-visa-and-foreign-ownership-rules/index.html.

Lewis, Paul, and S. Ramakrishnan. 2007. "Police Practices in Immigrant-Destination Cities: Political Control or Bureaucratic Professionalism?" *Urban Affairs Review* 42 (6): 874–900.

Longva, Anh Nga. 1997. *Walls Built on Sand: Migration, Exclusion, and Society in Kuwait*. Boulder, CO: Westview Press.

1999. "Keeping Migrant Workers in Check: The Kafala System in the Gulf." *Middle East Report* (211): 20–22.

Lori, Noora. 2011. "National Security and the Management of Migrant Labor: A Case Study of the United Arab Emirates." *Asian and Pacific Migration Journal* 20 (3–4): 315–337.

2012. *"Temporary Migrants" or Permanent Residents? The Kafala System and Contestations over Residency in the Arab Gulf States*. Center for Migrations and Citizenship, Institut Français des Relations Internationales, November. www.ifri.org/sites/default/files/atoms/files/notecmcnooralori1.pdf

2017. "Statelessness, 'In-Between' Statuses, and Precarious Citizenship." In *The Oxford Handbook of Citizenship*, edited by Ayelet Shachar, Rainer Baubock, Irene Bloemraad, and Marteen Vink. 745–763. Oxford, UK: Oxford University Press.

Lorimer, John G. 1915. *Gazetteer of the Persian Gulf, Oman and Central Arabia*. Calcutta: Superintendent Government Printing.

Lynch, Maureen. 2010. "United Arab Emirates: Nationality Matters." Refugees International, January 12. www.refugeesinternational.org/blog/united-arab-emirates-nationality-matters.

Mahdavi, Pardis. 2016. "Stateless and for Sale in the Gulf." *Foreign Affairs*, June 30. www.foreignaffairs.com/articles/kuwait/2016-06-30/stateless-and-sale-gulf.

Mahoney, James. 2000. "Path Dependence in Historical Sociology." *Theory and Society* 29: 507–548.

Maister, David H. 1985. "The Psychology of Waiting Lines." https://davidmaister.com/wp-content/themes/davidmaister/pdf/PsycholgyofWaitingLines751.pdf

Mann, Leon. 1970. "The Social Psychology of Waiting Lines: The Mammoth Waiting Line Is a Sophisticated Cultural Microcosm with a Unique Set of Social Rules and Behavioral Regularities." *American Scientist* 58 (4): 390–398.

March, James G., and Johan P. Olsen. 1984. "The New Institutionalism: Organizational Factors in Political Life." *The American Political Science Review* 78 (3): 734–749.

Marshall, T. H. 1950. *Citizenship and Social Class*. London: Pluto Press.

Martin, Philip L. 2001. "There Is Nothing More Permanent Than Temporary Foreign Workers." Backgrounder. Washington, DC: Center for Immigration Studies. https://cis.org/Report/There-Nothing-More-Permanent-Temporary-Foreign-Workers.

Martin, Philip, and Mark Miller. 1980. "Guestworkers: Lessons from Western Europe." *Industrial and Labor Relations Review* 33 (3): 315–330.

Mathew, Johan. 2012. "Trafficking Labour: Abolition and the Exchange of Labour across the Arabian Sea, 1861–1947." *Slavery and Abolition* 33 (1): 139–156.

Mau, Steffen, Fabian Gülzau, Lena Laube, and Natascha Zaun. 2015. "The Global Mobility Divide: How Visa Policies Have Evolved over Time." *Journal of Ethnic Migration Studies* 8: 1192–1213.

Mehta, Uday. 1997. "Liberal Strategies of Exclusion." In *Tensions of Empire: Colonial Cultures in a Bourgeois World*, edited by Frederick Cooper and Ann Laura Stoler, 59–86. Berkeley, CA: University of California Press.

Menjivar, Cecilia. 2006. "Liminal Legality: Salvadoran and Guatemalan Immigrants' Lives in the United States." *American Journal of Sociology* 111 (4): 999–1037.

Menz, George. 2011. "Neo-Liberalism, Privatization and the Outsourcing of Migration Management: A Five-Country Comparison." *Competition & Change* 15 (2): 116–135.

Middle East Monitor. 2017. "Saudi to Deport 5 m 'Illegal' Workers" (blog). March 7. www.middleeastmonitor.com/20170307-saudi-to-deport-5m-illegal-workers.

Migrants at Sea. 2011. "ECJ Rules Italy May Not Criminally Punish Illegally Staying Migrants Who Fail to Depart." April 29. http://migrantsatsea

.wordpress.com/2011/04/29/ecj-rules-italy-may-not-criminally-punish-illegally-staying-migrants-who-fail-to-depart.

Milanovic, Branko. 2016. *Global Inequality: A New Approach for the Age of Globalization*. Cambridge, MA: Harvard University Press.

Morris, Loveday. 2012. "UAE Deports Rights Activist Ahmed Abdul Khaleq in Clampdown on Dissent." *The Independent*, July 17. www.independent.co.uk/n ews/world/middle-east/uae-deports-rights-activist-ahmed-abdul-khaleq-in-clam pdown-on-dissent-7946871.html.

Mylonas, Harris. 2013. *The Politics of Nation-Building: Making Co-Nationals, Refugees, and Minorities*. 1st ed. New York: Cambridge University Press.

Najdmabadi, Shahnaz. 2009. "The Arab Presence on the Iranian Coast of the Persian Gulf." In *The Persian Gulf in History*, edited by Lawrence Potter, 129–146. New York: Palgrave Macmillan.

2010. "Cross-Border Networks: Labour Migration from Iran to the Arab Countries of the Persian Gulf." *Anthropology of the Middle East* 5 (1): 18–33.

Nagy, Sharon. 2010. "Families and Bachelors: Visa Status, Family Lives, and Community Structure among Bahrain's Foreign Residents." In *Viewpoints Special Edition: Migration and the Gulf*, February, 58–61. Washington, DC: Middle East Institute.

The National. 2010. "Committee Examines Claims of Children Abandoned Abroad." *The National*, January 16. www.thenational.ae/news/uae-news/c ommittee-examines-claims-of-children-abandoned-abroad.

Ngai, Mae. 2004. *Impossible Subjects: Illegal Aliens and the Making of Modern America*. Princeton, NJ: Princeton University Press.

Nicolini, Beatrice. 2007. "The Baluch Role in the Persian Gulf during the Nineteenth and Twentieth Centuries." *Comparative Studies of South Asia, Africa, and the Middle East* 27 (2): 384–396.

Onley, James. 2007. *The Arabian Frontier of the British Raj*. Oxford University Press.

2017. *India and the Persian Gulf: Trade, Society, and Empire across the Indian Ocean, 1507–1947*. Cambridge University Press.

Pan, Jason, and Hung Jui-chin. 2013. "Pingpu Registration Drive Starts in South." *Taipei Times*, November 9. www.taipeitimes.com/News/taiwan/archives/20 13/11/09/2003576493/2.

Paret, Marcel, and Shannon Gleeson. 2016. "Precarity and Agency through a Migration Lens." *Citizenship Studies* 20 (3–4): 277–294.

Parolin, Gianluca. 2009. *Citizenship in the Arab World: Kin, Religion and the National State*. Amsterdam: Amsterdam University Press.

Parussini, Gabriele. 2017. "India's Massive Aadhaar Biometric Identification Program – The Numbers." *WSJ* (blog), January 13. https://blogs.wsj.com/br iefly/2017/01/13/indias-massive-aadhaar-biometric-identification-program-the-numbers/.

Paul, Kathleen. 1997. *Whitewashing Britain: Race and Citizenship in the Postwar Era*. Ithaca, NY: Cornell University Press.

Pearson, Michael N. 1998. *Port Cities and Intruders: The Swahili Coast, India and Portugal in the Early Modern Era.* Oxford University Press.

2006. "Littoral Society: The Concept and the Problems." *Journal of World History* 17 (4): 353–373.

The Peninsula. 2010. "Laqum Al Qarar: Expatriates Are the Future Threat of the Entire Gulf: HE Dhahi Khalfan Tamim." December 29.

Petersen, Roger. 2001. *Resistance and Rebellion: Lessons from Eastern Europe.* Cambridge University Press.

2002. *Understanding Ethnic Violence: Fear, Hatred, and Resentment in Twentieth-Century Eastern Europe.* Cambridge University Press.

Peterson, J. E. 2013. "The Baluch Presence in the Persian Gulf." In *Sectarian Politics in the Persian Gulf*, edited by Lawrence Potter, 229–244. New York: Oxford University Press.

Pierson, Paul. 2000. "Increasing Returns, Path Dependence, and the Study of Politics." *American Political Science Review* 94: 251–267.

Piven, Frances Fox, and Richard A. Cloward. 1971. *Regulating the Poor: the Functions of Public Welfare.* 1st ed. New York: Pantheon Books.

Potter, Lawrence. 2009. *The Persian Gulf in History.* New York: Palgrave Macmillan.

Rahman, Anisur. 2010. "Migration and Human Rights in the Gulf." In *Viewpoints Special Edition: Migration and the Gulf*, February, 16–18. Washington, DC: Middle East Institute.

Rawls, John. 1999. *A Theory of Justice.* Cambridge, MA: Harvard University Press.

Ray, R. K. 1995. "Asian Capital in the Age of European Domination: The Rise of the Bazaar, 1800–1914" *Cambridge Core* 29 (3): 449–554.

Reuters. 2018. "Comoros Ex-President under House Arrest after Probe of Passport Scheme," *Reuters*, May 21. https://af.reuters.com/article/topNews/idAFKCN1IM0LT-OZATP.

Ricks, Thomas. 1989. "Slaves and Slave Traders in the Persian Gulf, 18th and 19th Centuries: An Assessment" 9 (3): 60–70.

Robertson, Geoffrey, Graeme Irvine, Catherine Oborne, and Ravi Naik. 2013. *Trial Observation Report: UAE 94.* Emirates Centre for Human Rights. http://echr.org.uk/sites/default/files/Trial-Report-UAE-94.pdf.

Ruhs, Martin. 2013. *The Price of Rights: Regulating International Labor Migration.* Princeton, NJ: Princeton University Press.

Sadiq, Kamal. 2005. "When States Prefer Non-Citizens over Citizens: Conflict Over Illegal Immigration into Malaysia." *International Studies Quarterly* 49 (1): 101–122.

2009. *Paper Citizens: How Illegal Immigrants Acquire Citizenship in Developing Countries.* Oxford and New York: Oxford University Press.

2016. "Limits of Legal Citizenship: Narratives from South and Southeast Asia." In *Citizenship in Question: Evidentiary Birthright and Statelessness*, edited by Benjamin N. Lawrance and Jacqueline Stevens, 165–177. Durham, NC: Duke University Press.

Salama, Samir. 2010. "FNC Urges Fast-Tracking on Demographic Council." *Gulf News*, January 6.

Salisbury, Peter. 2015. "Inside the $100 Million Scheme to Send the Middle East's Most Unwanted People to Africa." *VICE News*, November 19. https://news.vice.com/article/inside-the-100-million-scheme-to-send-the-middle-easts-most-unwanted-people-to-africa.

Sassen, Saskia. 1996. *Losing Control? Sovereignty in the Age of Globalization.* New York: Columbia University Press.

Schain, Martin, Aristide R. Zolberg, and Patrick Hossay. 2002. *Shadows over Europe: The Development and Impact of the Extreme Right in Western Europe.* 1st ed. New York: Palgrave Macmillan.

Schwartz, Barry. 1974. "Waiting, Exchange, and Power: The Distribution of Time in Social Systems." *American Journal of Sociology* 79 (4): 841–870.

1975. *Queuing and Waiting: Studies in the Social Organization of Access and Delay.* University of Chicago Press.

Scott, James C. 1999. *Seeing Like a State: How Certain Schemes to Improve the Human Condition Have Failed.* New Haven, CT: Yale University Press.

Seccombe, I. J., and Lawless, R. I. 1986. "Foreign Worker Dependence in the Gulf, and the International Oil Companies: 1910–50." *International Migration Review* 20 (3): 548–574.

Shachar, Ayelet. 2017. "Citizenship for Sale?" In *The Oxford Handbook of Citizenship*, edited by Ayelet Shachar, Rainer Bauböck, Irene Bloemraad, and Maarten Vink, 789–816. Oxford, UK: Oxford University Press.

2018. "The Marketization of Citizenship in an Age of Restrictionism." *Ethics and International Affairs* 32 (1): 3–13.

Shah, Nasra. 2008. "Recent Labor Immigration Policies in the Oil-Rich Gulf: How Effective Are They Likely to Be?" Working Paper 3. ILO Asian Regional Programme on Governance of Labour Migration. Bangkok, Thailand: International Labor Organization. http://digitalcommons.ilr.cornell.edu/intl/52.

Shah, Nasra, and Fargues, Philippe. 2011. "Introduction to Special Issue: Migration in the Gulf States: Issues and Prospects." *Asian and Pacific Migration Journal* 20 (3/4): 267–272.

Shevel, Oxana. 2011. *Migration, Refugee Policy, and State Building in Postcommunist Europe.* New York: Cambridge University Press.

Simola, Anna. 2018. "Lost in Administration: (Re)Producing Precarious Citizenship for Young University-Educated Intra-EU Migrants in Brussels." *Work, Employment and Society* 32 (3): 458–474.

Somers, Margaret. 2008. *Genealogies of Citizenship: Markets, Statelessness, and the Right to Have Rights.* Cambridge, UK and New York: Cambridge University Press.

Soysal, Yasemin Nuhoglu. 1995. *Limits of Citizenship: Migrants and Postnational Membership in Europe.* University of Chicago Press.

Spindler, William. 2008. "UNHCR Welcomes UAE Decision on Stateless People." UNHCR, September 23. www.unhcr.org/cgi-bin/texis/vtx/search?page=search&docid=48d8be5d11&query=UAE.

Spiro, Peter. 2014. "Kuwait Bulk-Orders Comoros Citizenship for Stateless Bidoon." Opiniojuris (blog), November 13. http://opiniojuris.org/2014/11/13/kuwait-bulk-orders-comoros-citizenship-stateless-bidoons.

Steinmo, Sven, Kathleen Ann Thelen, and Frank Longstreth, eds. 1992. *Structuring Politics: Historical Institutionalism in Comparative Analysis.* Cambridge Studies in Comparative Politics. Cambridge, UK and New York: Cambridge University Press.

Stevens, Jacqueline. 2011. "US Government Unlawfully Detaining and Deporting US Citizens as Aliens." *Virginia Journal of Social Policy & the Law* 18 (3): 606–720.

2017. "Introduction." In *Citizenship in Question: Evidentiary Birthright and Statelessness*, edited by Benjamin N. Lawrance, 1–26. Durham, NC: Duke University Press.

Štiks, Igor. 2010. "The Citizenship Conundrum in Post-Communist Europe: The Instructive Case of Croatia." *Europe-Asia Studies* 62: 1621–1638.

Štiks, Igor, and Jo Shaw. 2013. *Citizenship Rights.* Abingdon, UK: Routledge.

Suzuki, Hideaki. 2013. "Baluchi Experiences under Slavery and the Slave Trade of the Gulf of Oman and the Persian Gulf 1921–1950." *Journal of the Middle East and Africa* 4 (2): 205–223.

Thiollet, Hélène. 2010. "Nationalisme d'État et Nationalisme Ordinaire En Arabie Saoudite: La Nation Saoudienne et Ses Immigrés." *Raisons Politiques* 37: 89–102.

Tichenor, Daniel J. 2002. *Dividing Lines: The Politics of Immigration Control in America.* Princeton, NJ: Princeton University Press.

Tilly, Charles. 1989. "The Geography of European State-Making and Capitalism Since 1500." In *Geographic Perspectives in History*, edited by Eugene Genovese and Leonard Hochberg, 159–181. Oxford University Press.

Torpey, John C. 2000. *The Invention of the Passport: Surveillance, Citizenship and the State.* Cambridge University Press.

Trump, D. 2017. "Executive Order: Border Security and Immigration Enforcement Improvements." The White House. www.whitehouse.gov/the-press-office/2017/01/25/executive-order-border-security-and-immigration-enforcement-improvements.

Tsai, Kellee S. 2006. "Adaptive Informal Institutions and Endogenous Institutional Change in China." *World Politics* 59 (1): 116–141.

Turner, Jennifer, Nisha Varia, and Human Rights Watch. 2007. "Exported and Exposed: Abuses against Sri Lankan Domestic Workers in Saudi Arabia, Kuwait, Lebanon, and the United Arab Emirates." http://link.vpl.ca/portal/Exported-and-exposed–abuses-against-Sri-Lankan/zLRDfWgGTLc.

UAE National Bureau of Statistics. 2005. "UAE Employed Population by Nationality (Emirati/Non-Emirati) and Emirate (2005)." https://gulfmigration.org/uae-employed-population-by-nationality-emirati-non-emirati-and-emirate-2005.

UAE National Bureau of Statistics. 2010. "Methodology of Estimating the Population in UAE." http://fcsa.gov.ae/en-us/Lists/D_StatisticsSubject/Attachments/68/Population%20Estimates%202006%20-%202010.pdf.

UN High Commissioner for Refugees (UNHCR). 1974. *Report of the United Nations High Commissioner for Refugees*, 1 January, A/9012. www.refworld.org/docid/3ae68c3c4.html.

United Nations Department of Economics and Social Affairs, Population Division. 2010. *World Population Prospects: The 2010 Revision.* www .un.org/en/development/desa/population/publications/pdf/trends/WPP2010/ WPP2010_Volume-I_Comprehensive-Tables.pdf.

2017. *International Migration Report 2017: Highlights.* www.un.org/en/devel opment/desa/population/migration/publications/migrationreport/docs/Migr ationReport2017_Highlights.pdf.

US Citizenship and Immigration Services. 2016. "Consideration of Deferred Action for Childhood Arrivals (DACA)." www.uscis.gov/humanitarian/con sideration-deferred-action-childhood-arrivals-daca.

US Department of Homeland Security. 2016. *2015 Yearbook of Immigration Statistics.* Washington, DC: Homeland Security. www.dhs.gov/sites/default/ files/publications/Yearbook_Immigration_Statistics_2015.pdf.

US Department of State. 2013. "Country Reports on Human Rights Practices for 2012: United Arab Emirates." https://www.refworld.org/docid/53284a5310 .html.

US Department of State Bureau of Democracy, Human Rights, and Labor. 2008. "United Arab Emirates." https://www.refworld.org/docid/49a8 f143c.html.

US Energy Information Administration. n.d. "Total Petroleum and Other Liquid Production – 2018." www.eia.gov/countries.

Van der Leun, Joanne. 2003. *Looking for Loopholes: Processes of Incorporation of Illegal Immigrants in the Netherlands.* Amsterdam: Amsterdam University Press.

Van Hear, Nicholas. 1993. "Mass Flight in the Middle East: Involuntary Migration and the Gulf Conflict, 1990–1991." In *Geography and Refugees: Patterns and Processes of Change,* edited by R. Black and V. Robinson, 64–84. London: Belhaven.

1995. "The Impact of Involuntary Mass 'Return' to Jordan in the Wake of the Gulf Crisis." *International Migration Review* 29 (2): 352–374.

Varsanyi, Monica. 2010. *Taking Local Control: Immigration Policy Activism in US Cities and States* . Stanford University Press.

Vitalis, Robert. 2009. *America's Kingdom: Mythmaking on the Saudi Oil Frontier.* New York and London: Verso.

Vora, Neha. 2010. "Business Elites, Unofficial Citizenship, and Privatized Governance in Dubai." In *Viewpoints Special Edition: Migration and the Gulf,* February, 46–48. Washington, DC: Middle East Institute.

2013. *Impossible Citizens: Dubai's Indian Diaspora.* Durham, NC, and London: Duke University Press.

Waite, Urban. 2011. *The Terror of Living: A Novel.* 1st ed. New York: Little, Brown and Co.

Walzer, Michael. 1983. *Spheres of Justice: A Defense of Pluralism and Equality.* New York: Basic Books.

Warrell, Helen. 2012. "Court's 'Hammer Blow' to Migration Cut." *Financial Times,* July 12. https://www.ft.com/content/6d03a618-d103-11e1-8a3c-00144feabdco.

Wass, Laura van. 2010. *The Situation of Stateless Persons in the Middle East and North Africa*. UNHCR Research Paper. www.refworld.org/pdfid/4cea28072.pdf.

Watanbe, Akiko. 2010. "The Pre-Departure Orientation Seminars as a Way of Protecting Prospective Overseas Filipino Workers." Paper presented at the 2010 Exeter Gulf Studies Conference "The 21st-Century Gulf: The Challenge of Identity," University of Exeter, Centre for Gulf Studies, June 30–July 3.

Weil, Patrick. 2001. "The History of French Nationality: A Lesson for Europe." In *Towards a European Nationality: Citizenship, Immigration, and Nationality Law in the EU*, edited by Randall Hansen and Patrick Weil. 52–68. New York: Palgrave.

Weiner, Myron. 1992. "Security, Stability, and International Migration." *International Security* 17 (3): 91–126.

Willen, Sarah. 2007. "Exploring 'Illegal" and 'Irregular' Migrants' Lived Experiences of Law and State Power." *International Migration* 45 (3): 2–7.

———. 2010. "Citizens, 'Real' Others, and 'Other' Others: The Biopolitics of Otherness and the Deportation of Unauthorized Migrant Workers from Tel Aviv, Israel." In *The Deportation Regime: Sovereignty, Space, and the Freedom of Movement*, edited by Nicholas De Genova and Nathalie Peutz, 262–294. Durham, NC: Duke University Press.

Wolozin, Rebecca. 2014. "Citizenship Issues and Issuing Citizenship: A Case Study of Sri Lanka's Citizenship Laws in a Global Context." *Asian-Pacific Law & Policy Journal* 16 (1): 1–28.

World Bank. 2015. "Comoros—Second Economic Governance Reform Grant Project." 95824. http://documents.worldbank.org/curated/en/80202146817
2787445/Comoros-Second-Economic-Governance-Reform-Grant-Project.

World Economic Forum. 2017. "Travel and Competitiveness Report 2017: Safety and Security." http://reports.weforum.org/travel-and-tourism-competitiveness-report-2017/ranking/#series=TTCI.A.02.

Yanez-Pagans, Monica, and Gustavo Machicado-Salas. 2014. "Bureaucratic Delay, Local-Level Monitoring, and Delivery of Small Infrastructure Projects: Evidence from a Field Experiment in Bolivia." *World Development* 59: 394–407.

Youssef, Marten, and Kareem Shaheen. 2009. "UAE Urged to Find a Balance." *The National*, July 10, 2009.

Zolberg, Aristide. 1983. "The Formation of New States as a Refugee-Generating Process." *Annals of the American Academy of Political and Social Science* 467 (1): 24–38.

Index

Note: *Page numbers in italics indicate figures and tables.*

CPSIA information can be obtained
at www.ICGtesting.com
Printed in the USA
LVHW101308170822
PP17490900001BA/4

9 781108 705561